# *Finding A* "KEEPER"

## A HANDBOOK
## FOR SINGLE WOMEN OVER 35
## IN SEARCH OF MR. RIGHT

## MYRA KAPLAN

*The Harold Morris Publishing Company*
*Houston, Texas*

# Finding A "Keeper"

**Published by The Harold Morris Publishing Company**
P.O. Box 310033
Houston, Texas 77235
Visit us on the Web at www.findingakeeper.com
Email: myra@findingakeeper.com

ISBN: 0-9745802-0-1

Library of Congress Control Number: 2004111212
Category: Relationships

**Disclaimer:**
The author is not a licensed therapist or psychologist, and the information in
this book is not intended to replace professional counseling, therapy or any
other service rendered by a qualified practitioner of any kind. The stories in
the book are based upon true experiences, but in all cases except for anecdotes
about public figures or the author herself, names and other details have been
changed. Some situations or characters are composites.

Editing, page design/layout & cover design by Connie L. Schmidt & Ron Kaye
Schmidt Kaye & Company Professional Literary Services ~ Houston, Texas

Manufactured in the United States of America
First Edition

# TABLE OF CONTENTS

## Part One
## A "New You" State Of Mind:
## Small Changes For Huge Results

## Part Two
## *Finding Your "Keeper" (And Helping Him Find YOU)*

## Part Three
## *Lighten Up!*

# Part Seven
## Getting Serious

# DEDICATIONS

*This book is dedicated to…*

My sister-in-law and my nearly life-long friend, Linda, who was one of the first to tell me I had to write a book, and whose encouragement sustained me throughout this project

My beloved sister Rochelle, who is always there for me and with whom I continue to share "secrets" as only sisters can

My wise and wonderful mother, Anne, who is a true lady, a woman of such grace, intelligence and class, and a living example of everything she taught us — and who, in her ninety-first year, continues to teach us something every day

My wonderful children, Bonnie and Michael, who have taught me humility and diplomacy, have so willingly shared their lives with their father and me, and continue to bring us so much love, joy and pride

Our delightful new daughter-in-law, Julie, who quickly became part of our family and, even as this book was near completion, was still able to offer helpful suggestions

*But most of all…*

To Gene, my amazing husband, lifelong partner and best friend, who has always encouraged me to reach for the stars. I cannot thank him enough for the countless hours he has spent working on this endeavor with me. Creating a book has often been compared to having a baby, and I suppose it is in many ways. I do know that without Gene's help, love, encouragement and endless patience, this book would never have been "born".

*This book is also dedicated to our parents who are no longer living…*

Gene's mother and father, Betty and Moe, with whom we shared so many happy times

My dear father, Harold, who left us before his time, who taught me so much and gave me so much love

*All of you are gifts in my life, and I am truly thankful.*

# ACKNOWLEDGMENTS

It was my sister-in-law Linda's suggestion to write this book that spurred me to action, and once I began the project her encouragement never wavered. For all those countless e-mails, phone calls and even a trip to Texas to help with the first editing — I thank you. Your efforts were immeasurable.

The first person who suggested I needed to write a book, however, was my husband, Gene, and it was only after he convinced me I could do it that I sat down and began writing. Although there were times I was so absorbed in the book that he must have wished I had never begun it, he stuck it out with me. Gene, for your patience and support — not to mention your creative marketing ideas — I thank you.

Before I began this project, I spoke with my children, Bonnie and Michael. I asked them what they thought about it and listened carefully to what they said. With their support I began writing, but a few weeks later, I again asked what they thought because I wanted to know if they did indeed have any objections. Since they were both single at the time, I didn't know how they would react to my writing a book about finding a spouse. If they had objected at all, I would have ended it immediately. But they both told me unequivocally that I should proceed. They were encouraging and motivating, and said, "Don't wait, do it now!" Without their approval, I would not have been able to complete this book. I thank them both for their time and input, and most of all for their patience, while I was writing this. There were missed messages, interrupted phone calls, visits that were too brief, and times when I just couldn't break away to be with them. But Bonnie and Michael, you were always understanding and supportive. Thank you so much.

Our parents gave my sister and me the wisdom and fortitude to believe in ourselves. These are gifts that have served me well all of my life. My beautiful mother, Anne, has been an invaluable support for me since I began this project. She has listened for hours as I read excerpts to her late at night, always enjoying it, but never hesitating to suggest a word here and there! For months and months she continued to suggest titles, and it was she, together with my husband and I, who finally arrived at *Finding A "Keeper"*. Her only wish was for the book to be published while she was alive to enjoy it. I am happy to say she is here and this year celebrated her ninetieth birthday. Thank you, Mother, for being the person we all aspire to be.

There are many friends who I hope will forgive my frequent absence during the two years I spent writing this book. I did my best to keep connected with you, and I appreciate your understanding when my efforts fell short. I did not discuss the subject of the book before it was complete, and you were all considerate of that — thank you so much. I'm sorry for the many missed phone calls, visits, etc., but...I'm back!

My sister, Rochelle, had to listen to me read excerpts or talk about the book even when she didn't have the time. Rochelle, you have always been wonderful, and never more so than these past few months as I struggled towards the finish line. Thank you!

I must also acknowledge my most dedicated readers, Marlene Battle, Roberta Berk, Harriette Kurtz, our life-long friend, Dr. Mimi Scott, Esther Zalta and my dear cousin, Paula Winig. Thank you all for your efforts in helping to make this book even better!

I thank all the countless and nameless people I have talked with over the years. Thank you to the many Continental flight attendants on those long trips — you sure made the time fly! From our friends, to our children's friends, and all the strangers I met along the way, your stories are here, all incorporated into this book. I listened as you spoke and heard every word you told me.

And finally, thank you to my editors, Connie Schmidt and Ron Kaye, of Schmidt Kaye & Company in Houston, for their endless hours. They gave the book the shape it is in today, and I have no doubt that without them, I would not have completed it. I'll never forget that July morning sitting in that hot little bagel shop when the idea for the book's format was first suggested. Connie, all I had to do was say a few words and you read my mind. I could not have found another person more dedicated and committed than you have been. You are one in a million, and I cannot thank you enough. I used to wonder why authors spoke so fondly of their editors — I now know.

# WHY I WROTE THIS BOOK
## A Special Note From The Author

People of all ages have always found it easy to talk to me. Many of them have shared the relationship challenges they were facing, and when they would ask my opinion, I would always do my best to give them a helpful and honest answer. Although my opinion was not always what they expected or even wanted to hear, they often took my suggestions anyway, and would almost invariably end up thanking me.

One day my husband said to me, "Myra, what you say makes more sense than most of those relationship books out there. Why don't you write about what you've been telling me, and everyone else, for years?" At first I dismissed his remark. I had always thought that if I were going to write a book at all, it would be a cookbook. Not too long after that conversation with my husband, however, I was speaking to my sister-in-law about the problems single people have finding their mates — and she too suggested I write a book about it.

Even after these conversations, I never seriously considered my husband's or sister-in-law's suggestions, but one day I sat down at my computer, began to put down some thoughts on the subject — and before I know it, I had the beginnings of this book.

I am neither a therapist nor a relationship counselor, just a woman with common sense and a lifelong interest in people. Not incidentally, I also have a strong, solid marriage that has lasted more than forty years. Which brings us to the obvious question: Having been married so long, how could I possibly know what's going on with singles today? It's simple. Although I married young, I've always had many close single friends and I have been very aware of the singles scene throughout the years.

After I was married, one of my very first single friends was my husband's sister — yes, the same one who later helped inspire me to write this book. She is six years younger than her brother, and when she started dating he and I were already married. She and her closest girlfriends all had a hard time finding their Mr. Right; I guess they just went about finding husbands differently than my other friends and I did. Being privy to their adventures and misadventures, as well as those of countless other singles throughout the years, I began to make mental notes — and I never stopped.

No matter how old or how young they are, everyone has a story, and I have spent a lifetime listening to and learning about people. Frequently they told me how they found, or failed to find, true love, and I've shared many of these stories and their lessons in the pages of this book. (Of course, names and minor details have been changed to protect the privacy of all involved.)

So in the end, although my dear husband and sister-in-law gave me the final "push" I needed, the real inspiration for this book was provided by all those people over the years who shared their stories with me. I like to think that I helped many of them have a happy ending. And I sincerely hope that **Finding A "Keeper"** will help you have your own happy ending, or should we say — a happy beginning!

# INTRODUCTION

*I*f *you want to marry, you can marry* — and I don't mean just any man — I'm talking about a really great one. I hope that by the time you have finished reading this book, you will be as convinced as I am! By now you may have had your fill of disappointing relationships, and perhaps have even come to the conclusion that where single men are concerned, all the "good ones" are taken. This is simply not true. There are plenty of good men left, and one of them is waiting for you. It doesn't matter how old you are, it doesn't matter if you've never been married before, and it doesn't matter if you haven't even had a date in many years. If you really want a husband — not just the first available man who comes along, but one who is truly a "keeper" — you can find him.

You may believe that the odds are against single women marrying over thirty-five, since by that time, most of the good men really do seem to have disappeared. It is true that there are fewer choices, and many people in their forties and beyond have become set in their ways, making it easier to remain single than to marry. Then how can a woman "past a certain age" expect to find a husband, let alone a really great husband?

Not only is it possible, but it can happen to **you**. I will share many stories with you in this book, but there are hundreds more I could cite. True love has happened to so many women I've known, even women in their sixties and seventies, that I am firmly convinced it is never too late. People meet and marry every day at every age. I cannot say it too many times: **It is never too late to marry!** But you cannot just sit back and wait for it to happen. You have to take some initiative.

This book is for single women who genuinely want to get married. Although many people find it hard to believe, some women are happy single, and perfectly content to stay that way. I am assuming that you would not be reading this book if you fell into that category. I recognize that some of you may have mixed feelings about marriage, and we will discuss those feelings in detail. I have written this mainly for women who have never married or who had very short first marriages, but if you have been married before and are currently in the market for another husband, I think you will find it helpful as well.

*Finding A "Keeper"* is not a conventional 1-2-3 "how-to" book. There are enough of those on the market already, enough books that claim to tell you in so many "simple steps" how to get a husband. Real life, however, does not progress in simple, logical, 1-2-3 steps. Love rarely sticks to a "program", and the heart certainly doesn't pay much heed to "steps". (Besides, most of those "simple steps" really aren't all that simple for most people!) That's why I felt it more appropriate to write a "handbook" than an instruction manual. Think of this book as a "read it as you need it" guide; you can open it anywhere and begin reading. The chapters are short and easy to digest, and each one is self-contained. You don't have to read the chapters in order and you don't even have to read every one — I'll never know whether you do or don't!

Chances are, if you want to marry you will, with or without this book. In my experience, almost everyone who wants to marry eventually does; it just takes some longer than others. It is my hope that *Finding A "Keeper"* will make it happen more quickly for you, and with considerably less effort.

I wish you the best of luck in your search, and remember — the smallest changes can bring HUGE results! I'll be thinking of you.

Myra Kaplan
Houston, Texas

# BEFORE BEGINNING...

This book is about helping you reach your goal of getting married. As such, it is about today and tomorrow, not about yesterday. What you did in the past was not necessarily wrong — it just didn't work. We're going to help you make some changes in your life — nothing radical, just some subtle changes in behavior and attitude that will increase your chances that Mr. Right will find you. If you have made up your mind that marriage is definitely what you want, and you commit yourself to working with me to make these changes, we'll travel down the road together. Although you may doubt me now, by the time you've finished reading this book you will already be closer to your goal, and you will see that you really do have some control over how soon you reach it.

If you come home from work and do nothing different until you're ready to return to work the following morning, what are the chances of any changes coming into your life? Zero! If you do not bring change into your daily routine, the chances are slim to none that anything different is going to happen. Even the suggestions in this book won't help unless you make a commitment to yourself to bring some changes into your life.

As you read through the pages, try to imagine yourself making the actual changes. Picture yourself in the various situations. If you tend to be a bit shyer than you'd like, visualize yourself as the more confident, socially savvy woman you would like to be. Before long you will be that woman — and you won't even realize when the transformation took place. And if you're happy with yourself just the way you are, it still helps to envision yourself in the various situations. It will remind you how great you really are!

Being happy with yourself really is the key to success. If you're happy with *you*, you'll be much more likely to attract *him*. You can't be depressed and miserable and expect Mr. Right to fall into your life. It just doesn't happen that way. I've written this book in such a way that the chapters really don't have to be read in order, but if you're not very happy with yourself right now, I'd definitely suggest you begin with Chapter 1!

Every time you begin to feel sorry for yourself or doubt yourself, go back and read the *"Remember"* boxes in the chapters. If you think those reminders aren't working, return to the paragraphs you highlighted or earmarked. If you sense you may have been too critical in the past, perhaps looking for Mr. Perfect when in fact no one is perfect, picture yourself more open-minded, a little less judgmental.

As I said in the introduction, this book is for single women who are reasonably certain they want to get married. However, if you're feeling a little ambivalent about marriage, do know that you're not alone, and this book is for you too. One of the points I stress is that marriage does not mean you're giving up everything you've worked hard for while you were single. Nor does it mean you have to settle for someone that you wouldn't have turned your head for years before. What it means is you've found someone with whom to share your life, someone whom you deeply care for and someone with whom you've fallen in love. And isn't that what you want?

I am convinced your Mr. Right is out there. Just as many men as women desire a life-long relationship, one that's filled with love, trust, respect and fulfillment. And even if you are in your forties, your fifties or older, it is not too late. **It is NEVER too late.** If you're sitting here reading this, I am asking you to believe that marriage is possible for you, it is real, and this book will help you make it happen. All you have to do is make up your mind to expect great things.

The one gift we are all given is life. What we do with it is up to us. It would be wonderful if we could rewrite history, but since we can't, we must take the energy spent thinking about yesterday and focus on tomorrow. We really do have some control over what tomorrow can bring, and it is my wish for you that all of your tomorrows will be yesterday's dreams coming true.

So let's get started...today!

THE MOST IMPORTANT
RELATIONSHIP
YOU WILL EVER HAVE
IS THE ONE YOU WILL HAVE
WITH YOUR *SELF*.

# A New "You"
# State of Mind:
## Small Changes
## For Huge Results

# "LOVE THY SELF" —
# BE PROUD OF WHO YOU ARE

o you know what's so extraordinary about you? You're you, you're unique! And unless you have an identical twin, there isn't another person like you. That's what makes you so wonderful. If you're convinced that you're the best thing going and that you sincerely do "love thy self", then you can probably skip this chapter. But if you have any doubts whatsoever that you are the very best, read on.

Although you've heard it for years, perhaps you're not quite convinced that you should love yourself. It was probably one of the first lessons we were taught, and rightly so. The way we feel about ourselves affects every aspect of our personalities. All of our relationships, from our girlfriends to the men we date, are a reflection of what we think of ourselves. It's the number one, most important signal we send to other people. If we love and respect ourselves, we will attract people who feel the same way about us. Without self-love and self-respect, we will attract the wrong kind of people — if we attract anyone at all!

I'm sure you have also heard that you cannot really love someone else until you love yourself. Yet throughout this book I talk about the importance of putting the other person first in a relationship. It truly is a paradox that you cannot love someone else selflessly unless you love yourself. You can be a martyr or a masochist, but that's not the same as loving selflessly. For example, staying in a classic "codependent" relationship with a practicing alcoholic or drug abuser is not a sign of selfless love. Nor is it selfless to remain with an abusive partner because "I know he/

she doesn't really mean it." It's not too much of a stretch to speculate that most people who stay in codependent or abusive relationships, and don't try to do anything to improve their situation, really do *not* love themselves. Undoubtedly they are convinced they love their partner, but because they don't love themselves they don't understand the true, healthy definition of loving selflessly. You cannot give love to another if you don't love yourself first. And if you do love yourself, you won't passively stay in a relationship that makes one or both of you miserable. Your level of self-love, then, really does determine whether or not you will have happy, healthy relationships.

While most of us can accept the importance of self-love, many people have trouble taking the concept to heart. Therapists work at this all day long with their patients, hoping that at some point the patient will wake up and say, "Of course, I get it. It's simple. I can do anything I want to, I'm great, I'm wonderful, I really do like me!" That is the foundation of self-respect, self-esteem, self-worth — in short, self-love.

We hear so much about self-esteem these days, but have you ever wondered why some people have more self-esteem than others? It isn't because their mother told them every day, "You can be whatever you want to be," or because they were good ball players or had high IQs. It's because they like themselves. They may not like everything about themselves, but they love the person beneath it all. That attitude of self-assurance, self-worth and self-esteem sends signals, both verbal and non-verbal.

What about you? Do you love and respect yourself? Do you appreciate your uniqueness? Or are you grumbling, "Well, if I'm so wonderful, how come guys don't seem to realize it?" If the latter sounds more like you, chances are those guys don't realize how terrific you are because you're not quite convinced yourself. Maybe you're the type of person who is always looking in the mirror, or looking at your own life, and finding a long list of things you don't like. Under those circumstances, it's difficult to love yourself or convince someone else that you're loveable.

Unfortunately, women are often too self-critical. But think about this: Would you criticize your best friend as harshly as you do yourself? Your task is to learn to become your own best friend. Ease up on the self-criticism, and loving yourself will naturally come. Once you stop being so self-critical, you may notice a marvelous side effect: you'll stop being so critical of others too. What we fail to accept in ourselves is generally what we find so intolerable in others, and if we accept ourselves, we'll be much more tolerant of other people's imperfections.

It should be noted that loving yourself does not mean you have to love *everything* you were born with. It does mean you've learned to accept those things you're not necessarily happy with and you love yourself in spite of them. When you find Mr. Right, he's not going to be perfect, since "perfect" doesn't exist in real life. You will accept and love him for his uniqueness. The same principles you apply to accepting him apply to loving yourself. What you don't like, and cannot change, you must learn to live with and accept. This message is of such great consequence that it is often repeated throughout the book, because it applies to so many aspects of learning to love and be loved.

## Remember...

hat we fail to accept in ourselves is what we find so intolerable in others. Once we accept ourselves, we will be much more tolerant of others' shortcomings.

Some people might argue that there is too much self-love in our culture. After all, we live in a self-indulgent (some would say decadent) society where everyone is supposedly looking out for number one. The "Me Decade" has lasted much longer than ten years! Self-love, however, is not the same as self-indulgence or selfishness. You can "indulge" yourself all year round with the fanciest spa treatments, the latest techno-toys or the most expensive designer wardrobe, and still not love or even like the person you are. You can be a profoundly selfish person, always looking out for your own needs first — and still be filled with self-loathing. Self-love is something that goes much deeper than the outer trappings of our lives.

Self-love begins with embracing our uniqueness, which is difficult at best when we're very young. One of the virtues of maturity is "growing into ourselves". When we were young, most of us looked at other kids in school and wished we were like they were. Perhaps there were girls we envied because we thought they were prettier or more popular. As we grew older, however, we came to appreciate our differences, and we realized that if we set realistic goals, we could be whatever we desired to be. Just think of the young girl with curly red hair. She hated it; the kids teased her and she was miserable. As she matured, she learned how to manage her curls, lightened or highlighted her hair — and now gets compliments on her gorgeous hair! She grew into herself. Or consider the shy, rather plain girl who was the class "brain". The less academically inclined kids always made fun of her. But no one's laughing at her now that she's grown up and has won worldwide recognition for her contributions to cancer research. Without a doubt, she too grew into herself.

---

# Remember...

*hat you don't like about yourself and cannot change, you must learn to live with and accept. Self-acceptance is the key to self-love.*

---

By now, it is hoped, you have grown into yourself as well. You have learned to accept that which cannot be changed and are continuing to work on areas you can change. You have realized that almost everything you wished for when you were young is really within reach now. If you were terribly shy, you've overcome your shyness or are working on it. If you wanted to be more popular, you've discovered there are many ways of making new friends, and good ones, too! (In Chapter 35 we discuss ways to systematically expand your circle of friends.) If you wanted a fulfilling career, you've worked hard to make it happen. Hopefully you have gained confidence in your ability to make at least some of your dreams come true.

Self-love comes from within, but it can always use a boost from outside sources. Generally speaking, everyone has some good qualities — each of us is unique and we can stand on our own. But this does not mean we shouldn't constantly seek to expand our knowledge and interests and add new dimensions to our lives. It makes us more fascinating and can be lots of fun. It's like adding the frosting to an already delicious cake! Besides, it's nice to stand out from the crowd, to be a little bit more informed on issues than others are. And lest we forget, we never know who we may meet along the way. In other chapters we talk about physical activity, personality enhancement through courses and clubs, and the myriad of other opportunities that are available. Don't be afraid to explore any of these. All can boost your self-confidence, which in turn can increase your self-esteem — and as your self-esteem grows, so will your core sense of self-worth. The more interest*ed* you become, the more in-terest*ing* you become to others. Developing your interests and talents is part of developing your *self* and becoming a whole person — which will ultimately attract another whole person, providing a foundation for a healthy relationship.

Of course if you really have an issue with self-loathing, or you just don't like yourself very much, all of the classes and activities you could cram into your week won't be of much help. Consider discussing your issues with a qualified therapist or counselor; it will be well worth it.

Whatever you do, never underestimate the power of self-talk. If you tell yourself something long enough you will believe it. So instead of criticizing yourself, tell yourself that you're bright or pretty, or anything else that will help give you the self-confidence to go forward. Before long you may begin believing these things. The truth is that you can be or do just about anything you want to, as long as you believe in yourself.

Loving yourself is crucial to your happiness. If you love and respect yourself and are proud of the person you are, despite your "imperfec-tions", I guarantee that some man someday is going to look at you and decide you are the most wonderful person he has ever met. And he'll be right!

# DON'T SELL YOURSELF SHORT

ne of the most important messages of this book is that you don't have to "settle" for a life or a partner that is less than you deserve. Unfortunately, too many women sell themselves short and marry someone who is all wrong for them, perhaps because they fear they won't get another chance.

Other women pass up a successful, attractive man because for some reason they don't think they're "good enough" for him. Maybe they don't believe they're attractive enough, smart enough, or sophisticated enough for this great man. They automatically assume his standards are too high for them to live up to, so they "reject" themselves before he has a chance to make up his own mind. It is distressing to see women with this kind of defeatist attitude. They are their own worst enemy.

Why would you want to settle for a man who is less than what you deserve? Of course you want to get married, but don't you want to marry someone with whom you'll be happy? If you settle, you won't be happy and most likely you won't even be content. If, for example, you marry a man because you think he has little if any expectations of you, you might believe you're in for an easy time, but you will wake up one day knowing you made a big mistake. Either you will come to discover that he has expectations after all (which may not be at all compatible with your own), or you will become bored or disgusted with him because he expects *too little* of you and the relationship. Ideally love is unconditional, but we are all human, and we all enter relationships with expectations and needs, some of which are realistic and some of which are not.

In a healthy, loving relationship, both people learn to compromise on some of their expectations, but they also make an effort to live up to some of their partner's expectations of them. When Jack Nicholson's character said to Helen Hunt in the movie, *As Good As It Gets*, "You make me want to be a better man," she was genuinely moved. I think that's one of the things love is about — becoming better for each other. If you marry a man who has no expectations, or whose expectations are completely unrealistic or contrary to yours, sooner or later you may come to realize that you could have done better. In either case, you will be so unhappy that ultimately your marriage will end in a divorce — not because your husband changed, but because *you* did. If you refuse to sell yourself short in the first place, you won't settle for a marriage that's little more than a divorce waiting to happen.

## Remember...

*on't settle for a man who seems to expect little of you just because you assume that you won't be able to "live up to" the expectations of a more attractive man. If you do you will only be unhappy and so will he. Refuse to sell yourself short in the first place, and you won't have to settle for a life or a partner that is less than you deserve.*

The truth is that if you have self-confidence and strong convictions, you can do whatever you desire to do — and this includes finding a great husband, even if the odds don't seem to be in your favor. One of my girlfriends growing up chased her future husband all through high school and college. Everyone used to say behind her back that she was wasting her time, he'd never marry her. He was better looking than she and certainly he had better looking women pursuing him. We all felt sorry for Ellie, fearing one day he'd break her heart. She stuck by her convictions, though, and eventually he asked Ellie to marry him. That was over forty years ago, and to this day, we're still amazed that the marriage lasted that long. Ellie had the self-confidence to hang in there — and sure enough he came around.

Similarly, Nancy, the daughter of a friend of ours, started dating her future husband in college. At the time he had no idea he'd be marrying her one day, but she wanted him and she was going to do everything she could to get him. He was brilliant, and his friends all thought he'd either marry another physician-to-be like himself, or perhaps an attorney or another well educated woman. Nancy, on the other hand, was just a mediocre student who spent more time in the bars than she did in the classroom. After college, the young man moved to Philadelphia to attend medical school. Within a short time Nancy followed him there, without any promises from him that he would eventually marry her.

Nancy was smart. She went into one of the neighboring towns, rented an apartment, found herself a roommate, and before long, had made a life for herself. She found a job, enrolled in a local college for some graduate courses and even ended up taking some yoga and martial arts classes. Meanwhile, her boyfriend was so busy with medical school he had little time for anything else, certainly not enough time to go around looking to find any new girlfriends. Nancy stuck it out; she had self-confidence and the conviction that she would one day be this man's wife. She wasn't the smartest, the prettiest or the richest, but she was determined and she persevered, which is what she needed in order to get what she wanted. She could easily have sold herself short by having the attitude that she was not up to his standards, but she didn't. She continued her classes, eventually enrolled in a master's program and ended up getting a master's degree in education — not bad for a gal who was only a mediocre student and liked to party. By the way, they've been married for eight years, have three children and apparently have a wonderful marriage.

Those are only two stories of women who believed in themselves when they easily could have sold themselves short. We have all heard stories like these over and over again. There's an old saying, "She chased him until he caught her!" Well, that's been going on for a long time. This is not to imply that the women are in complete control and the men are helpless. Obviously the men must have also seen something in these women that they thought was worth hanging around for. But if the women had not had the self-confidence and determination to convince the men that they were truly special, more than likely the men never would have given them a second thought.

Whether you are about to look for a new job or a new boyfriend, do not sell yourself short. You can do anything you set your mind to, as long as you believe in yourself, believe in your ideals and have the fortitude to persevere. There is no reason for you to ever settle for less than what you deserve. ♥

# 3

# CREATE A "BETTER REALITY" FOR YOURSELF

*E*verything in life is a state of mind...a half-empty glass is always half full...when one door closes, another opens. Do these sayings sound familiar? You may want to dismiss them as clichés, but there's a reason they became clichés in the first place. Parents, teachers and psychologists use these metaphors all day long, and rightfully so, because how we perceive life determines our happiness (or lack thereof). It also tells others a lot about us, so it's important to convey the message that we're positive and upbeat!

There is much in life we can't control, and positive thinking alone won't alter the course of certain external events. It won't bring peace in the Middle East, stop global warming or solve the traffic congestion on crowded freeways. But every one of us can control how we interpret and react to what life dishes out. Our own personal state of mind about what happens has more effect on our happiness or unhappiness than the actual events themselves. We live in a world of duality — there's no doubt that both good and bad exist, but we can always choose where we focus our attention.

This is what the New Agers really meant when they said, "You create your own reality." If the reality you've created isn't to your liking, you need to realize that you have the ability to create a better one by changing your perceptions and transforming negative situations into positive ones. It takes some practice, but it's worth it, for not only will it do wonders for your romantic life, it can help your career and all your other relationships. This is not to suggest that positive thinking by itself will get you a husband (or a promotion), but it is a crucial first step.

Your perceptions of the past and the present, and your feelings about how life is treating you, become part of your persona. This is important to know, because the kind of people that you want to attract will be far more drawn to you if you think in the positive mode. Notice how good you feel when you're around people who have a bright outlook on life. It's contagious! You want to talk to them, and they make you feel good. There's plenty in life to be depressed about, but if you focus on the positive, you will lift your own spirits and those of the people around you as well.

Once you've become adept at changing your perceptions, you'll be surprised at how easy it is to transform virtually every negative situation in your life into a positive one. This is not to suggest you should look at life through rose-colored glasses, nor is it meant to diminish the severity of a physical illness or a tragedy. This is strictly about assessing a situation and choosing to see that something good can come from it. Problems arise every day, from the most serious crises to small annoyances, but you don't have to let them bring you down. Instead, you can be someone about whom others say, "She always sees the bright side, no matter what the situation is!"

Let's look at a few examples. Due to distance or heavy traffic, you have a long drive back and forth to work each day. Have you considered using that time to catch up on your "reading"? There are so many books available now in audio format that it makes coping with slow traffic almost tolerable. When you try it, don't be surprised if some days you end up wishing the traffic didn't move so quickly! The next time you're looking at new CD's, consider audio books instead. Better yet, check out all the available audio-book clubs and have the selections sent to your home. You'll always be ready for your next car ride, and you'll also have something refreshing and new to talk about — the latest book you just "read".

Here's another example. There has been an indication at work that your job may be at risk. Instead of waiting to become a "victim", you can begin the process of searching for a new job immediately. Who knows, you just may get a better job offer. (I'm not suggesting you resign prematurely, just be prepared so you're a step ahead.) Or perhaps you receive a notice that your monthly parking fees for your office building are increasing. You may want to consider car-pooling, park-and-ride buses or mass transit, if available. Not only will you be turning your situation around, you'll be saving money, and you never know who may end up sitting next to you!

Suppose your computer is out for repair, or you're waiting for a new one. Take out those photos you've been holding on to and update your picture frames. If you don't want to put the remainder of the photos into albums, organize them according to dates and put them in a photo box. Cleaning out a closet or two or reorganizing drawers are other great choices. They may seem insignificant, but because you're making them at a time when you could be angry or disgruntled, they can make a re-markable difference. Once you begin to practice these alternative choices, it will become automatic. You may not notice a difference at first, but I guarantee you other people will. Learning to look at the positive makes us happier and healthier — and more appealing to others.

Some people blame their unhappiness simply on bad luck, but that's nonsense. Positive people know that we make our own luck. Without a doubt, some people are luckier than others, but if you knew all the cir-cumstances behind their good fortune, you would probably find that most of them did have some control over the matter. Even winning the lottery is a matter of luck if there ever was one — but it does require buying a ticket! This is not to suggest that you rely on winning the lottery to turn your own luck around, but to make anything happen you have to get out there, change your routine and do things you haven't done before. You have to venture away from the comfortable you, take a risk and not be afraid to try something different.

I'm very aware that life sometimes blindsides us with tragedies, ca-tastrophes, or just plain bad luck that no amount of positive thinking can alter. The examples above are about "everyday life" situations that we all encounter in one form or another. Unfortunately, many people suffer from serious depression that makes it difficult to see the "bright side", even if there is one. However, even in the worst situation there is always a way out. There is help to be found if you seek it. If you suspect depression is your problem, an appointment with a qualified healthcare professional can help put you back on the path to a happier life. Counseling and/or medication can do wonders. There are agencies, organizations and nu-merous other resources to help with problems such as financial stress, health issues, addiction and abuse. But you have to reach out for assis-tance, and you have to believe things will get better. Even in the worst crisis, you can work on changing your perceptions and you can transform negatives into positives. In some cases, just a little outside help may do it. I'm assuming, however, that most of you reading this book are not faced with catastrophic situations or clinical depression. You are simply experiencing "divine discontent", and that can be very healthy. It's a sign that you need a change!

So what does all this have to do with finding a husband? *Everything.* When you're able to turn negatives into positives, it makes you a more confident, appealing person. This one change alone can make the difference in whether or not you find Mr. Right. The connection becomes clear when you remember that finding a husband is about you, not about the man. Altering your perceptions will change you in ways you can't even imagine — wonderful ways, making you more attractive to the sort of person you want to attract.

## Remember...

*ocus on the positive. In many instances it's not the situation that's bad or good — it's how you look at it.*

This ability to transform negatives into positives is essential to your happiness even after you have found Mr. Right. The relationship will go much more smoothly if you always try to be positive and upbeat, not just at the beginning when you're trying to impress him, but as time passes and the two of you become more serious.

Maintaining a positive attitude can be a challenge once the initial thrill of the relationship is over and you begin to discover your differences. Both of you have been independent for most, if not all, of your adult years. Chances are you're both set in your ways and neither one of you wants to change. Your attitude will have a major effect on how well your relationship develops. At least be willing to meet him halfway. Naturally, you should expect the same from him.

What do you do if he has a passion for outdoor sports and you'd rather stay inside? Instead of looking at this as a problem, look at it as an opportunity to put the principles we've been talking about into practice. If you try hard to reach out and turn what you perceive as a negative (not sharing the same interests) into a positive (the opportunity to learn about something new), you might actually find yourself enjoying his passion.

That doesn't mean you have to love hunting and fishing. But in all fairness, if he asks you to try golfing, boating or skiing, why not give it a try?

What if he lives for his football games and wants you to join him, but you just never got into football? If that's the case, then wake up! Be happy that this man wants you to be with him. Bring along a book or a magazine, or use that time to make out your "to-do" lists for the coming week. The two of you get to be together, he's happy, and you even accomplish something. Do you see the picture? You've turned a potential negative into a positive, you've negotiated — which is the most valuable "tool" for any relationship — and it wasn't terribly painful. (Just be thankful that football season isn't twelve months long!) In turn, you will see that this positive approach will benefit you in the long run. Your Mr. Right won't have to think too hard before he agrees to do something that pleases you. After all, aren't you there for him?

## Remember...

 *on't automatically dismiss his interests or passions just because you don't share them. It's easy to transform this potentially negative situation into a positive one if you think of it as an opportunity to learn about something new. Who knows, you might become as much of an enthusiast as he. But even if that doesn't happen, you're still spending time together, and he will appreciate your efforts.*

Relationships are not about you alone — they're about the two of you together. To build the foundation for a relationship, you need to continue to have the desire to be together, sharing different experiences. Of course, that should not be at the expense of pursuing your own interests. But your time together can't just be a night or two a week of dinner, a movie or sex. It's important to show enthusiasm, interest in and support for each other. Even when you disagree about what you want to do, think of how you can turn that situation into something positive, and not only will you avoid a fight, but your relationship will be stronger than ever. Together with love and respect, you need to be able to communicate, negotiate and compromise. If you can do those well, you have the formula for a long, happy marriage. Don't wait for Mr. Right to practice on. Begin it *now*, because this formula works for all relationships.

Changing your perceptions is a small step towards building a new life. It will lead to larger steps and will make finding a husband, as well as every other facet of your life, easier and a lot more enjoyable. Learning to transform negatives into positives, whether on the job, on the road to matrimony, or just living life in general, is the best gift you can give to yourself and to the people around you. ♥

# CHANGE YOUR ATTITUDE
# AND YOUR HABITS

ttitude. No doubt about it, attitude has received a lot of attention in the past few years. These days, the very word *attitude* is all but synonymous with defiance or cockiness. For many years, "attitude" was a catch-all concept used by teachers and bosses alike, often in a negative manner. "I don't like your attitude, Missy!" "Mary's organizational skills are excellent but she needs to work on improving her attitude." And, of course, the self-help gurus have been telling us for decades that we need to have a positive attitude. By this point in your life, you may be so sick of hearing about attitude that the very word makes you want to head off to the nearest bar for their "attitude adjustment hour"!

Throughout this book we talk about change and how important it is to try something new if what you've been doing hasn't been working — and we can't talk about change without talking about attitude. I realize that sometimes change seems like a formidable task, especially if you've been doing things a certain way for many years. But let's face it, you really are ready for changes in your life, as small as they may be, or you wouldn't be reading this book. No one expects you to make major changes overnight. Take it one step at a time by making small changes.

In Chapter 3 we talk about altering your perceptions and transforming negatives into positives, which are the first steps to changing your life. Your perception of a situation, and how you react to it, have more of an effect on your happiness than does the actual situation. But there's more to making changes than just changing your perceptions. You also have to work on — yes, you guessed it — your attitude. Although they are related, perception and attitude are two different things. Your attitude is actually the outward reflection of your perceptions. That's what others see, and this is why it's so important that you project a positive attitude.

In fact, it might be argued that the most important change you can make to alter the direction of your life is to change your attitude. Attitude is everything in life — it affects us professionally as well as socially. And if you're arguing that you still don't have a social life, hang on, that's about to change.

As I've said before, everything is a state of mind. Many years ago I attended a lecture on identifying Type A and Type B personalities. The message in the end was that if you are not happy with your type of personality, you can change. I recall leaving the lecture saying, "How can people change? They are what they are!" Well, live and learn! Today we're all smarter and we know people *can* change — if they want to. They can even change their personality "type".

---

# Remember...

on't try to make large, sweeping changes in your life all at once. That's too intimidating for anyone. A series of small, simple changes, one step at a time, is the key to success.

---

Along with changing your attitude — the outward manifestation of your perceptions — you will almost certainly want to work on changing some of your habits. NBC's *Today Show* weatherman Al Roker decided he was tired of being overweight and had a gastronomic bypass. In his interviews, however, he said the surgery alone wasn't totally responsible for his losing all the weight. He still had to alter his eating habits and he could no longer be sedentary. He started an exercise routine almost immediately after his surgery, and continues to exercise daily. He said that only the combination of sensible eating and exercise could have produced such wonderful results. Before he changed his habits, however, he first had to change his attitude.

Mr. Roker's example is rather extreme, but all of us can make even the most profound changes if our desire to change is strong enough. Once you've begun to change your perceptions and your attitude, you need to start changing your actions, which, as Al Roker discovered, probably means getting rid of some bad habits and developing good ones to take their place. In fact, the best way to stop a bad habit is not just to stop it, but to *replace* it with better ones.

Consider, for example, someone who is trying to give up smoking. It isn't only the craving for nicotine that makes them smoke, although that's an undeniably powerful addiction, as nicotine is a drug that affects virtually every part of the body. It's also the physical movement of the hands, fingers and cigarette to the mouth — the whole scenario of smoking. Just taking the cigarette out and lighting it provides a satisfaction to the smoker. So when a smoker quits, the entire process is missed, not just the actual inhaling of the lit cigarette. There has to be a pretty powerful incentive to give up all of these things. The smoker has to want freedom from the habit more than he or she wants the nicotine rush and the entire experience of smoking. Developing other pleasurable habits to take the place of smoking will make it much easier to become and remain a nonsmoker.

When people with an incurable sweet tooth want to lose weight, they have to want the weight loss more than the taste of that Snickers Bar. They have to want to lose weight more than they desire the cool feel of ice cream in their mouth every night at ten o'clock. They know they have to eliminate those wonderful "comfort foods" that are evil to dieters. Going to the freezer, scooping out the ice cream, putting on a topping, then sitting down in front of the television...well, what isn't wonderful about that? It's good and satisfying to the soul as well as the taste buds, but it's not on the new healthy eating plan. Again, the desire to change has to be *greater* than the satisfaction felt when indulging in old habits.

It is easy to see why many people fail at dieting. Next to alcohol, nicotine and other drugs, food is without a doubt one of the most powerful addictions. Advertisers spend millions of dollars touting weight-loss programs, and the public is there listening, wishing, hoping that maybe this one will work. From organizations to individually prepared meals, from special frozen foods to protein drinks, there will always be opportunists promoting something new and different. When there isn't anything new on the market, they return to the old commercials and just refresh them with a beautiful person who has a to-die-for body. People spend millions of dollars, believing what they hear and see on television. Sure, some diets work — for a while anyway — but the only way to lose weight and to keep it off is to change your eating and exercise habits.

That is the same formula for life, for anything we want to change. It takes the same energy to do something one way as another. It's just a matter of getting used to a different way. Of course it won't be easy in the beginning — it's uncomfortable, unfamiliar and perhaps less satisfying, but if you can keep drawing on the strength of your desire to change, remembering what you really want, you will begin to see changes. The first few days are the most difficult, because everything you are doing is foreign to you, and old habits die hard. But we are human, with large brains and the ability to change if our desire is great enough. It all begins with a change in attitude.                    ❤

---

## Remember...

*Although change is difficult and often uncomfortable at first, if you can keep drawing on the strength of your desire to change, and a vision of what you really want, you will begin to see changes. It will get much easier as time goes by.*

---

# LOVE YOUR BODY

What can you do to improve yourself physically? In other chapters we discuss the emotional, behavioral and environmental changes you may need to make, but don't forget that your physical self is also part of who you are. When you feel comfortable with your body it's much easier to radiate the confidence that will attract men. This has nothing to do with beauty; a self-confident woman exudes something men love! They will be drawn to you, perhaps without even realizing why.

So just how comfortable *are* you with your physical self? Do you love your body unconditionally, or does the very question make you cringe? Or do you fall somewhere in between those two extremes? It doesn't matter how old or how young you are, if you're a woman in our culture, you have probably struggled with your body image at one time or another. Maybe you think your thighs are too big or your breasts are too small, or perhaps you fret over cellulite or wrinkles. Your body-image issues may be a minor annoyance, or you may have let them eat away at your self-confidence, even to the point of preventing you from getting close to a man.

Many women look in the mirror and instead of seeing their body as the marvelous, miraculous instrument it really is, they see a long list of flaws that need "fixing" with crash diets, rigorous exercise, expensive beauty treatments or even painful cosmetic surgery. Martha Beck, author of *The Joy Diet*, wrote about this topic in O Magazine. For the first half of her life she set about "breaking" her body as one might break a horse, subjecting it to all sorts of discipline in order to make it conform to the cultural ideal of beauty. She writes, "I was chronically ill before it occurred to me that anyone caught treating a beast of burden the way I treated myself would be arrested for cruelty to animals." Harsh words, but not too much of an exaggeration.

What Beck learned to do was listen to her body in much the same way that the famous horse trainer Monty Roberts, known as the "Horse Whisperer", learned to listen to horses. She began to take a kinder, gentler approach to her body — listening with care, interpreting its signals and treating it with respect. Instead of "punishing" it, she learned to praise it. As a result she became more comfortable with her physical self and healthier as well. In other words, she learned to love her body.

You can learn to love your body too, by using the same simple but powerful technique we've discussed in other chapters — focusing on the positive. Instead of criticizing your flaws, find something to praise. Learn to appreciate your body for all of the wonderful things it can do. More than likely this won't come naturally at first, but practice! Instead of cursing your thighs for being flabby, praise your legs for being strong and sturdy, allowing you to run up a flight of stairs or walk out to the mail box. Rather than moaning about your crow's feet, praise your miraculous eyes that let you take in the beauty of the world (even if you do need glasses or contacts to see it clearly). You may be heavy, but have pretty hands, or you may be blessed with strong, healthy finger nails. Every time you begin to criticize your body or face, stop and turn your thoughts around. If you continually give yourself positive reinforcement, you may begin to see your physical self in a new light.

---

## Remember...

 ou can learn to love your body by focusing on the wonderful things it can do, rather than on real or imagined "flaws". Loving your body unconditionally is part of loving yourself — and it all adds up to making you much more attractive to Mr. Right.

---

Loving your body does not mean there's something wrong with wanting to refine, enhance or improve it. There's always room for improvement. Even the smallest change for the better will work wonders for your morale. As long as your underlying motive is self-love rather than self-loathing, and as long as you don't do anything that will compromise your physical or emotional health, there's absolutely nothing wrong with making an effort to become fitter and more attractive. Even cosmetic surgery is fine as long as your motivations are right and your expectations are realistic.

There is much you can do to improve your health, enhance your looks and boost your morale without resorting to plastic surgery, and that's what the rest of this chapter is about. This is not a diet, exercise or beauty book, but I want to share a few thoughts on these subjects.

Let's get the obvious issue out of the way first. If you're overweight, I am sorry to have to be the one to inform you of this, but you are no longer allowed to use that as an excuse for still being single. Just go to the malls and look at all the heavy women who are married and have families. You can't help but think to yourself, *hmmm, there really is a match for everyone...* and there is! People can come up with all sorts of reasons for not finding a mate, but most of these are just excuses. The truth is that not all men like skinny women, and many overweight women were that way before they got married. I can't say it too many times: If you want to marry, you can marry, and your size and shape are not the reason you haven't found a "keeper".

Unfortunately, it is a fact that most women are not happy with their weight. After all, we live in a society that blasts us with the message that thin is in and the thinner the better. That's why we're seeing eating disorders in girls as young as eight or nine. However, we also live in a society where obesity has reached an all-time high, and with obesity comes a host of other health problems. So just because you love your body, and just because many overweight women have found their Mr. Right, this doesn't mean you should give up your efforts to manage your weight, or lose weight if your extra pounds are compromising your health. (It should be noted that not all overweight people are unhealthy, and some are very fit; many other factors besides weight determine health.)

If you do decide to embark on your weight-management routine, do it for a positive reason rather than a negative one. It's also important that you do it for *you*, not for your mother, your best friend or that ex-boyfriend who was always nagging you to lose weight. Needless to say, don't begin any weight-management program, whether it is an eating plan, an exercise routine or both, unless you've consulted with a qualified healthcare practitioner first and have had a thorough checkup.

If you want to lose a little weight and are finding it difficult, take heart. A few small modifications to your diet and activity level can quickly add up to a five-pound loss. That might not seem like much, but just pick up a five-pound weight and you'll see it's not light! Six to eight pounds is a dress size, so if you can lose just five pounds, your clothes will fit better and you will feel better.

The diet gurus know best: Reduce calories and increase exercise, and you will lose weight. "Yeah, right," you may be saying. "I've tried that and it just doesn't work!" I know that decreasing your intake and increasing your output is sometimes more difficult than it sounds, and I don't want to seem as if I am over-simplifying. Furthermore, if you are seriously overweight or obese, and have sincerely tried and failed with a variety of reduced-calorie/increased-exercise plans, please seek medical help. Today there are many fine and compassionate physicians who specialize in weight management, and every day science is learning exciting new things about the causes of and treatments for obesity. Don't be afraid to seek help; it could save your life.

Most people, however, can achieve pleasing results by watching calories and increasing physical activity. Finding exactly what works for you is the trick. It's not always easy because there is so much confusing and conflicting information out there. For example, for decades the experts have argued back and forth about which element is most important to weight management; is it exercise or diet? Or are both equally important? Some say diet, some exercise, but the vast majority of weight-loss programs today include both an exercise and a diet plan. I'm no expert, but common sense tells you if you burn up more calories than you take in, you're going to lose weight. Whatever you do, set small attainable goals so you won't be discouraged.

It is far beyond the scope of this book to recommend any eating plan or exercise regimen. The real message here is that you need to do *something*. Even if you are satisfied with your weight, a balanced diet and the right amount of physical activity are important to help you maintain that weight. If you're not satisfied with your weight, or anything else about your body, you have the power to change it. But *you* have to make the effort, because nobody else is going to do it for you!

Before we leave the topic of health and beauty, don't forget that your hands, feet and nails are part of the person you are, an extension of yourself. If you don't take the time to make your hands and feet look nice, it says you're lazy about yourself and you don't care. Therefore, manicures and pedicures are a must. They are really just part of good grooming. If you can't afford to have them done professionally, do them yourself. It's not that difficult.

As a matter of fact, feet can be very sexy, and not just to foot fetishists. Millions of dollars are spent yearly on products to enhance them, but it is unnecessary to buy expensive products in order to have nice feet. Have you ever wondered how some women can have such pretty feet? Unless they sit still all day and do little or no walking or standing, and never wear shoes, those women aren't sharing their secrets with you. You can be quite sure they treat themselves to regular pedicures and perhaps other procedures as well. The good news is that you can have pretty feet too, even if yours are misshapen and you think they're ugly. By the way, if you think the problems with your feet are unusual and you're embarrassed to have a pedicure, trust me — manicurists and pedicurists have seen it all. There is nothing to be embarrassed about.

Maybe you're convinced you need more than a pedicure to get your feet in shape. One of the hottest new trends in plastic surgery today is reconstruction of the feet and toes, for correcting hammertoes, removing bunions or simply making feet pretty. If you have been hiding your feet because you are ashamed of them, you may not have to any longer. A consultation with a podiatrist or an orthopedist will bring you up to date on all the advances that have been made in foot surgery. There are many different procedures available, and they may be more affordable than you think.

Please note that, as in many areas of health and beauty, there are people who are less qualified than others. Be sure you get recommendations from patients who have used the doctors you may be considering. There have been incidents where the doctors were not properly trained in the surgery they were performing. Carefully check them before you agree to have any kind of surgery — on your feet or anywhere else.

Once you get your feet in relatively good shape, it doesn't take much to keep them looking nice. The best spa pedicurists will tell you there's only one way to have pretty, soft feet; the dead skin has to be removed. That's where a pumice stone can work miracles. For those of you who are unfamiliar with a pumice stone, they are those rough stones, made from volcanic rock, that you rub on the bottoms of your feet to remove the hard skin. Tweezer Man ® makes a pretty, hand-held pumice stone that is awesome. It's fairly expensive but well worth the money. Put it in the bathroom or on your night table, and use it every night before you go to bed; it takes just a few minutes. Then rub your feet with a good foot cream. You will notice a difference immediately, and in no time you will have feet that feel like a baby's. You will never snag another pair of hose, and when you go bare-legged and wear open-toed shoes or sandals, your feet will always look great! And remember, someday someone may be asking you for a foot massage...and afterwards, you won't hesitate to say, "It's my turn!"

Few of us have bodies like the models in the *Sports Illustrated* swimsuit calendar or the *Victoria's Secret* catalogue. But they are our bodies, and we can always improve parts of them. We can do a lot to make them fit and healthy. Most importantly of all, we can learn to love them unconditionally. If we love our bodies, Mr. Right almost certainly will too. 💜

# 6

# LEARN FROM YOUR DATING HISTORY, BUT REMEMBER THAT IT'S "HISTORY"

t's often been said that those who don't learn from history repeat it. That's true, but it's also possible to spend too much time dwelling on the past. If you are going to find happiness, you need to find a happy medium. You can look at your past mistakes as lessons to keep from repeating them, but don't make the even bigger mistake of using your past as a blueprint for the future. Even the most persistent patterns can be changed.

Let's take a quick glance back at your dating history — but only to learn from it, not to dwell on it. Very simply, if you've been dwelling on the past, it's time to stop. Fixating on the past accomplishes nothing and does little to make you feel good. I am sure you've relived your relationships — especially those you would like to forget about — over and over again, wondering what went wrong. You can easily drive yourself crazy doing this, and it won't undo the past.

A terrific, little-known movie called *Seven Girlfriends* tells the tale of a man in his mid-thirties who has reached a crisis point. Plagued by his inability to maintain a successful relationship, he decides to go back and visit several old girlfriends, find out what went wrong, and possibly "fix" the mistakes he made. As you can imagine, things don't turn out at all the way our hero had hoped. He doesn't really find out much about what he did wrong, and he certainly doesn't undo his past mistakes. He does receive a few difficult and embarrassing lessons along the way, and yes, somehow ends up finding love anyway, but not at all in the way he had planned.

In reality, few of us are able to actually go back and confront our past that way, and probably many of us wouldn't want to. A better strategy is to make up your mind to make peace with your past. This isn't always easy, but you can do it. Do not feel bad or beat yourself up about anything you did (or failed to do), or the decisions you made. At the time you thought it was right or you wouldn't have done it. If you did something and knew it was wrong at the time, but did it anyway, you still don't need to beat yourself up. Just recognize that you need to listen to your inner voice and exercise better judgment in the future.

What if you have little or no dating history? Believe it or not, you're not alone. More women and men than you might imagine have rarely if ever dated — and it doesn't mean they are gay, unattractive to the opposite sex, or socially dysfunctional. Often it just means their priorities had been on other things besides their social lives. Perhaps this describes you. You may have been concentrating on your education or your career, and you probably never had the opportunity to meet anyone with whom you really connected. Or perhaps you weren't sending out the right message to the men you met, or weren't accurately reading the messages the men were sending to you. (Learning to send and read messages and "signals" is a vital part of successful relationships, and is discussed elsewhere in this book.) Whatever the reason for the brevity of your dating history, you need to stop dwelling on it. Why waste time obsessing over what hasn't happened, especially when you have the power to *make* it happen?

Some of you with short dating histories may nevertheless have had someone special in your life at one point. For one reason or another, the relationship didn't last, and you may still be questioning, "What went wrong?" No doubt you've made fewer mistakes than the women with longer dating histories, but you still may be asking yourself, "Did I do something wrong?" "What could I have done differently?" Even if you feel you did nothing wrong — at least not so wrong that you let some great man slip through your fingers — it's pretty hard not to doubt yourself.

If you did have a special relationship that failed, don't spend time torturing yourself about what you could have done differently. Just tell yourself it wasn't "meant to be." For various reasons, people are sometimes attracted to the wrong people. It happens to everyone, but perhaps it's just taken you a little longer to get over it. (On the other hand, if you are one of those people who are repeatedly attracted to the "wrong type", you need to become aware of this and work on breaking this negative pattern. We'll talk about that in Chapter 40.)

Dwelling on past relationships, whether sweet or bitter, can compromise your chances with any potential Mr. Right you meet. Bringing your past into a present relationship is one of the worst mistakes you can make. That nice guy you just met may very well be as terrific as the demigod who left you years ago, but you'll never see him for the person he is if you're still obsessed with Mr. Wonderful. Similarly, the jerk who hurt you years ago isn't the man sitting across from you now, but the latter will never have a chance if you are so caught up in past hurts that you take it out on every man you meet.

I know it's sometimes hard to let go of your past, but you have to do it if you ever want to enjoy your life. In fact the main problem with dwelling on the past, particularly on a past failed relationship, is that it keeps you from *having* a life. When I was growing up, our family had two female friends who had never married. Today there are many more single women at every age, but years ago it wasn't as common. Both women were intelligent and well-read, and were savvy in business. I cannot remember their being around my father and not talking about the stock market. That too was unusual in those days.

As successful as they were in their business lives, their personal lives were a different story. One of the women, Barbara, or Aunt "B", as we called her, had been my mother's girlfriend since they were young girls. She came to visit us every summer, and every summer my mother and she would have the same conversations. Nothing seemed to change because Aunt B lived in the past, so she never had any new stories. I suppose because she was unmarried and never dated, she must have felt the need to talk about her "old boyfriends", but the truth of the matter was that these men had been in her life when she was eighteen or twenty. She spoke about them as if she had seen them yesterday, when in fact she hadn't seen them for forty or fifty years. There was one man in particular that she never failed to talk about. She said he had been madly in love with her and wanted to marry her, but she just didn't love him. She never would say his name.

Aunt B never did marry, and the last time my mother saw her, she had the beginnings of dementia. She again repeated the stories, but since her memory was fading, she forgot to fudge some of the facts. When she invariably mentioned the man who had loved her so passionately, my mother once again asked who it was and the truth came out at last. "You remember him, it was Jack!" said Aunt B. Actually, Jack had dated her when she was seventeen, but of course that relationship had not lasted and Jack had been married to someone else his entire adult life. In fact he was our uncle, my mother's brother. Poor Aunt B had no life — she lived in the past obsessed by a "grand romance" that was grand only in her own mind.

And what about that other unmarried female friend I mentioned? Her name was Mary, and I'll share her story in another chapter. For now I'll just say that unlike Aunt B, Mary lived for today instead of dwelling on the past — and she really did find her Mr. Right later in life!

And so can you, and you don't have to wait until "later". But you have to get over your past in order to create your future. No matter how much or how little "history" you have, your task is to let it go. What we can't change, we must accept and go on from there. There is no other way to look at life. We cannot rewrite history (though poor Aunt B surely did try).

What we do have some control over is the present and the future — the things we can do today or tomorrow. Of course, we don't quite have the measure of control depicted in the TV show *Early Edition*, in which the Good Samaritan saw the headlines in the newspaper a day beforehand and was able to prevent a tragedy — in other words, rewrite the future. Maybe it would be nice if we could all do that, but nevertheless, there is much we *can* control. Those things we can control are what this book is all about. The mindset we create in the present can affect our future.

The next time you start obsessing about all the things you did wrong, or agonizing over what you *haven't* done…**STOP!** Remember that your future is not dependent on some dating "credit bureau" that will deny you your Mr. Right just because you have a "bad history" or "no history". Fortunately, love doesn't work that way. The only person who has the power to deny you happiness is you, but you also have the power to grant yourself happiness. After all, you deserve it. So what if you made mistakes yesterday? You can't change what happened, and as long as you are willing to try something different *today*, you are putting yourself onto a positive track. Now is the time to acknowledge your past, learn from it, and then say goodbye to it. The past has passed — it's gone, history. We're going to focus on now, the present — and the future.

---

## Remember.....

 o not dwell on the past. What you did wasn't wrong, it just didn't work! You cannot change what happened, but as long as you are willing to try something different today, you are putting yourself on a positive track.

---

# DROP YOUR BAGGAGE —
## AND DISCOVER THE JOYS OF
## "TRAVELING LIGHT"

n Chapter 8 we talk about physical clutter, but here we're going to tackle emotional clutter or "baggage", as it is commonly called. Everyone has baggage, so why not look around and see if you can discard some? The less you carry around, the happier you will be — and I guarantee you will be much more appealing to men.

The airlines announced after September 11, 2001 that passengers would have to reduce the amount of luggage they carried on board the planes and security would become much tighter. People adjusted. Traveling became more of a hassle, but nevertheless we adapted. We either packed differently or just left some things behind. That's what is so wonderful about people — we adjust to change. Change is good, and the more flexible we are, the more easily we adapt.

If you're carrying around a lot of baggage from your past, you need to drop it. In other words...lighten up! Lightening up can involve only minor adjustments in your beliefs and attitudes, or it can mean a major overhaul in your thinking. It's not always easy, and I'm not pretending it is. Particularly if you've had many disappointing dates and relationships, it's understandable if you've acquired a hard edge. Who wouldn't have? But you need to shed the hardness a bit and try to be a little more easygoing. Walls that are created as protection all too easily become the walls that keep people out.

Part of lightening up is the ability to laugh at yourself, but many people don't know how to do this. They take life too seriously, and they take themselves *much* too seriously. If they make a mistake they're mortified. We all make mistakes, and we're all occasionally clumsy or awkward, because we're all human. When we mess up we have a choice: We can either berate ourselves or laugh at ourselves. People who know how to enjoy a good laugh at their own expense generally find life much more enjoyable than the humor-impaired. They're also a lot more fun to be around!

---

# Remember...

 alls that are created as protection all too easily become the walls that keep people out. If you've acquired a hard "edge" due to past dating experiences, you need to do whatever is necessary to shed it.

---

As you'll read in Chapter 35, we should always be increasing our circle of friends and acquaintances. The benefits go beyond our imagination, since we never know who or what we may encounter as a result of those new relationships. Occasionally these acquaintances develop into a new "best friend". That's how Diana came into my life. My husband and I were on a cruise a few years ago and before the ship ever departed, we had met and become friends. Diana's early dating history typifies what can happen to women when they approach the dating scene laden with baggage. In Diana's case, that baggage resulted in her continually being attracted to the wrong kind of man.

Diana had grown up thinking she had to marry either a physician or an attorney. Although she didn't realize it for many years, the men she dated in those professions made her angry. The doctors made her feel as if she knew very little, especially in the field of medicine, which in fact she didn't know since she'd hated biology and chemistry. Attorneys made her angry too, and after having dated one for over two years, she realized she could never date another attorney because if she ever married one, they'd spend their entire married life fighting, or she would always feel as if she were on trial. Yet she could not seem to let go of her obsession with doctors and lawyers, and she had one unhappy relationship after another.

She finally moved away and took a sabbatical from dating. When she was ready to begin going out again, she had enough sense to readjust her thinking. Maybe there were some good single physicians and attorneys out there, but the thought of them instantly made her angry, and she knew she had to get away from them — she had to drop that baggage — in order to reveal the fun-loving, lighthearted person she really was. Today she blames her mother for her former fixation, because Mom always told her she had to marry a doctor or a lawyer. When she tells me that, I laugh. Maybe her mother was partially responsible — our parents definitely help pack those "suitcases" when we're younger. But once we've grown up, we get to decide what to keep and what to discard. Blaming Mom and Dad won't get us anywhere. In any case, Diana took the time to reevaluate her ideas about what she was looking for in a husband. Soon after she did, she began dating people who were entirely different from the lawyers and doctors in her past. After a couple of years, she met a terrific guy, a computer professional to whom she has been married for sixteen wonderful years. They have two children and a great marriage.

We carry other kinds of baggage besides our past dating histories or our preconceived notions about the type of man we "have" to date. Just about any negative attitude or behavior is baggage. Envy is one example. As an adult I have come to the conclusion that some people are just inherently more envious than others. Envy is unhealthy and does nothing to make your life better. Being envious of your old girlfriends who are married and have beautiful families will not get you married. Being envious of the co-worker who is less qualified than you but earns more money will not get you a raise. Things always happen for a reason. Your girlfriends probably had different priorities than you. Your co-worker could have more seniority than you have, or someone just gave her a break that you did not get, or perhaps she was just in the right place at the right time. Whatever the reasons are, let them be. Don't hold grudges and don't let them eat away at you. Go on with your life, because everyone's time comes. Yours will come sooner if you do not fall prey to self-destructive emotions such as envy. (In case you're still not convinced, read Chapter 25.)

Conceit is another form of baggage; I suppose you could say it is the other side of low self-esteem. There are plenty of single women who fit this description — they just seem to think they're better than everyone else. The attitude could stem from their education, their income, even their family background, but something has given them a feeling of exaggerated self-worth. Some of these women are true narcissists. I'm sure you are not like this at all, but if you see anything of yourself in these descriptions, it's definitely time to drop that baggage. Don't let your sense of "self" be so dependent upon superficial criteria. To put it bluntly, that advanced degree or blueblood family tree hasn't landed you a husband to date, so why not try to show who you really are beneath all those impeccable credentials? Drop the veil and be the nice, caring woman you really are. This will impress a potential Mr. Right far more than your pedigree. If you have any doubts, just look at the image of the "girl next door" who isn't rich, gifted or brilliant —just an all around great gal who feels comfortable with everyone.

Self-centeredness is yet another form of baggage. We all have our selfish or self-centered moments, but if you're always focused on your own wants and needs, you're probably going to have a hard time attracting another person. You have lots to give, but if you're completely consumed with "I...Me...My..." the other person will never know. When you meet a prospect show interest in him, and remember that people like to talk about themselves. We'll go into more detail about that in other chapters.

I believe that neediness is a type of baggage too. These days there are lots of single women who are "high-maintenance". Most of us think of a "high maintenance" woman as being materially demanding, and of course there are many who fit that description — they're more focused on what is in a man's bank account than what's in his heart. Then there are those "frou-frou" women who need constant pampering and can't seem to do anything for themselves. What I'm talking about here, however, are women who are *emotionally* demanding. Perhaps without realizing it, these women are looking for a man to fulfill all of their emotional needs. Their neediness comes across in all of their words and actions, and most men hate it. To many men, an emotionally needy woman is even more frightening than a gold digger. Certainly you want a partner who will be a lover, a companion and a best friend, and who will meet many of your needs. But if you look to a man to make you emotionally complete, or to be your *only* friend, you will be disappointed. It isn't fair to expect another individual to be your "everything". Even though that notion may sound romantic, it just doesn't work in the real world.

Sometimes women are emotionally needy when they're rebounding from a relationship, and the condition is temporary. But some women are chronically needy. If you think you are one of these women, it's very important that you work on discarding that "baggage". Ask yourself why you're so needy. Men are not naturally drawn to a woman with such great needs. Why would they be, when there are so many "lower-maintenance" women around? Just remember the acronym "KISS" ("Keep it simple, stupid!"). Lighten up and try to be a little more easygoing.

If nothing else works, try reversing the roles. (By the way, this is a handy tool to use with other negative traits as well — it can be very effective.) Simply ask yourself if you would want to be in a relationship with a man whose needs are so great. Probably not! If you're in a relationship with a man who thinks you are too needy or too demanding, consider the possibility that he is right. Then think about this: If he walked out the door and began dating your best friend tomorrow, wouldn't you wish for the opportunity to behave a little differently? Do something about your neediness now; it's easier than suffering rejection and loneliness later. And remember, there's nothing wrong with seeking professional help if you can't do it yourself.

Well, you get the idea. There are probably as many kinds of emotional baggage as there are brands of luggage. It's time to let go of all that unnecessary matter and start traveling lighter. You'll get where you're going a lot faster.

When you meet a man for the first time, whether on the phone, on the Internet or in person, think about what you're going to say *before* you talk to him. Men do not want to hear about your past bad experiences. More than likely they already assume you're single and tired of the hopeless dating scene. They know what the score is from all the other women they've dated. After all, unless they are recently divorced or widowed, they have been dating a long time as well. If all you can talk about is your unhappy past, that's a clear indication you're still stuck. There are plenty of positive things to talk about, and if you've made an effort to expand your horizons, you won't run out of things to say. (And remember, when in doubt you can always ask a man questions about himself.)

Also keep in mind that many, if not most, of the women that your Mr. Prospect has been dating are also carrying a lot of baggage. Many single women become desperate over the years. Time is passing quickly, and they aren't any closer to marriage than they were ten years ago. That alone is depressing. Men can sense that anxiety, and it's not exactly a turn-on for them. But you are going to be *different* from all of those other women!

If you find yourself feeling negative, depressed or desperate, stop before you pick up the phone or go out to meet someone. Put a smile on your face and rehearse what you're going to say, then think about it and practice it. What if you suddenly get a phone call from an old friend that you haven't spoken to in ages? Your voice would immediately show excitement, happiness and pleasure. So why not transfer some of that lightness to your voice all the time? Remember, what you are aiming for is to be entirely different than all those other single women this particular man may have been dating. You are going to be you — a refreshing and wonderful woman who's content and happy and living in the present, not the past. If he doesn't want to get to get to know you, it's his loss.

---

## Remember...

*hen you're meeting or talking to a prospect for the first time, it's particularly important that you not bring your baggage with you. Don't hit him with your entire dating history or with anything negative. Remember he's probably tired of dating baggage-laden women, so show him you are different!*

---

After the initial contact with a prospect, if he asks you about your dating history, you can be honest without going into too much detail. Everyone likes to know the dating history of the people they're going out with (particularly now that "safe sex" is a paramount concern), but believe me when I tell you that there's little to gain by complaining about your disappointing experiences. Once you've been dating someone for a while, you can begin to talk about some old relationships, as long as you don't dwell on them, and as long as the subject comes up naturally in the course of the conversation. However, it's much better if you put those old relationships to rest and bury them, particularly if most have been "duds". Why shouldn't your new prospect think there are many good men that have tried to win you over, but you just didn't think you had met Mr. Right yet? Looking at it this way will make you much more appealing to him, and will make you feel a lot better about yourself. When talking about your past, it is always best to err on the side of discretion, but if you must say something about your past lovers, say something positive!

Not too long ago, I met a woman who had recently married for the first time at the age of forty-six. She was attractive, bright, and personable, and was in really great shape. I couldn't figure out why she had stayed single for so long. She didn't seem to be overly consumed with her career, she had a pleasant personality, and I thought many men would have found her appealing. Without my asking, she offered an excuse about why she hadn't yet married. She told me there had been plenty of good men who wanted to marry her, but she didn't think she had met Mr. Right, until she met her husband a year earlier. She continued her story, telling me that her husband had indeed been worth waiting for and she was only sorry they hadn't met earlier in life. I haven't a clue whether or not she told me the truth about her dating history, but it sounded believable, it made her look good and who knows, it may have been true!

No one needs to know the truth about your dating history but you. Certainly you don't want to lie or exaggerate, nor do you want to volunteer a lot of background information to a man you've just met, but sooner or later he's probably going to ask. Be prepared with a "positive spin" on your history; you'll look good to him and feel better about yourself.

Whenever you're about to meet someone new, whether in person, online, or on the phone, put on your best smile and try to be upbeat and refreshing. If you're feeling depressed, stay home and avoid getting on the phone with anyone new. You have to psych yourself up to meet others. If you just can't manage to do that, stay home and "recharge". When you are ready to venture out again, literally or virtually, leave your baggage at home.

---

## Remember...

 o one needs to know the whole truth about your dating history except you. Of course, if you're dating someone he'll want to know about your past sooner or later. Don't lie or exaggerate, but be prepared with a positive "spin" on your history. You'll look good to him and feel better about yourself.

---

I'll admit that dropping baggage can sometimes be a challenge. It might not be so difficult for those who are relatively young and haven't had all that many life experiences yet. In fact, it could be argued that the lack of baggage is one trait that makes younger women so appealing to many men. Don't let that discourage you if you're not on the younger side. Not all single men are looking for younger women. In fact, many men find a woman more interesting if she has a lot of experience. It's how you use your experience that counts. It is important to put the past in perspective and live for today. Continue to remind yourself that what was, *was*. Yes, we are what we are because of all we've experienced — but we don't have to wear it. So keep conversations light and happy, be yourself and smile! Think of it this way: If you're not loaded down with baggage, when you meet Mr. Right you will be able to welcome him with open arms. Learn the pleasure of traveling light, and before you know it, you won't be traveling alone. ♥

# RE-FEATHER YOUR NEST
## (CHANGE, LIKE CHARITY,
## BEGINS AT HOME)

Your home is an extension of your self, and for better or worse, it tells people a lot about you and your life. It also reflects, and influences, how you feel about yourself. Making small improvements in your home environment will boost your morale along with your self-confidence. Think of it as another one of the small changes for big results that we discuss throughout this book.

Your home should always be prepared for company. That doesn't mean living as if it is going to be featured in a lifestyle magazine; it just means your home should reflect a life with some semblance of order. There are extremes on both ends of the spectrum. Some people exist in total disorder, and some live with so much order that their home looks as though no one is living there. Most of us live somewhere in the "middle of the road" — and that's perfectly okay. There are efficiency experts and psychologists who advise people on how to remove clutter from their lives and get organized, and perhaps in another lifetime, I'll be able to live exactly the way these experts advise. For now, though, I just try to live my life as most people do, with as much order as I can manage. It really is much easier than living in disorder.

If your home environment is leaning precariously towards the "disorder" end of the scale, you definitely need to take action. It is not mentally or physically healthy to live in a cluttered home or climb into a cluttered car. Clutter is a neon sign that something isn't quite right. The effects of living and working in disorder are far reaching. First of all, clutter wastes time that can never be recovered. It can cost you money, it's distracting, you're always looking for something rather than being able to find it quickly — and you can't get it off of your mind because you're always thinking you will tackle the mess tomorrow. When tomorrow comes and you haven't touched it, you feel even worse. You're ashamed for others to come into your home. Ultimately, it can be very depressing.

Even if ridding yourself of clutter doesn't come easily to you, you can and should learn to do it. But be warned, it is an ongoing process, though well worth the effort. Everyone who has mastered the art of living clutter-free will tell you they feel as if they've been reborn. Not long ago, I reorganized a room in our home and turned it into my office. Everything in this room is designed for efficiency. My current files, along with everything I need, are close to my desk and chair; the old files and supplies are stored in the closet. I still have a ways to go to live clutter-free, but I've made a lot of progress and it's a wonderful feeling.

Living a more organized, less cluttered life really is healthier. It definitely saves you time and money in the long run, and it reduces stress. It's also energizing; you don't feel so overwhelmed, and you love yourself for having become organized. De-cluttering is probably one of the best gifts you can give yourself, and perhaps one of the least expensive. It may not cost you much more than a few boxes and files.

## Remember...

 *iving a more organized, less cluttered life is healthy for you physically, mentally and emotionally. It saves you stress and money in the long run and you'll feel good about yourself.*

You might be thinking that all this "stuff" around you is actually necessary, and the real problem is that your house or apartment isn't big enough to hold it all. What you really need is a larger place, which will happen as soon as you get that big bonus or raise, and then the problem will be solved. The truth, however, is that the more space you have, the more you collect. Unless you mend your "pack rat" ways, *there will never be enough space*. It's kind of like the government: The more money they have, the more they spend. There will never be enough. You can't do much about the spendthrifts in Washington, but you can do a lot about your junk surplus and space deficit. So why not just work with what you have now?

If you think you need expert help or advice, you could hire a professional organizer. Or you could do some reading on your own. There are dozens of books about simplifying your life and de-cluttering. Don Aslett, professional cleaner and "dejunking" expert, has written several books on the subject, such as *Lose 200 Lbs. This Weekend: It's Time To Declutter Your Life!* and *The Office Clutter Cure.* But you don't have to spend money on experts and books. You can do it on your own — if you really want to.

So where and how do you start? If the job seems too overwhelming, break it down into segments. Begin with just one room, or just a corner of a room if need be. Remember, this is all about making *small* changes. Think of an area in your home or apartment that particularly bothers you. It could be your computer area. It could be the place where you keep your mail, the daily newspapers or catalogues and magazines. It could be that stack of stuff on your kitchen counter — all those recipes that your mother, grandmother and girlfriends have so nicely shared and you have little time to experiment with. Or perhaps you have a closet shelf that's crammed with piles of sweaters and tank tops that you have to sift through for fifteen minutes to find the one you're looking for.

What about all those photos that you have been promising yourself you will put into albums? Instead of berating yourself for not having gotten around to doing this task, just buy photo boxes or use old shoe boxes, and put the photos in there for now. Then label the boxes and put them away.

Maybe it's your makeup area that's driving you nuts. Go into your bathroom, dressing table area, or wherever you put on or keep your makeup. Look at it, and if you haven't used it in twelve months, throw it out! Makeup is not intended to last forever, and colors are always changing. Take a small mug from your kitchen. Sharpen all your make-up pencils that you can't part with and put them into the mug. Use them up, and when they're down to stubs, discard them and don't buy any new ones until that cup is empty. If you clean up your cosmetics area, you'll see how much easier it is to apply your makeup when you're in a rush.

Take an afternoon or evening and organize that single room or area — you will be glad you did. I recently bought a versatile magazine/newspaper holder that can attach to the wall, freely stand up or fit snugly into a corner. It is one of the best, handiest pieces I've ever seen. It takes up so little room and accomplishes so much. I am still amazed and pleased whenever I put the "stuff" in there and see the order it brings to the room. A little thing like that brings lots of pleasure, and best of all, it gives you the incentive to do more and more cleaning, organizing and tossing out.

If you find you are having trouble parting with some of your "stuff", I feel your pain. I used to be the same way and still am on occasion. But by hanging on to things that you can't use, you are adding to your stress level and possibly depriving others of something useful. Not long ago, I was looking for something in the garage and I came upon a closed box. Not knowing what was inside, I slowly opened it, only to find some old clothes of mine that I had been unable to part with a few years ago. They were still neatly folded and now covered with mildew. I knew when I put them there I'd never wear them again, but I still couldn't bring myself to part with them. Someone could have worn those clothes then, but now, unfortunately, they went directly into the trash. We all need occasional reminders. Go into your closets and dresser drawers; if you haven't worn something in three years, the chances are you won't. Either donate the clothes or take them to a resale shop. (Just a note here: Most cities have organizations that help battered women get back on their feet again. Many of these women have walked out of the house with only the clothes on their back and they have to start from scratch. If you have clothing in good condition, these women are desperately in need of it. They can use all the clothes, shoes and even makeup that you can spare.)

Recently a cousin and her family were visiting us from Vermont. She didn't like my oven mitts because in her opinion, they didn't offer much protection. When she returned home she sent me a wonderful present: the most fabulous oven mitts and pot holders ever made. There isn't a time I use them that I don't feel happy. They're not only safer than my old ones, but they remind me of the wonderful time we had with our cousins. I have to confess, however, that I wasn't able to part with my old oven mitts. They still looked new and they were pretty, and I continued to use them occasionally, though I didn't need them. My cousin was right about those mitts, though, because one day I was using one and my hand burned right through the mitt. Ouch! At that point I took all my old mitts and trashed them. They had become clutter, they had out-lived their usefulness, and yet I was unable to part with them. It took a painful wakeup call to make me get rid of them, but it was such a good feeling to throw them out. There was that much less to fill up the kitchen drawers.

You can do this with so much around your own home. Look around you; if you don't use it and you just can't part with it, box it up and store it. Better yet, take the plunge and give it away (or throw it away). You will never miss it, and you will love your new found space. Believe me, I know how hard it can be to part with "stuff" — but if it doesn't serve you in some way, or have sentimental value, you need to get rid of it.

Don't forget that your car is part of your personal environment too. I used to be one of those people who kept an "office" in the car. I no longer do, and what a pleasure it is to open the door and not see my files, tape measures, fabric samples (I'm a perpetual redecorator), sun visor and headphones for walking, and an extra workout towel. Now I keep all those things neatly in two containers in the trunk. When I need to use the trunk, all I have to do is lift them out and everything is ready. It was just a matter of taking the time to ask myself, "What do I need in the car and what can I discard?"

If your car is filled with half-empty water bottles, running clothes, old gum wrappers, empty soda cans, papers and the like, it all reflects who you are. All those things should be thrown out or put away. Your car should be clean and neat so that if anyone at any time gets into your car, you are not ashamed or embarrassed. After all, no one, including your girlfriends, wants to get into your car when it looks so messy. If you're in doubt, ask yourself how it feels to get into someone else's messy car — it's rather unpleasant! It's nice to step into a neat, clean automobile.

Once you've cleaned up your act, so to speak, it's time to get to the fun part, decorating your home. You don't have to go to a lot of trouble and expense...remember, *small changes!* Even if you are living in a tiny one-bedroom apartment, you can make your home comfy and presentable. Don't wait, rationalizing that it's foolish to spend the money now because you haven't anyone special in your life today. You do have someone special in your life — you — so make your surroundings as beautiful as you can for yourself. Surround yourself with an environment that makes you feel good. The smallest apartment, even a one-room efficiency, can be made over into a fabulous place. It just takes some imagination and a little bit of time and effort.

I love our home; it makes me feel good when I walk through the door. Yet if I had to move into a one-bedroom apartment, I know I could turn it into a home that would make me feel the same way. You don't have to have a lot of space, or spend a small fortune, to make a terrific home. For example, I have a girlfriend who lives on the upper west side in Manhattan. She's a playwright, actress and director, and frequently has rehearsals or writing sessions in her two-bedroom apartment. Every weekend she went to the flea market and furnished most of her apartment from there. She bought old furniture, painted it, and added some cheerful fabrics and pillows.....and voila! She transformed an old apartment into a beauty. Her apartment is so cheerful you can't help but feel happy when you walk through the door.

Your home should make you feel good too. It is the place where you relax, daydream, and make plans. Most of your greatest decisions are made in your home. If you are surrounded by clutter, shabby furniture or just a plain dreary apartment, you will feel the same. Without spending a fortune, you can make your apartment look like it's had a make-over, and you will feel as if you did as well!

Pick up some handy do-it-yourself books or magazines at your local home improvement store. They're filled with ideas; many have weekend projects you can easily do. Perhaps you can paint a room; ask a friend or two to help and promise to help them in return. Or change your window treatment. Today you don't have to be able to sew; the people in the fabric stores or window covering department in other stores offer all the help you need. A swag over an attractive pole changes the look. If you have a skirted table alongside your bed, buy a new square of fabric to use as a topper. Tie tassels on the corners, add some new picture frames, buy a new plant or two — anything to give your home a refreshing new look, or as the interior designers say, a bit of a punch.

When you have created a home that reflects the best in you, you will be proud instead of embarrassed to share it with others. When someone says, "Let's get together!" you can be the one to say, "Sure, come on over!" And someday soon, that "someone" you invite to your beautiful re-feathered nest could very well be your future husband.

# 9

# "REFRESH" YOURSELF
## BY TRYING OR LEARNING
## SOMETHING NEW

et's take a look at your personal lifestyle. The "same old same old" may be working, more or less, but it hasn't helped you find Mr. Right, so what better time than the present to get refreshed? Even the word "refreshed" is refreshing! It connotes happiness, enlightenment, even pleasure. So ask yourself, what is it that really makes you feel good? What puts a smile on your face? Whatever it is, *do it!* Whether it's going for a walk in the park, horseback riding, a walk on the beach or a Sunday drive out into the country, do something for *you* that will make you feel good. You'll be happier, more relaxed, more confident, and altogether more appealing.

While you're taking that walk, or that drive out into the country, try to do some soul searching. Start making some mental notes. What makes you tick? If you used to be an avid reader but you haven't stopped in at your nearby Barnes and Noble lately, it's time to return. How about joining a book club? Ask your friends if they would be interested in forming one. If you have no success with your friends, check the message boards in the book stores or the library. There may be people in search of new members for already existing book clubs, or others also looking to form a new club. You can also post your own message there, as well as at work or at your gym. If you're not sure how book clubs work, someone at the bookstore can help. Most of the clubs meet monthly, at each member's home, on a rotating basis. In some clubs the members are asked to research different books and make recommendations for future selections.

Other clubs may have different members buy a few books each month that rotate through the group.

If exercise is something you've been putting off, consider joining a walking or jogging club. Check your local newspapers or parks. There is usually a place where they post notices in the parks, giving times and places where these clubs meet. Is biking something that might make you feel good? Perhaps you have a bike stashed away that you keep telling yourself to either sell or use. Now is the time to dust it off, put air in the tires and go for a short ride. If you don't have a bike, maybe you can borrow a friend's to see if you enjoy it. There are many weekend bike clubs. Just check in the bicycle stores; they should have all the information. And don't be surprised when you see how many single men are in these clubs.

Have you been telling yourself you should be going to the monthly meeting of any group? There's no better time than now to go. Many professional groups and women's organizations have early breakfast meetings for business/professional women. Some organizations have "brown bag" meetings at lunchtime; you bring your own lunch and they provide drinks. Evening meetings of social organizations are still the most popular, and since you're probably working days these may be the most feasible for you. Try to join a group in which you think you will have some interest. There are so many women in the work force today that there's a group for anything you can imagine. If you don't see one that fits your interest, begin one yourself.

Volunteering as a docent in a local museum is also a great way to get out and meet people. Docent hours are flexible and short, and museums are thrilled to have new volunteers. It doesn't even have to be one of the big city museums. There are many different types of centers and homes which also provide tours and are always looking for volunteers. Some entertainment venues, such as local theatres or performing arts centers, use volunteer ushers. Try it once or twice and you'll be hooked. It's fun, and you never know who you're going to meet. It could be your next girlfriend, your future sister-in-law or your next prospect!

I can't say enough good things about volunteering. Even if you don't view it as a means of meeting prospects, volunteering is a wonderful way to give back to others. Life is the greatest gift we have. Even if our lives are not quite as we would wish, it is our responsibility to give back. It is also one of the most deeply satisfying things we can do.

What other interests can you explore? Have you considered gardening? Although the majority of single women don't have homes with large yards, the home and garden section of newspapers frequently offer gardening tips. There are garden clubs and they too have meetings. Just recently I read in our local newspaper that free bulbs were offered to those attending a yard and gardening seminar. Is there anything more pleasing than looking outside and seeing flowers in bloom? You really don't need a yard; many bulbs and plants can go right into pots on your patio or deck, or just outside your front door. Speaking of flowers, check out your local markets or flower shops. They usually have specials when flowers are in abundance. Pick up a bunch, put them in a pitcher or vase, and see if that doesn't put a smile on your face.

Photography is another hobby you might consider. Take a photography class and then find a club that sponsors lectures and slide shows. I think you'll find many men share this interest. You don't have to spend a lot of money on equipment unless you want to. Who knows, you may discover a new passion.

Don't overlook the multitude of classes offered in adult education learning centers or community colleges. They are as varied as people's lifestyles — you'll find classes in everything from Yoga to the Kabala, computers to car repair, foreign languages to local, national or international politics, modern art to world history. If you're lucky you'll even find some basic classes in the theatre arts, ranging from set design to lighting to acting.

The latter is a particular love of mine, and if you have never taken an acting class, I strongly recommend that you sign up for one, and do it today! There are countless benefits, and you will have so much more fun than you ever imagined. Also look into your local theatres or community theatre groups. They are always seeking new faces, and it doesn't matter if you have little experience. They need volunteers in every department: sound, lighting, ticket sales, costumes, props and actors — and the actors don't necessarily need to be experienced. In small theatre groups that are perhaps less established, they are usually desperate for newcomers, and you will be welcomed with open arms.

Many years ago, one of my closest friends, a professional actress, suggested I try out for a play in one of our local theatre groups. I hadn't acted since I was a pilgrim in a play in elementary school, but at the last minute I decided to go. I had never read for a part for a play and wasn't sure I wanted to do so now, but I listened as a few others read — and before long I volunteered to read also. To my surprise, I not only got a part, but it was the female lead in the play. I remained in theatre until I began selling real estate, and there just wasn't time for both. The friends I made in the theatre were from every ethnic, religious and social group. It may sound like a show-biz cliché, but theatre people are the most wonderful people you will ever meet. If you are the least bit shy and would like to overcome it, I can't think of a better, or more fun, solution. (And by the way, most actors and actresses will tell you that they all have a shy side too.)

Dancing is another wonderful way to increase your self-confidence and social skills. If you have two left feet, if you have no rhythm, even if you have never ballroom danced, sign up for a series of classes. If you have any doubt about the benefits, many dance studios offer a free trial lesson. (Take advantage of those freebies; if you don't see one advertised, ask for it when you call the dance studio.) A series of dance lessons may seem a little expensive, but it's worth every dollar spent — the benefits will be enormous! Dance studios also offer weekly dances, and you never know who may be taking classes on your off nights. Many single people are in those classes, and the purpose is for you to enjoy them so you will sign up for future classes. The instructors are always there, so if there's no one else to dance with you, they will. If you have tried dancing and were unhappy with one studio, try another. What if you don't want to go alone? Consider asking another single friend to sign up as well, and if you don't have a friend who is interested, ask a co-worker. You don't have to be best friends with them; you don't even have to like them that much. It's just someone with whom to share an activity. I have never heard anyone say they were sorry they took dance lessons. Do not hesitate — sign up for classes now.

And now for my personal favorite — cooking! Even if you don't cook, don't want to cook, and haven't any interest in cooking, how about just attending *one* class in how to use your kitchen knives? What? You don't own any decent knives? That's all the more reason to find a store offering classes in using basic knives. A whole new world could open up for you. There's something about learning new things that really boosts your self-confidence. And who knows, the class might spur you to explore an actual cooking class. Classes are easy to find; begin by checking the weekly food section of your local newspapers. There are always a variety of classes at venues ranging from your local department stores to the finest restaurants, but the kitchen stores have the best. Specialty stores such as Williams-Sonoma are always offering classes, and many larger cities have upscale supermarkets that hold a wealth of classes as well. Many individuals who run cooking schools frequently give classes and workshops too. Just remember, if you haven't spent much time in the kitchen, beginning classes are best. And if you do cook but aren't in love with it, the classes might change your mind. Your entire outlook on your home and entertaining could change.

Best of all, there are often a lot of single men in these classes. In fact, what better place could there be to meet a prospect than in a cooking class? If you sincerely do not care for cooking, that's not a problem, because you may meet someone who loves to cook. If you both enjoy cooking and especially entertaining, you have a common interest and automatically have something to talk about. If a particular cooking class doesn't interest you, try another one, at another location. At least consider taking a class; you won't be sorry. Even if you never become a gourmet cook, the self-confidence you gain can be immeasurable.

What if you're hesitant about clubs, classes or other activities because you don't have a friend to accompany you? Don't be intimidated by the prospect of going somewhere alone. Provided you take reasonable safety precautions, there is nothing to fear. And you don't need a friend to attend a class with; you can make friends in the class. That's one of the great things about these classes. You might be a little timid at first, but remember, changing your life for the better often involves stretching beyond your comfort zone. Besides, it should be easy to make new friends, since you already have a common interest.

Will taking a power Yoga class or a course in Thai cooking help you find a husband? You never know. Any activity you choose could lead directly or indirectly to that walk down the aisle. Even if it doesn't, you could end up having a good time. But you'll never find out unless you go out and start trying new things. Almost anything is better than sitting around doing nothing but fretting because you don't have a husband. Don't be afraid to spread your wings. If you try something and don't like it, there's no law that says you have to keep at it. Try something else. And if you don't like that, then try something else again. I can't promise you that you'll meet Mr. Right in your kayaking class or Tai Chi group, but you *will* be refreshed and renewed in body, mind and spirit — and that will make you all the more alluring when your future husband does come along. ♥

---

## Remember...

f you have been doing something and it doesn't work, try something else. Don't be afraid to experiment. Each new pursuit helps us differentiate what we do like or don't like. And when you find a lasting interest your energy and vitality will expand. There's a whole world of things to try, so get started now!

---

# BECOME AN EXCEPTIONAL CONVERSATIONALIST

reat conversational skills will do more than just about anything else to help you attract the kind of man you want to marry, and keep his attention once you have it. Everybody knows how to talk, but few seem to really know how to *converse*. In fact, so many people have developed poor conversational habits that a genuinely skilled conversationalist is the exception rather than the norm today. Let's work on making you exceptional!

Even if you think you are already a good communicator, there's always room for improvement. There are many books on the art of conversation, so I'll just give you a few basic pointers here. Then go out and practice, practice, practice on everyone you meet in person or speak to on the phone. I think you will see an improvement in all of your relationships — business and personal alike.

Being a good conversationalist has a two-part structure: listening and talking. We need to be both good speakers and good listeners in order to be good communicators. Let's talk about listening first, since without an audience, there's no need to talk! When I was very young I had a teacher who understood the importance of listening. She asked the class this question: "Why do you think we were born with two ears and one mouth?" I have never forgotten that teacher! Unfortunately, many people carry on conversations as if the reverse were true, but they're only cheating themselves. You can learn so much by just listening, and it is one of the surest ways to win people over and make friends. Besides that, it's a wonderful form of entertainment. Once you really learn to listen to other people, I bet you will find listening far more enjoyable than talking about yourself.

My husband always says I walk out of the house and return with a story. That's true, I usually do, because I easily communicate with people. I'm a "talker", no doubt about it, but when I talk I am usually focused on finding out about the other person. I wasn't a born communicator; it's just something I developed over the years. I'm sure my years in real estate also helped. My success depended upon finding the home that best met my clients' needs. We had to first qualify our clients to be sure they could afford the price range they requested. We learned to ask questions and carefully listen to the answers. That's a useful skill whether or not you're a Realtor!

Years ago, before I pumped my own gas, I could tell you everything about the gas station attendants. I'd roll the window down, and while they were cleaning the windshield, we visited. The man who owned my local gas station had a heavy accent, so one day I asked him where he was from. I couldn't have asked a better question. It turned out he was from Greece, and each time I pulled into his station I learned more about his wonderful country and his family members who were still there. He loved talking about it, and we soon developed a nice relationship.

Just remember that everyone has a story to tell. Some tell it better than others, but we all have stories, and we all love to tell them. In the beginning, you need to set your own stories aside, because you want to hear other people's stories. You'll soon find that when you seek others out by asking them questions, you are the person who actually reaps the benefits. When you show interest in people, they will respond sincerely and return that interest, because you made them feel good, which makes you feel good — and so your self-confidence grows. Everyone wins. Even if you are innately shy, you can learn to be a great listener and a good conversationalist. After all, the spotlight isn't on you, it's on the other person. All you have to do is encourage him or her.

Do more than simply ask questions; you have to listen *carefully* to the answers. When someone is talking, don't try to jump ahead, thinking how you're going to respond. Just listen, and if necessary repeat what they said, so you fully understand what they did say. That lets the other person know you are sincerely interested, and almost immediately a closer relationship begins to develop. Success breeds success, and your responses will come more and more naturally as you practice listening and asking questions.

One caveat: Being a woman, you might find that giving a listener your total attention can be a challenge if there are other conversations going on around you. This is not to sell the men short, but many women are able to multi-task; we can talk to someone and listen to an entirely unrelated conversation which we're not even a part of. It's just one of our special gifts. I was astounded years ago when I realized that most men haven't a clue how to do it; this may be because women's brains really are "wired" differently than men's. At any rate, if you are one of these women who can perform such phenomenal feats when you're talking with some-one, you must learn to tune out the other conversation. Give your lis-tener your total attention — the same respect you would like in return.

Another element of good listening, and good speaking as well, is learning not to interrupt. We are all taught this rule as children, but as adults we sometimes forget. We become impatient when we want to say something, so we just blurt it out. Listen to any group conversation and you'll hear people breaking in on others constantly. Or try watching TV shows such as the ABC morning talk show *The View*; hosts and guests alike are rarely allowed to utter a complete sentence without someone interrupting and then someone else interrupting the interrupter. Wow, talk about confusing and frustrating! During everyday conversations, many people, even when they're not interrupting, are focused so intently on what they're going to say next that they miss most of what the other person is saying. Interrupting may be necessary at times, but most often you can and should avoid it. Learn to catch yourself when you start to interrupt.

You can go a step further and demonstrate how great a communica-tor you really are by allowing *yourself* to be interrupted occasionally. If you're talking and see that your listener is anxious to jump in, offer an opening: Look at the person and say, "Did you want to say something?" This shows that you're paying attention to your listener and open to con-versation. Of course, if the person simply wants to dominate the conver-sation, that's a different matter. You might need to assert yourself, but don't turn it into a competition.

Now that we've covered listening, let's tackle the other aspect of conversation, talking. When you speak, try to listen to yourself. Be aware of what you are saying, how it comes across, and how your audience is responding to what you have said. The number one mistake women make when they meet a new prospect is trying to keep the conversation going.

They get nervous and end up babbling on about nothing, and the situation gets out of hand. This is a turnoff for most men. When talking, try not to ramble on. Make your story short and concise, and let him talk.

Paying attention to the response you're receiving and knowing how to read others is a great step towards better communication. Think about your subject matter before you begin talking, and pay attention to your listener's cues once you start. That way you won't waste time and energy going on and on about something the other person cares little about. It isn't just the subject matter that may be a turn-off, it's also the message that person is sending. Anyone who rambles on about something in which his or her conversational partner obviously has no interest comes across as painfully self-absorbed. This does not make for good date material, to say nothing of marriage.

So watch for cues in people as you're speaking. They will let you know immediately if they're interested in what you are saying. *Learn to read the signs.* If they look bored, if their eyes wander the room, if they fidget or show restlessness in any other way, change the subject immediately by asking a question and putting the ball back in their court. Should it be obvious that they are still disinterested, excuse yourself and find someone who is more responsive. Unlike the poor stand-up comedian who has to finish the show even if the audience is yawning or jeering, you can move on.

You need to fine-tune your ability to read people. Often the signs of disinterest are quite subtle. Your conversational partner may have enough manners not to appear disinterested, but in fact he has heard enough of whatever it is you're speaking about. If he hasn't come out and said that he also shares the same interest, or he hasn't at least encouraged you to tell him more, assume he's not interested in anything more than an overview. If someone is genuinely interested in what you are talking about, they will ask many questions and appear to mirror your excitement when they respond.

# Remember...

 art of being a good conversationalist is knowing when to stop talking! Many women go on and on about a topic, without paying attention to whether or not their listener is really interested. Whether this is from nerves or simply a lack of anything else to talk about, it's definitely a sign of poor conversational skills. If you fine-tune your ability to read people, you will be able to detect signs of disinterest (or interest) — and you'll be well on your way to being an excellent conversationalist.

Skill in the art of conversation will take you far beyond that first meeting. Let's say you've been to a party, met a possible prospect, and exchanged names — and to your delight, he calls the next day. Well, hold on. It's almost always best to end these initial conversations before they've worn themselves out. In fact, the biggest mistake you can make is to talk too long. Unless you sense that he is truly exceptional and neither he nor you have ever experienced anything remotely like this before, be ready to end the call sooner than you'd like to. People want what they can't have — it's human nature. If you finish the conversation before you are both talked out, chances are he'll want more. Don't be rude, but be ready with a reason or two why you have to hang up. Go over those reasons in your mind repeatedly, and remember them.

There's another point to consider: Where is it written that you have to tell your whole life story to this almost total stranger? You owe him nothing, so just tell him enough to keep him coming back out of curiosity. Is this playing games? Absolutely not! It is controlling your nervous habit to chatter. Chatter doesn't lead to anything positive.

Besides, he should be asking you out, and if that's not happening, then you certainly don't want to prolong your exchange. It's far better to cut the conversation off than to keep it going, hoping that eventually he will get to the point of asking you out. If he does want to ask you out, cutting the call short may be just the ticket to make him say what he was attempting. So think of something plausible; tell him you would love to chat but you were just walking out the door, or just about to return a business call, or you have to get to bed early since you have an early morning meeting. Or simply say, "It's been fun, but I have to go — busy day ahead!" This should spur him to get to the point, if there was indeed a point. If not, you're doing yourself a favor by hanging up.

If he does ask you out, good conversational skills will carry you through that first date as well as the second, and the third...and with a little effort, you'll never run out of things to talk about. Don't be afraid to do a little research if you need to. Read the newspaper or listen to CNN or C-SPAN before you leave for a date. If you're going for Japanese food because he said it's his favorite, and you have never tried it, stop in at the closest sushi bar or Japanese restaurant and familiarize yourself with the menu. Take a friend with you who perhaps knows something about the food, and you can learn a little in a very short time. The same thing goes for theatre, art, music. If you're going to a play, find out something about the actors; are they well known? Read a synopsis; you can usually find that online, and try to offer something, positive or negative, about the performance afterwards. No one wants to be around someone who hasn't an opinion. If you think the way to get a man is by being completely agreeable, it isn't. You won't come across as congenial, just desperate.

No doubt you've heard the expression, "I've never met a stranger." This can be a description of you if you practice your communication skills on everyone you meet. We may not all be natural-born orators, but anyone can learn to be a good conversationalist. The suggestions here will do much more than get you through a party or a first date; they are key elements to improving your self-confidence. And they are really quite simple. Use these hints in all your conversations, and practice, practice, practice, until you are not just a good conversationalist but an exceptional one. I promise you will get wonderful results, and sooner or later, Mr. Right will hear you loud and clear. ♥

---

## Remember...

*The key to being a good conversationalist is to focus on the other person. Ask questions of others and let them lead the conversation. People love to talk about themselves, and if you encourage them to do so, they'll love talking to you!*

---

# 11

# CULTIVATE A NEW APPROACH
## AND USE IT EVERYWHERE

et's say you've been working on changing your perceptions, transforming negatives into positives and altering your attitudes and habits. Good for you! These are all steps to cultivating a new approach that will not only make your life much more enjoyable, but will help you attract Mr. Right.

When it comes right down to it, this entire book is about your "new approach". In this chapter, however, we're going to look at some everyday situations where you can put that approach to work. You need to practice and keep practicing, until it becomes so natural to you that you won't have to think about it. As with anything new or different, the more you do it, the better you'll get at it.

Before we go any further, let's take some time to talk about nonverbal signals, specifically body language, because this is a crucial part of your approach. If you aren't already aware of your own body language, you need to develop this awareness. Your body language is as important as what you say, sometimes even more so. Coupled with your physical appearance, it forms the first impression you make on someone. That is significant, because you only have *one chance* at a first impression. You can be standing talking to someone and, consciously or unconsciously, someone else may have already formed an opinion about you — just by a quick glance.

I cannot overstate the importance of nonverbal signals we all send. For example, if you're at a party and a man sees you standing with your arms folded, not smiling, looking like you had a bad day at the office, he won't even take notice of you, other than to say to himself, "Forget this one!" If you're stooped over with rounded shoulders and your head is down, you don't look like a happy camper. What does that say? It says, *This person is carrying a heavy load.* Again the man will move on. But if the same man looks at you and sees you standing with a friend, talking, smiling and looking relaxed, he will be much more likely to give you a second glance and maybe even walk up to you.

Posture is most important to your overall demeanor, as well as being crucial to good health. When we were quite young, my mother taught my sister and me the importance of good posture. My mother is five feet one-and-a-half inches tall, but people have always thought she was much taller. She walks into a room and commands respect. My mother was right to place so much emphasis on good posture because your posture is part of who you are. If it's poor, it says you don't think much of yourself. It conveys a negative impression. If it's good, it says you have self-confidence, you like yourself, you're proud of who you are! If you're in doubt about your posture, just remind yourself to put your shoulders back. Your head will automatically come up, your stomach will pull in, and you're ready to go on your way. Practice that and then promise yourself you'll never slouch again, whether you're sitting in a restaurant, riding the subway or standing up at a cocktail party. Just remember, "SB" — Shoulders Back!

## Remember...

*Y*our posture is important to your overall demeanor — it's part of who you are. Good posture sends a powerful non-verbal message of self-confidence.

Be aware of how you stand, how you hold your purse and what you do with your arms, legs and body. That folded-arms stance mentioned above can send any number of negative messages — that you're aloof, guarded, disapproving, or perhaps just chilly. Some people stand with their arms folded because they're ill at ease or don't know what to do with their hands. If you're unsure what to do with your hands, try simply clasping them in front of you. That way you'll avoid the defensive folded arms position, and your hands won't be flying nervously around your face. If you're at a social gathering, try observing others who seem to be at ease and having a good time, and see if their stance appeals to you. (If all else fails, a drink in the hand is a time-honored "prop".)

When you're talking to someone and your head is bobbing around trying to see if the grass is greener elsewhere, the person observing you has already made a decision about you. You're sending a signal to this person that you either have low self-esteem or you're an opportunist, and neither one is a positive message. If you're talking to someone, look them straight in the eye and make them feel as if they are the most important person in the room. If it's someone you want to escape from, when there's a break in the conversation, simply say it was nice meeting them and excuse yourself.

Being conscious of your body language without becoming overly self-conscious may take some practice, but as you gain more confidence, positive body language will come naturally. The trick is to learn to see yourself as others see you. If you're walking by an office building, notice your reflection in the windows or doors as you walk by. Try to catch a glimpse of yourself wherever you can, because that's what others see. Ask yourself how you feel about the person you see reflected. Do you like yourself? Of course you do — it's your "new you" state of mind! Let your body language mirror it.

Don't forget to pay attention to other people's body language too, as quite often it will tell you more than words about what's going on. For example, I'm sure you've observed two people talking while standing face to face, quite close to each other. Their body language says they're having a serious conversation. You probably know instinctively not to interrupt them. On the other hand, if they're standing half-facing each other but with their bodies turned slightly away, they're inviting anyone else to come and join in their conversation. This is just one example, of course. There are many books on body language, but careful observation will teach you just about all you need to know. So whenever you're at a party or any other gathering, pay attention to nonverbal signals.

---

# Remember...

onverbal cues such as body language are extremely important because often they are even more revealing than words. Always pay attention to your own body language, and make sure it says something positive about you. Of course it's important to learn to read other people's body language as well.

---

Now let's "walk" through a social situation where you can try out your new approach. You've been invited to a party at which there will be many single men. Put on your favorite little black dress, leave all your "baggage" at home and step out with a smile. Think of yourself as a newcomer to town, the person everyone wants to meet (even if they don't know it yet!).

If the party is in a restaurant or other public place, you might want to first stop by the restroom to check your hair and put on fresh lipstick. If it's in a home, do that just prior to arriving. Before you enter the room, pause for a second and remind yourself that you don't enter a room as if you're fearing the unknown! Try transforming your fear into anticipation and excitement, and then it will be easier for you to enter with self-confidence. Check your posture, take a deep breath... and now you're ready. You smile, make eye contact with the people standing closest to the entrance, say hello whether you know them or not, and then carefully look around to see in which direction you want to head. (Forget the back door, you came for a reason!) Tell yourself you have walked into that room full of wonderful people who are all eager to meet you.

Once you've entered the room and have greeted your host or hostess, do a quick overview. You're casing the room for potential prospects, but you're doing it differently this time. Forget looks, size, and height...even hair. I know you've done this a zillion times before, but remember, you promised you'd set aside all your history and try a new approach. You're even going to talk to some of those guys to whom you wouldn't ordinarily give a second glance.

Let's say you've been mingling and you end up engaged in conversation with a friend from work. While you're talking, a prospect happens to catch your eye and smile at you. What do you do? It's very simple, just smile back — not a broad grin, but a subtle smile, perhaps even a raised eyebrow. He'll walk over, guaranteed! Now you can really start putting your new approach to work. If you've read Chapter 10 on the art of conversation, you know you are *not* going to spend the entire night talking about yourself. Nor are you going to ply your new acquaintance with obvious questions such as, "So, what do you do for a living?" You are going to keep your conversation light, refreshing and non-threatening. Ask questions, of course (just not "obvious" ones). If you get stuck, it's okay to ask what he does, but take your time before you do.

If the men who interest you are too shy to come over to you, go over to them. Let's say you see a single man walk up to the bar, or go into the kitchen to pour himself a drink. Walk up alongside him, but not too closely, and start a conversation. You don't even need to make eye contact; you're just sending out feelers. Glance at him for a second, turn away and then, almost as if you're talking to yourself, make some sort of small talk: "Great party.....do you see any Diet Coke?" Or make some other light remark that indicates you find him interesting enough to engage in conversation.

If you can't think of a specific topic to get the conversational ball rolling, don't worry. You don't have to be clever or scintillating in order to get a man's attention. If you're at a party hosted by an individual, you can begin simply by introducing yourself and asking him how he knows the host or hostess. Even if it's a party sponsored by a business, association or other organization, you can ask him about his connection. The rest will fall right into place.

Whatever you say, make it friendly, light, engaging — but again, not obvious. You don't want to be accused of coming on to someone's husband since you haven't a clue whether this man is single or not. And he doesn't know whether you're married or not...but you're a female and all heterosexual men are interested in women. Just get his attention and he'll respond, even if non-verbally. If he says nothing, don't let it bother you, just think of it as a signal to move on to the next one. You gave him the opportunity to talk, and if he had been interested he would have taken it. Don't waste time with the uninterested.

# Remember...

*You don't have to come up with a clever opening line or a scintillating remark to get the conversational ball rolling with a man. Keep your remarks friendly and light, and he'll respond if he's interested. If he doesn't respond, don't let it bother you. Just think of it as a signal to move on to the next one.*

If he does respond, keep the conversation light. Smile and be friendly, but be prepared — he still might walk at any moment. Besides, at this point, you still don't know if he's single. If he's married, well, you kept it light and practiced your new approach. If he's single and interested, he'll let you know pretty quickly. Fortunately, you probably won't be kept guessing for long about whether or not he's interested. Most men aren't great at playing games; they can't hide their feelings as well as women. (There are, of course, exceptions — some men are excellent actors — which is why you need to hone your "people reading" skills.) Sometimes men's responses can be hurtful if they are profoundly indifferent or look as if they can't get away quickly enough, but at least they're being honest. That's why what you first say is so important. You want to throw out the bait and see if he bites. You've either piqued his interest or not. If he is intrigued enough to find out more, he will let you know.

Let's suppose your prospect has responded favorably to your initial remark. At the very least you can see he is interested in continuing your exchange. Now what? Turn, look him in the eyes and ask him a question or make a direct statement. If you haven't done so already, simply introduce yourself, and if you have a free hand extend it forward and shake his hand. Then, if you haven't done this already, you can ask if he is a friend of the host or hostess. He'll answer, but keep in mind that he still might pivot and leave at any second, so be prepared. Turn as though you're about to walk away yourself, but still continue to engage in some conversation. Remember that smiling is important, and it goes along with light conversation — nothing serious yet. Be sure to follow his lead, however. If he's brief, you be just as brief. If he really opens up and starts talking, enjoy!

On the other hand, what if his response to your initial comment is indifferent or even rude? Does that mean you are striking out? Not at all, it's his loss, not yours! If it's obvious that he wants to cut the exchange short, give him what he wants — move on. You gave it your best effort. Besides, when someone snaps back with a rude comment, who wants to talk to him anyway? He could have easily been polite, but he wasn't, so don't waste your time. You were ready to walk anyway, so move on.

You'll have a lot more fun at parties if you are not attached to the outcome of any exchange. If your first effort doesn't bear fruit, more than likely you'll see several other interesting guys and you will have plenty of other chances to try out your new approach. Just realize that you have a better chance at grabbing a man's attention when he is alone or talking to another man, than when he's sitting between two women on the sofa, or engaged in a group conversation. If you see a single man talking to a couple that you happen to know, go up to the woman and start a conversation with her. If she has any social graces, she'll introduce you to the new man.

However, if the opportunity to approach a single man doesn't present itself, don't be afraid to join in a group conversation if the group contains a likely prospect or two. If you see there isn't a chance for you to get a word in, scan the room and move on. An interested man will remember your face and seek you out. You may have the opportunity to meet him later on, but why stand there if there are other interesting possibilities? Finding a prospect might take time, but if you keep in mind that this is just one evening out of many, and refuse to take it too seriously, you won't feel rejected if someone doesn't "take the bait". You won't be spending the evening lamenting that you're meeting nothing but losers. And you also won't come across as desperate, which is the biggest mistake some single women make.

# Remember...

*W*hen searching for a prospect at a party or other gathering, be optimistic but keep an open mind. Don't feel rejected if a man doesn't show interest, and don't think the evening was a complete failure if you don't meet any prospects at all. Part of your "new approach" is not being too attached to the outcome in social situations. Even if nothing comes of the evening, it's a good opportunity to practice your social skills. You may or may not meet Mr. Right, but you can have fun anyway!*

There are plenty of other places to try your new approach besides at parties. Let's say you're at the supermarket, in the produce department, and...hmmm, those apples sure look good. While you're trying to select a few, you notice a gentleman standing alongside you. You can say, "Who said picking apples was easy!" or "This store has the best produce!"...and who knows, if he puts only a couple of apples into the bag he just might be single. Do not confuse this exchange with flirting; it is just friendly conversation. It's the same light approach you tried at the party, and even if nothing comes of it, it's good practice for future encounters. A woman I know recently married a man she met while standing in the checkout line of a supermarket. She's a physician and he's an attorney. Who spoke first? She did — of course! Meetings like this happen every day, but you have to seize the opportunity when you see it. Of course, don't forget to use discretion. Don't just talk to anyone standing next to you — you still must exercise good judgment.

Whenever the opportunity presents itself, try to be "on" — you don't have to go all out, but just be a bit friendlier than you previously may have been. And always remember to smile. When someone smiles at you it's natural to want to smile back. Always make an effort to say something light and refreshing, whether you're standing next to someone at the dry cleaners, picking up food at the local take-out restaurant, or waiting at a car dealership for your car. Practice being friendly; you'll see how many people are receptive. Most people are really shy and welcome warmth and conversation, especially in a waiting situation — it helps pass the time. But again, you don't want someone to follow you home, so always use discretion and be cautious when leaving.

Recently I was in the Newark Airport waiting for my flight and had gone to one of the quick-serve counters for something to drink. In one hand I had my purse and a shopping bag, and I was unable to get a tight grip on the cap to open the bottle of water. I turned to the male pilot standing next to me and said, "Can you please open this for me?" He responded, "I'm sure you did all the work for me!" He smiled when he returned the opened bottle, and I smiled back when I thanked him. He then said, "Where are you headed?" We had a nice conversation. All right, so you're thinking pilots are always on the make...but aren't most men? He was young enough to be my son, but that doesn't stop people from being friendly or flirty. It was a pleasant exchange for both of us, and it wouldn't have happened if I hadn't made the initial effort.

Every day you have opportunities to practice your new approach. If you are in sales, then you're already ahead of the game. But if you are sitting inside a cubicle or an office ten hours a day, it's pretty difficult to meet new people, so try doing whatever you can to change your routine. Bring walking shoes and take a ten or twenty minute walk at lunch time if you can. It can do wonders for your psyche. Just being outside, if possible, lightens your mind and clears it for the afternoon. Seek out some new places for lunch and try to meet as many different friends as possible. Look around, even at your co-workers. There may be some you haven't really gotten to know. Stop at their desks and see if they want to go to lunch one day or join you for a walk.

Whenever you get to the gym, visit the juice bar or water fountain and find someone who looks "normal" — and start up a conversation. When you're walking into the gym, look around; if someone looks interesting, non-threatening, or friendly, why not smile at him and say "Hi!" Or when you're leaving and you happen to notice someone also walking out, all you have to say is, "Did you have a good workout?" Smile — it doesn't matter if he's married or single. If the latter is the case, you just never know; you could be talking to your future husband!

# Remember...

*ook for opportunities to try your new approach every day – whether at work, at the gym, or at the supermarket. You don't have to go all out — just be a little more "on" than you're used to being. Remember, small changes can bring huge results!*

Also consider a "change of venue" once in a while — a different coffee shop than the one you're used to, a different bookstore, a new supermarket — just to get out of the same old grind. If you're a little short on ideas, there's a list at the back of this book to get you started.

One more point: Although you may not have given it much thought, you should apply your new approach to phone conversations as well as personal contacts. Sometimes a single woman living alone will answer her phone in a quiet, sheepish manner, as if she is apologizing for taking up space in the world, or as if she's fearful of what she's going to hear on the other end. Others use a cold, business-like voice. Your telephone presence is part of your persona. As we discussed in Chapter 7 on shedding "baggage", negativity of any type comes across loud and clear over the phone. But so does a positive, cheerful, confident manner — so put a smile on your face before you pick up that receiver. Don't be phony and overly cheery, but do sound as if you're *happy* to be you, and glad to be speaking to the other person. Practice your "Hello!" until it sounds friendly, upbeat and confident — and remember, **SMILE** when you speak so you sound friendly and inviting. It's not that difficult!

Make sure that your message on your answering machine casts you in a positive light as well; this is more important than you may realize. After all, this is the very first impression that many people will have of you, and it can literally make or break your chances with a prospect. I have seen it go both ways — I've seen singles who were completely turned off by a cold or mediocre recording, and others who were captivated by a pleasing message — so I know what a difference this can make. Listen to your message as objectively as you can, and if you sound too business-like, timid, breathless, whiny or nasal, re-do it. Even if you have to record and re-record it a dozen times till you're satisfied, take the time to create a message that reflects the confident, warm, optimistic woman you are.

# Remember...

*Y our telephone presence is part of your persona — and it's more important than you may realize. Make an effort to sound confident, warm and positive when you answer the phone, rather than cold and business-like, or sheepish or fearful as so many single women do. Put a smile in your voice, and people will want to hear more from you.*

What if you're having trouble putting your new approach into practice because you're shy? Let me be blunt: shy does not work when you are a mature adult, particularly when you are competing with other single women. Shyness can be perceived as being snobbish or even selfish, whether you're talking to someone in person or over the phone. It makes the person you're talking to have to carry the conversation. If you don't respond, the person will feel as if he's talking to himself. He will very likely perceive you as disinterested, and will move on in search of someone who's more responsive.

Look, there's a lot of competition out there and you have to grasp every opportunity to be friendly and charming. It isn't hard! Most men are really quite easy to get along with and if you're nice to them, they'll respond in kind. The ones who don't...well, you don't want them. So shed your old style and see where it takes you. You just might be surprised. Remember that this is all about trying something new and doing things differently from the way you've done them in the past. It may not be natural for you, but try to be a bit more assertive than you have been. You don't have to be the life of the party — just open up a little. However, if your shyness is severe, or if you think you may have what is currently known as "social anxiety"— in other words, if it's a real problem — talk to a therapist.

Whether we're naturally shy or are born extroverts, most of us can always improve our social skills. There's always something we could be doing a little differently in order to get better results. Chances are you're not happy with the results you've had up to now, but you can change that. If you practice your new approach everywhere you go, you will not only increase your chances of finding Mr. Right, you will also make some wonderful friends and acquaintances along the way. And I just bet you will have the time of your life! ♥

# 12

## TAKE A CUE FROM WOMEN WHO HAVE TAKEN THE LEAP

*H*ave you ever wondered why a woman who's been married once, even for a short time, will find another husband before the woman who has never been married? That isn't a coincidence — it happens over and over again.

You may be thinking, "That's obvious, she's done it once, so it's easier the second time!" After all, history repeats itself, doesn't it? Getting married becomes sort of a "default mode" for these women. Actually, however, that has little if anything to do with the phenomenon I'm talking about. While it's true that many things are easier to repeat if you've done them once, marriage is not necessarily one of those things. Women who marry again have something else going for them besides the mere fact of having walked down the aisle before. Yet if you were to ask them what they do, they probably couldn't give you an answer.

If you cornered them, most would probably tell you they're just being themselves. A little further questioning, however, might reveal something else: *They are not afraid they won't find another husband.* In fact, if you were to sit down and talk to them it would be obvious that most of these women simply have the self-confidence to find another husband. Whether this confidence is the cause or the result of their unshakeable belief that they will marry again, I couldn't tell you. What I can tell you is they absolutely know that they will get married again. It isn't a question of *if* they will remarry, it's just a matter of who and when. And the latter are details they're not particularly worried about.

You still may not be satisfied that I've answered the real question we're asking, which is why some women can get a second or even a third husband when others — you, for example — can't get even one, at least not a "keeper"! For that matter, why do some people appear to sail through life, while others seem to stumble and then pick themselves up, only to stumble again? Perhaps you think these are questions that really have no answers. Maybe you're thinking that life is just unfair and we should let it go at that.

I say that's a cop-out. Life may sometimes seem "unfair", but that doesn't mean you can't do something to make your life a lot better. Be assured that all those women who get second and third helpings of matrimony are not any prettier, sexier, richer or smarter than you. Rather, they instinctively know how to get a man. (Obviously, some of them don't know how to keep one...but that's the topic for another book!) Furthermore, those people who seem to sail through life aren't necessarily smarter or luckier; they simply have better judgment than those who are less successful.

The good news is that although it may not be natural for you (at first, anyway), you can learn the techniques of those confident women we've been talking about. The ability to exercise good judgment can also be learned.

First you must learn to examine what these women are doing that may be different from your own approach to similar situations. In this book we discuss many ways to change your perceptions, attitude and approach. But the book is only a beginning, since the best way to learn married women's "secrets" is to go straight to the source. As we discuss in the following chapter about how to acquire a "married woman" attitude, observation is crucial. You need to observe married women up close, even women who have been married many times. All can give you some valuable insight. Make friends with them, watch them, listen to them and don't be afraid to pick their brains!

Even if you have never married, you can develop the kind of self-confidence enjoyed by women who have successfully taken "the leap". Once you've developed that confidence, it's really quite easy to reach the point where you have an unshakeable belief that you will get married. You will have lost the fear that you'll never walk down the aisle.

# Remember...

reviously married women who remarry have at least one thing going for them that many never-married women lack: an absolute certainty that they will wed. This certainty gives them the confidence to go out and meet their next "Mr. Right". Even if you have never married, you can develop this kind of self-confidence.

Previously married women in search of another husband seem to have an attitude about them. Of course they're scared the first time out on a date in twenty or more years, or the first time they go to a singles party. And singles web sites didn't even exist when they were married years before. The best they can do is set their fears aside, and they quickly do, as soon as they've had a few dates. Truth is, you're a step ahead of them. Most of you in search of your Mr. Right have had at least a few dates in the last twenty to thirty years! What sets these widowed or divorced women apart is that they have their minds made up they want to marry, and they're confident that they will. Furthermore, they are not afraid of marriage, as some never-married women are.

By making minor changes in behavior and attitude — by observing and emulating women who have achieved the results you want — you will see that you can get similar results. With practice and perseverance you'll be well on your way to your own success. ♥

# 13

# LEARN TO PROJECT A "MARRIED WOMAN" ATTITUDE

*E*verything about you displays your attitude, which can work for you or against you when you're looking for a husband. Although attitude is discussed at length elsewhere in this book, here we're going to focus on a specific *type* of attitude. I'm talking about a "married woman" attitude, and it's important to cultivate one even though you're single.

At some point after you've met a man who seems right for you, you will no doubt begin to think of him as a prospective spouse, and if he's the kind of man who wants to marry, it's very possible he's thinking of you in the same way. In this respect, men who desire to marry aren't any different from women. If you want to be sure your potential Mr. Right sees you as a possible future wife, help him out by thinking of *yourself* that way, and projecting the attitude of a married woman.

When I was talking about this chapter to my husband, he was puzzled. "How can a woman act married if she's never been married?" he asked. That's a fair question, but there is a subtle shade of difference between what he was talking about and what we're talking about here. It's really not about "acting married" as much as it is about *imagining* yourself as a married woman, and adopting some of the mannerisms and habits that will help smooth the way to your making your imaginings a reality.

Before we go any further, I want to clarify that projecting a "married woman" attitude does not mean you are being manipulative, pushy or phony. Nor does it mean you are living in denial or being delusional. All you are doing is making your state of mind work for you. Think of it as a form of positive visualization, of "acting as if" something has already happened. Visualizing alone won't make something happen, of course, but will facilitate it. If your goal is to find a man with whom to share your life, ultimately ending in marriage, you have to envision that it has already happened. The super-athletes who have trained most of their lives for the Olympics have to visualize themselves winning. This is the same concept. If you can create in your mind a picture of yourself as a married woman, you will *automatically* change your attitude, and your actions will follow. It's "just" a state of mind — but isn't that *everything*?

So how do you go about it? This can be tricky because there are dozens of subtle and not-so-subtle ways in which a married woman's attitude differs from that of a single woman. Of course there are exceptions; some married women (and men) never get over feeling and acting single, but they need to grow up.

Creating a married woman attitude begins with using your imagination. If it's easier, *pretend* that you have a husband already, or perhaps that you're looking to replace the one you already have. Any game you play in your mind that will work for you is fine. What you are trying to create is a sense of strength and security, which will make you much more attractive to a man who is looking for a wife.

To aid your imagination, consider what a married woman does with her day. Married women have to change their hats all day long, and a woman who has a husband and children, and works outside the home, wears at least three hats. She's a wife, she's a mother, and she's whatever her job demands her to be. When she walks into her office each morning she is the professional worker. Of course she's concerned about her children, husband and home. After all, the children are home with the sitter, or perhaps her husband dropped them off at day care. Or they're in school, but nevertheless she's thinking about them. She's also thinking about her husband — it's only natural for a husband and wife to think about each other during the day. Naturally, she can't share that with her co-workers or boss, since they expect to get 100% of her attention while she's working. When she returns home at night she's a wife and mother — but probably still thinking about her job as well.

This shouldn't be so difficult for you to imagine since you too wear many hats and probably just never really thought about it. You work full time and you're a single woman. And who said single women don't have a life? (If you don't, it's because you have chosen not to.) Are you a jogger or serious tennis player? Do you volunteer, belong to any organizations, or sit on any committees or boards? If so, it's not that much of a stretch to imagine yourself adding more roles to your life. Many single women are in dance groups, teach Sunday school or are members of their church choir. And don't forget the hat worn as a *friend* — just being a friend can be demanding. Lunches, dinners, an occasional afternoon of shopping — all those plans made with your girlfriends. You're probably wearing more hats than you thought.

Now you have your imagination fired up, and are really beginning to see yourself as a married woman. That's a good start, but projecting a married woman attitude is about more than visualizing yourself as married. It is also about changing your mannerisms and your speech patterns. This is where it really helps to *listen* to your married female friends and co-workers, and see how their conversation differs from yours. The first observation will probably be that they usually don't talk just about themselves. They have matured beyond the young single life, so if you're still thinking of the singles bars, singles parties or singles anything, forget about it. This may have been fine when you were in your twenties or maybe very early thirties, but now it's time to break out of that mold. This is not to say that all single people are shallow or self-centered. Being single does leave time for interesting pursuits, and many singles can converse about a variety of topics. However, as a rule single people tend to be self-absorbed in ways that married people aren't, and this is only natural. Unfortunately that self-absorption can come across in your attitude, and can be a real disadvantage when you're trying to find a mate.

What do married women talk about? Naturally they talk about their husbands and children. Of course, you can't talk about your husband and children when they don't exist, but if you keep your subject matter to a mature level that everyone can enjoy, you'll be ahead of the game. You can talk about current events, the latest research on health and nutrition, the international music festival your city is sponsoring, or any number of other topics. If in doubt about how to start a conversation, just ask questions. It works 95% of the time. (In Chapter 10 we dig a little deeper into the art of conversation.)

Another point to consider is that when a married woman is ready to leave a party or meeting, she doesn't hang around. She has to leave. You need to have that same mindset. It's easy to say, "Well I have to get going....I have an appointment." Discipline yourself not to linger too long at any gathering. Remind yourself to do this before you leave your home, before you walk into the party and during the party as well; after all, you have places to go and people to tend to. (This also gives you good practice for being the first to end a date, which, as we discuss in other chapters, is recommended early in a relationship.)

Visualizing yourself as a married woman won't change who you are, but if you do this exercise correctly it will boost your self-confidence, and this will be evident in your speech, your mannerisms, and your attitude in general. If you imagine yourself returning home to a husband and family instead of your cat and a bunch of house plants, you will come across entirely differently from a desperate or depressed single woman.

Okay, let's say you've mastered the attitude, met a potential Mr. Right and are itching to take that "married woman" approach a step further. No, we're not talking about sex here (that's another chapter); we're talking about...food! After the second or third week of dating a prospect, the thought may occur to you to invite him to dinner, bake him some brownies or do something else that shows domesticity. It's natural to want to do this, and a little bit of domesticity and nurturing is an important part of the married-woman attitude you're trying to project. But if you decide to invite a prospect over for dinner, do *not* go overboard. Yes, the way to a man's heart is through his stomach, but first make sure you really want to get to his heart. Every man out there is not right for you. Be selective, take your time, and don't run to cook dinner for a man unless you feel is a potential Mr. Right. Unless you're a professional chef and you cook gourmet meals every night anyway, it's too much work for a mere prospect, and if you go through all that effort and nothing develops, you will not be happy with yourself. And you may come across as "desperate" even after all the work you've done projecting your confident married-woman attitude.

Just a few words about caring. Without being oppressive, or over-bearing, there are ways to display concern for another person. No one wants to be smothered or overly attended to, but there are ways to show concern and caring that make another person take notice and make them feel good. The very least you can do is to show you're sincerely interested in him and that you care about his well-being. At the same time, you will also be demonstrating that you have something substantial to bring to a marriage. Again, however, you have to be careful not to smother him.

# Remember...

*urturing and domesticity are an important part of the "married woman" attitude you want to project, but you absolutely must not go too far with it early in a relationship — especially if you're not certain this man is really a good prospect. Even if you think he has potential, you don't want to "smother" him with your domesticity; that's a great way to scare him off.*

Once you are really able to think of yourself as a married woman, your whole mindset will change. Instead of feeling burdened, frightened or doubtful about the concept, I bet you will actually feel as if a weight has been lifted from your shoulders. This will enable you to become the desirable woman a man is seeking. In fact, this attitude we've been talking about is part of the reason that a woman who has previously been married will remarry before the woman who has never been married. It isn't just because she has the experience of having been married (as in the case of a divorcee or widow); it's because of the way she perceives herself. Even if a woman's marriage has failed, her mind is generally tuned into a different frequency than the young single woman who hasn't a clue as to what marriage is all about. Some people don't need the experience of marriage in order to be able to tune into this frequency; it just comes naturally to them. Everyone else can learn to do so.

At first, this positive visualization technique may seem strange to you, but it works. Learn to think of yourself as a married woman, and you will project the right attitude to any man who's looking for a wife.

PART

Two

# FINDING YOUR "KEEPER"
## (AND HELPING HIM FIND YOU)

# 14

# STOP BELIEVING THAT "THE GOOD ONES ARE ALL TAKEN"

When it comes to marriageable men, the pickings are pretty slim for women over thirty-five. Or so it would seem when you look at the numbers. At the time of this writing, the number of single women thirty-five and over in the U.S. has reached an all-time high of nearly 30 million, and that number is growing. This is actually not too surprising when you consider that the youngest members of the huge and influential baby boom generation are now over forty. Defying a decades long tradition of marrying soon after high school graduation, millions of baby boomer women chose to wait to get married until after they finished college or were established in their careers. A couple of decades later, many are still waiting.

The statistics I've cited above can be discouraging. In fact, you may very well be thinking, "That's right, we're all single because there aren't any good men left. The good ones are all taken and what's left is not marriage material." If that's what you're thinking, I have a surprise for you. There really are some good men out there. Okay, let's get the obvious "yeah-but" question over with first: "If there really are so many good men, where are they, and why haven't I been able to find them?"

You probably think you have an answer to that question already. Maybe your town is too small, and you need to move to a larger one. Or your city's too large and it's easier to meet someone in a smaller town. Or the few "good" men who are left are moving in different circles than you and you'll never run into them.

Finding a prospect used to be much easier. When you were younger, singles were everywhere, and if you didn't like one group, all you had to do was turn around and there was another group to hang with. Everyone was friendly then, everyone was out having a good time. One by one, couples met and paired off — everyone, that is, except you. Or so it seems. What it all boils down to now is that the single men may be there, but you sure can't find them, and it's not for lack of effort on your part.

In the pages of this book we're going to find them together, and you might discover that it's easier than you think. As I've said before and will no doubt say again many times, with some changes in your behavior and attitude (and in most instances, only minor changes), you can remain the same person you are and still find your Mr. Right.

Please know that I'm not trying to oversimplify, nor am I trying to sugarcoat the realities. There are many men in whom you'll have no interest whatsoever. Not all of them have potential just because they're single. In fact, some of them are single precisely because they have no potential. Some are absolutely hopeless (we'll talk about those elsewhere in this book). Not even all of the "good" ones are right for you. But what about the others? How will you find them?

You will find them by changing the way you look *for* them, a topic we'll discuss in more detail later on, and the way you look *at* them, which we'll talk about in this chapter. If you haven't been successful so far in finding the "good ones" — to say nothing of "the" one — it only makes sense to do something different. After all, the chance of Mr. Right just falling into your lap is pretty slim. Why wait for that remote possibility?

Starting today, when you are introduced to a man — or even when you encounter someone you've known for a while but who didn't interest you in "that way" — instead of writing him off immediately, see if you can approach him in a different manner than you have in the past. If you would normally have given him the cold shoulder because he didn't meet your criteria (e.g., he wasn't good-looking enough, or you didn't think he earned enough), take another look. Ask yourself what this man is all about. Does he make good eye contact with you? Does he smile? Does he seem genuinely interested in talking with you? Forget his physical features for a moment; is he well groomed and neatly dressed? If he didn't turn you off immediately, then he's worth a few minutes of your time. Lighten up and give him a chance, because you may have something more in common with him than you initially thought.

If the problem seems to be that he isn't all that interested in you, look more closely. If he's truly turned off by you, or totally uninterested, he'll probably make it pretty obvious. Most men aren't all that great at hiding actual distaste. But if he just seems a little hesitant or evasive, or isn't very talkative, consider the possibility that he may simply be shy. Some men are. I know it's hard to believe that of a man in his forties or fifties, but it's true.

If shy men aren't your cup of tea, it might be time to expand your tastes. Granted, the aggressive, outgoing man may be more appealing. He'll probably take care of you (whatever that means these days) and he very likely is in pretty good shape financially. Well, consider this: The shyer man is probably equally stable, but never gained a lot of self-confidence with women. That doesn't mean he doesn't have a lot to offer the right woman. Most likely, he's been working for years, has saved his money, and is ready — emotionally, financially and every other way — for a serious relationship.

And he just may turn out to be a tiger in bed (in case you're looking for something more than mere stability). When you were twenty-five you probably wouldn't have given this shy guy the time of day. When he was twenty-five he might have been a real geek. But he may very well have grown into a wonderful man. Don't be afraid to give him a chance just because he's shy.

In fact, virtually every single man you meet is a prospect. Again, this doesn't mean that every unmarried heterosexual man you encounter will be marriage material or even a dating partner. You can still be choosy, in fact you should be. Just don't go overboard, since there are, after all, fewer men to go around than there were when you were twenty-five. Try to keep an open mind. My first suggestion is that if you think he's decent — if he is sincerely interested in you and isn't self-centered, egomaniacal or narcissistic — give him a fair chance. If you don't speak to a man because his looks don't appeal to you, you may be the one who's losing out. Beneath that not-so-sexy exterior there might be an intelligent, funny, good-hearted man — who could very well become better looking to you over time!

# Remember...

ou must keep an open mind — don't automatically reject someone because he doesn't meet your list of criteria for Mr. Right. A single man is a "prospect until proven otherwise".

A young woman I know was introduced to a man who was half a head shorter than she, was bald and had a slight stutter. I couldn't possibly tell you how many times she used to emphatically state that she would never date a man shorter than she. I always gave her the same answer, "Never say never!" Of course you know the end of the story — they married!

There are hundreds of stories like this. Attraction works in strange ways, and contrary to popular belief, it isn't *always* instantaneous. Love doesn't always pound on the front door, sometimes it just stands outside waiting for you to open the door and invite it in. Give it a chance and by all means give the next single guy you meet a chance — and you just may be very pleasantly surprised.

If you continue to believe the myth that the "good ones" are all taken, you are severely limiting your chances for finding a husband. You have all but admitted defeat. There are still good men out there and you can find them. You may have to change your search criteria, and you will almost certainly have to change your own perceptions as well as your behavior, but your happiness is worth all of your best efforts. ♥

# 15

## THROW AWAY
## ALL OF YOUR "LISTS"

*H*ow many women do you know who say, "I have a list"? Whether it's mental or written, they have a list of qualifications for their future mate. He has to be in good shape, intelligent, be a professional, make upwards of $100,000 annually and — this one is my favorite — he'd better have hair on his head! If you're one of these women, the first thing you must do is throw away all of your lists, written and mental. Don't panic, I didn't say give up chocolate or sex. I just said to throw out your lists!

I know it's hard; you've had those lists in your mind for a long time. And perhaps you've always heard that whenever you want to make changes in your life you need to set specific goals, which means making lists. It's true that list making can be helpful for some aspects of self-improvement, and without a doubt, lists are crucial for running your daily life — shopping, packing for a trip, daily reminders and the like. But they do *not* work for finding a husband.

If you have a list, the chances are slim that you will find your mate. If you want marriage and still want to keep a list, then go back to the store and ask for your money back, because this book will definitely not work for you. This is about finding a husband, a really great one — but *Mr. Perfect doesn't exist.*

# Remember...

*ists work well for everyday functions in life, such as shopping, planning for a trip, or daily reminders. They're useful in self-improvement programs as well. But they absolutely do not work for finding a husband. If you insist on a list, your chances for success are slim.*

Our children's friends have always been close to my husband and me. Many of them married soon after graduating from college, then another group married when they were well into their thirties, but others never married at all. From college to graduate school to the real world, I listened to these perpetually single young people and I heard every excuse possible. By far the most common reason was, "I just can't find the right person." Upon questioning them, I found their expectations were often unrealistic. Obviously, one thing they weren't doing was looking in the mirror. Were they perfect? Of course not, but they thought they would find the "perfect" person nevertheless. Believe me, the men were as bad as the women, if not worse. To this day, some of them are still searching.

Years ago we went to a family wedding. My cousin, whom I hadn't seen in a few years, ran over to me and said, "I wanted to warn you, Cindy (a girl we'd gone to high school with) is here — and you won't believe her husband!" Cindy was one of the girls all the guys wanted to hit on. She was very tall and attractive and had a great body. We had all gone off to college, her family had moved away, and no one had seen her since. Now there she was, happily married to a man who was only four-feet-something tall. But he had a giant of a personality, and the last I heard, they had a family and are still married. Who knows why anyone chooses the spouse they do? For whatever reason, it worked for Cindy. You can be sure she didn't set out to marry a four-foot-tall man, nor am I suggesting you look beyond the norm — I'm just saying lists don't work.

A girlfriend of mine, Rachel, is in one of the best relationships of her life. Years ago she wouldn't have looked twice at Mark, but after years of bad experiences with sexy "ladies' men" who fit the criteria on her own list, she found Mark's kindness and sense of humor very refreshing. No, he isn't as stunning as some of the men she's dated in the past, but he treats her well and she thoroughly enjoys his company. If she hadn't been willing to throw away her list, she would never have given this great guy a chance.

I sold residential real estate for years. More often than not, prospective buyers would tell me all the criteria they desired in their new home. For example, they wanted a traditional two-story home with the master bedroom down, three additional bedrooms, no pool, etc. The lists usually went on and on, but the few items on the top of the list were the only ones that mattered. Once I'd hear what their basic requirements were — location (for work/schools), a good school system, number of bedrooms and of course price range, they didn't need a list. Everything else was negotiable. Frequently within the first or second time out with a couple, I knew which house they were going to buy. Of course I never told them, but thirty homes later, they'd return to the second or third house I had shown to them. The reason was simple: this home fit their needs. It was somewhat like trying on shoes; they either fit or they don't. All of the other amenities were just details.

All of us have walked into a store looking for something specific. Let's say you have your heart set on buying a pink double-breasted wool blazer for your winter wardrobe. You look all over, but this particular season there isn't one to be found in the stores. You have a choice. You can either choose something else or do without. In other words, you can't buy what isn't there. Suppose you broaden your parameters just a little, and decide this season you're going to buy a nice looking, versatile wool blazer or jacket. You may not have found what you originally set out to buy, but I bet you'll love it just as much, if not more.

In Chapter 12 I discuss some of the traits you can pick up from women who have married before. Besides self-confidence, there is one other common denominator they share — an open mind. They never say, "He has to have this," or "He can't be like that." In other words, they never keep "lists".

When I was young, I thought I would marry a tall, thin, dark haired, older man. If I had gone through life obsessed with that image, I would still be single, because what we conjure up in our minds simply doesn't exist. What we want and what we get are two different things. On the other hand, if you play it right, once you get it, it *is* what you want, just plus or minus a few things here and there!

We all have a tendency to form a picture in our minds, and perhaps our subconscious continues searching for it. Maybe it is time for you to change the picture. Understand that you are not lowering your expectations, you are expanding them. You're not going to "settle", but neither are you going to limit yourself with arbitrary lists.

## Remember...

 *hrowing out your lists does not mean you are lowering your expectations — you are simply expanding them.*

Believe the pros who say it won't happen when you're expecting it to. They're right! After you've made the small changes we discuss throughout this book, you need to go on about your life — without that shopping list. Of course there are certain basic requirements on which you should *never* compromise, such as compatibility in core values, which we discuss in Chapter 19, and abusive or addictive personalities, discussed in Chapter 44. As for all of the other details, let them take care of themselves. Lighten up, and keep your eyes open, because when you least expect to meet him, you will. But if you cling to your shopping list, you may never know he's the one — and you may have passed up the greatest "find" of your life. ♥

# *16*

## ACCEPT IMPERFECTIONS (YOURS AND HIS) — "SECONDS" CAN BE FIRST-RATE!

*H*ad you ever considered that Mr. Right could be Mr. "Right Under Your Nose"? Is it possible that you've been passing up exactly what you've been looking for? Don't overlook the possibility that your future husband could be traveling incognito. He may be the man to whom you've never given a second glance, simply because he didn't measure up to your idea of husband material. But you could be making a mistake.

As you know if you've read Chapter 14, I completely disagree with the idea that after a woman reaches the age of thirty-five or so, "the good ones are all taken". It just isn't so. There are still some good single men available at every age. How do I know? I hear of women meeting and marrying these great men nearly every day. In case you're still not convinced, let's look at this issue from another angle.

Our culture is obsessed with notions of "perfection", particularly when it comes to physical beauty. Thanks to clever marketers and advertisers, we're so used to airbrushed, retouched perfection in everything from food to cars to people that we often carry these unreal expectations, consciously or subconsciously, into our everyday life. It's only natural to want a mate who is physically attractive, but some people are so set on finding someone with flawless looks (and, perhaps, a "perfect" career and income level as well) that they overlook some truly wonderful prospects. Maybe we need to take a lesson from apple growers.

Apples are picked and graded according to size and quality, then put into storage and from there they are shipped to the wholesalers. Many apples fall to the ground before they have a chance to be picked. Those perfectly good apples cannot be sold as "firsts", but they aren't discarded. They're called culls and are gathered up and sold as "seconds". Out of a whole bushel of those "seconds", there might be a dozen or more that are just a little bit less than perfect. A slight imperfection, however, doesn't make an apple inedible. Even an apple that isn't perfectly symmetrical but may be otherwise good is definitely worth a try, or better yet, a bite! Sure, they're slightly imperfect — but who's perfect, right? When it comes to men, those "slightly imperfect apples" are what you're looking for. Naturally, that doesn't mean you're going to "settle" for someone less than you had hoped to marry. You're not going after the rotten apple just because the shiny, flawless one is beyond your grasp. You're not going to pursue Quasimoto just because you can't have Tom Cruise. If you've read Chapter 15, which discusses throwing away your "lists", you will know that I am not asking you to lower your expectations, just to expand them. Change your perception, and perhaps you will begin to see some men differently.

Some of the most amazing relationships have involved women who picked "imperfect apples", sometimes against the advice of family and friends, or the expectations of society. A young woman I know fell in love at the age of twenty-six with a man who had just been diagnosed with a malignant brain tumor. Although her family thought it was going to be a long road without a happy ending, she accepted his proposal of marriage. Most people would say that was just a heartbreak waiting to happen. Indeed, after ten years he lost his battle with the disease — but when I spoke to her soon after he died, she said she had absolutely no regrets. They gave each other the love and strength that they both desired and she has ten years of wonderful memories. Many weeks and months were spent helping him convalesce over the years, but she was thrilled to have made his life better, and when he could manage it he was the most wonderful, devoted husband. Her marriage was a wonderful experience and she said she hopes to remarry. I know she will, because with that attitude she won't have any problem finding another husband. And if she hadn't had such an open mind and heart, think of the joy she and her late husband would never have known. This is a rather dramatic example, but I think it's a great illustration of how love can thrive against terrible odds.

Meredith Viera, co-host of the ABC morning show *The View*, married her husband when she was still in her twenties, knowing he had already been diagnosed with multiple sclerosis. She fell in love with him and married him regardless of his disease. Of course she knew that life wouldn't be easy for them, but does anyone know what may lie ahead? Their marriage has endured many hardships but their love is stronger than any disease. Sure, life would have been easier without it, but in a recent interview she stated that their love has been strong enough to sustain them through all their problems. Love...that's what you want, someone to love you, and for you to love him, unconditionally, regardless of either your imperfections or his.

---

## Remember...

on't hold out for Mr. Perfect, because he doesn't exist. Take a closer look at the not-so-perfect guys you meet; some of the most amazing relationships have involved women who picked slightly "imperfect apples".

---

Often the "imperfections" in your potential Mr. Right aren't physical. A friend of mine had a short first marriage and then was single for many years. Tammy was in her late forties when she met the love of her life. Unfortunately, his first marriage had been so bad that he was, to put it mildly, a little gun-shy. To make things worse, his children sided with their mother, and his relationship with them at the best was strained. Many women would have said, "Forget it!" But Tammy loved this "bruised apple" and continued to date him. Though it seemed unbelievable to those who knew them, there came a day when he changed his mind about marriage and proposed. They were wed and had the most wonderful marriage. Please know that it is rarely advisable for a woman over thirty-five to "hang in there" for extended periods of time if she definitely wants to get married and the man is obviously not interested in marriage. In most cases, when a man says he doesn't want to marry, you have to believe him! Tammy's case was an exception because marriage was not her number one goal. While of course she would have liked to marry again, she adored this man and enjoyed his company so much that she didn't particularly care if they married or not. When they finally did marry, it was just the icing on the cake for her.

Up to now we've been talking about "imperfect" men, but what if you are a "slightly bruised apple" yourself? You should never feel that your quest for a husband is hopeless. So what if you don't live up to the image of perfection you imagine most men seek? The reality is that not all of them are looking for stunning beauties; most men are more realistic than that. And even if you have a physical handicap, birth defect or other cosmetic problems, there are still men who will appreciate you for who you are. Yes, your prospects may be fewer, but if you want marriage you can find it. People fall in love with another because of who that person is. Believe me, I have seen firsthand some astonishing cases of men who have fallen for women who had severe physical problems. It happens all the time; it has even happened in my circle of family and friends. And think of former Beatle Paul McCartney and his lovely wife, Heather, who is an amputee. The man who falls in love with a woman who has a disfigurement simply does not care. He has fallen in love with her for the person she is.

---

## Remember...

 on't use your own flaws and imperfections as an excuse for not finding a husband. Even if you have severe physical problems, there are men who will love and appreciate you for who you are.

---

There are, of course, some men who are looking for the "perfect apple", even as there are women who are holding out for the same, but my guess is that they're *all* going to have a pretty long wait. Single men who think Ms. Perfect may still be around the corner should look in the mirror and ask themselves, "Are *you* perfect?" Okay, a few of them really may think they are, but many more will be hesitant to definitively say, "Yes!"

To everyone who is looking for that flawless mate, I ask you to think ahead. What if you did find your Ms. or Mr. Perfect, and then something happened to that flawless spouse a few years into your marriage — an illness or accident, for example? You wouldn't walk, would you? For that matter, what happens when you have your first disagreement and your shining knight's armor begins to look a little tarnished? Will you leave? If you think you might call it quits for any of the reasons above, perhaps you need to look in your heart and decide if marriage is really what you want. After all, marriage is for better or for worse.

Let's face it, few of us measure up to the "ideal" female or male. There are so many factors that are incorporated into who we are. As I read in a cookbook recently, "Don't judge an apple by its looks alone; the best tasting ones are often not the most beautiful." Keep this in mind when looking for a mate (and when evaluating yourself as a potential mate) and you just may have some golden, delicious experiences! ♥

# DON'T LET AGE
# (YOURS OR HIS)
# BE A BIG ISSUE

ge is a state of mind — it's just a number. We've all heard that before and it's difficult not to become a bit cynical, especially since everywhere we turn we are met with another reminder of how our culture values youth. In a world that seems to place so much importance on outward appearances, it's often difficult to focus on the fact that at forty-two or forty-eight, you really don't *feel* any different than you did at thirty-two. It's true that although the mirror image may have changed a little, you're still the same person inside.

Still, age is an issue in our society, and sometimes we just can't escape it. It is almost certainly an issue for you if you're over forty and unmarried — particularly if you've never been married before. Things weren't that bad when you turned thirty-five and were still single, but I'm willing to bet that turning forty was difficult. It's not just because you expected to be married well before that age, but some of you may also have felt increased pressure from family members and friends who wondered why you'd never settled down. If you're like millions of other women, the greatest pressure comes from within. You're constantly asking yourself why you haven't been able to find that special someone, and you're continually reminding yourself that you're not getting any younger.

This is understandable, since age seems to be such a big deal for so many people. It doesn't have to be a big deal for *you*, however, and it certainly doesn't have to keep you from finding Mr. Right. Apart from childbearing (which may or may not be a concern for you), age isn't a real issue unless you allow it to be. In fact, in some ways being over thirty-five can be an advantage, not a disadvantage, when you're looking for love.

"On what planet?" you might be asking. Well, this one. Consider the high divorce rates, for example. Divorce statistics in this country are sobering, but the good news is that *most couples who marry over thirty-five have a better chance of their marriage surviving than the couples who marry in their mid-twenties.* The plain truth is that overall, people who marry after thirty-five have a lower divorce rate.

That's not surprising. By the age of thirty-five you know a lot more about the person you are, and what you want in a partner, than you did when you were in your early twenties. More than likely you're established in your career and are more aware of what you want out of life than you were when you were younger. At the very least you have a broader perspective on life; a woman I know refers to it as "gaining altitude". What she means is that you have a better view of the landscape from "up there" than you did when you were younger.

The downside is that you are probably more set in your ways. Change may seem more daunting now than it was fifteen or twenty years ago. But think about it — initially, nobody really likes change, even if the change is for the better. It has been said, and rightfully so, that "The only person who likes change is a wet baby!" Just own up to your reluctance, and realize that if you want to change, you can, and it doesn't matter how old you are.

Every day we read about eighty-year-olds who are learning to swim, going back to college, running marathons, even finding true love. You can be sure that every one of these people had to make a conscious decision to make a change in her or his life; they weren't all former Olympians. Instead of just sitting around growing older and griping about the weather or life in general, these people went out and did something challenging and fun. If octogenarians can do it, there's no reason you can't make a few changes in your own life.

Also remember that this is all about making a series of *small* changes — not a wholesale revamping of your life in one fell swoop. Don't forget that even a subtle change can make a significant difference. If you're still reluctant, remind yourself that change is good for everyone, no matter how young or how old. Whether it's moving furniture around, making a new friend, or just taking a different route home from work, change adds a different perspective. It's enlightening and most of all, it's *refreshing.* And it helps keep you young, mentally and physically.

You might have to work at turning off that inner voice (or tuning out those outer voices) that say you're "too old" to try something new. You can continue listening to those negative messages, or you can take a lesson from Plato. The story goes that when he decided to take up flute playing late in life, someone told him he was too old to learn. He replied, "At what other age can I begin?"

---

## Remember...

urn off that inner voice, and tune out those outer voices, that say you're "too old" to try something new. Learning new things keeps you young mentally as well as physically, and helps you get to the point where age really is "no big deal"!

---

In another chapter I mention that when I was growing up, our family had two unmarried female friends. One of them, Barbara or "Aunt B", lived in the past, obsessing over boyfriends she'd dated as a teenager — and she died unmarried. The other friend, Mary, didn't live in the past; she lived for today. Her story is one of my favorites. Mary had single friends, married friends, divorced and widowed friends. While working full time, she was an active member of many organizations, and always managed to stay connected with countless people. For many years she didn't have a husband, but she had everything else going for her.

When Mary was in her early sixties, a friend of my mother's died and a few months later Mother introduced the widower to Mary. He was a nurturer by nature, and loved taking care of Mary, and she loved the attention. Like Mary, he was a people person, and before long they were engaged and then married. Although Mary didn't wed until she was sixty-two, she was madly in love. He treated her like a queen, and they had a wonderful twenty-four years together.

No matter how old or how young you are, your attitude is more important than your age. Mary knew this, and so did an aunt of mine. Even at the age of ninety-four, she was still attractive, and I recall her story of a time when a charming man came up and began flirting with her, completely ignoring her daughter, also an attractive woman, who was standing alongside her. The difference was that my aunt caught his eye and smiled at him. She was a remarkable woman, and many men were drawn to her because she had a twinkle in her eyes and she knew how to get a man. She outlived two husbands and a boyfriend. The only reason her boyfriend didn't marry her was that he figured she'd outlive him as well. He was right — she did!

Never think that just because you're no longer twenty-five, you can't find true romance. Love happens at every age and stage of life. Just go to any senior living center and you'll see many people who have lost their lifelong spouses but have found love once again. If Mary at sixty-two, or a ninety-year-old in a senior center, can find her Mr. Right, you certainly can.

Are you still not convinced? Are you protesting that Mary and my aunt are the exceptions and that for everyone else it's just harder to find a partner once you're over thirty-five? Okay, the statistics don't lie — as noted in Chapter 14, there really are fewer single men your age now than when you were in your twenties. But in truth there are desirable single men in every age group. Besides, who says you have to confine your search to a man who is your age or older? Why not consider a younger one? There's no reason not to. Years ago it was unusual for women to marry men younger than they; today it is much more acceptable. When a woman pairs up with a younger man, many people will say, "Good for her!"

There's still a bit of a double standard, of course, and people still seem to be more accepting of age discrepancies if the man is the older party, particularly if the age gap is more than ten years or so. For example, the media seemed much more tolerant of the romance between Harrison Ford and Calista Flockhart (a twenty-two-year age difference) than of Demi Moore and Ashton Kutcher (a fifteen-year difference). Why let the critics dictate to you? There are many advantages to pairing up with a younger man, and if you and he truly love each other, your marriage has at least as good a chance as more traditional match-ups…maybe even better! New York writer and critic Lynn Snowden Picket is blissfully married to a man who's fourteen years younger than she, and in an article in O Magazine she wrote, "Women who reject younger men could be denying themselves the most wonderful relationship of their lives." She says she and her younger man are constantly learning from each other and are fascinated by their differing perspectives. Age *is* sometimes an issue in their relationship — but according to her it's a positive one!

So don't waste any more time despairing because you're thirty-eight or forty-two or fifty-three or older, and aren't married. The next time you start fretting about your age, do three things:

1. *Think of all those happy couples who married after the age of thirty-five.* They're out there. And it's my guess that these couples once shared the same doubts you have, but they didn't give up, and they eventually found a person who was worth waiting for. So can you.
2. *Remember that you can choose to make changes in your life no matter how old you are.* So what if you're not twenty anymore? There really is no set timetable for finding happiness. A few years ago therapist and career counselor Barbara Sher wrote a book about finding fulfillment in the second half of life. I think the title says it all: *It's Only Too Late If You Don't Start Now*. Don't ever think you're "too old" to try anything new.
3. *Realize that if you don't let age be a big issue to you, it won't be a big issue to your partner.* He may be older than you, he may be younger, or he may be your age, but if you love and accept yourself as you are, so will he. And if he doesn't, he's not for you.

Desiring to share one's life with a partner is just a natural part of being human, and the basics of a good relationship — love, trust, respect and fulfillment — are the same no matter how old you are. When it comes to what's really important in life, age really *isn't* a big deal. Further, there are advantages to waiting later to get married. From a biological (i.e., childbearing) standpoint, the optimal time for a woman to get married is in her late teens to mid twenties. But from the standpoint of emotional, sexual and spiritual fulfillment — and the long-term success of the marriage — "better late than never" could accurately be revised to simply, *"better late"*! ❤

# 18

# OPPOSITES ATTRACT —
## CELEBRATE YOUR DIFFERENCES!

*I*f you study married couples, you'll find that most people tend to marry someone who is similar to themselves in many respects, such as socioeconomic background, education level and the like. Even if there are differences they are usually superficial. For example, a man grew up in an upper-middle-class home in a Chicago suburb, while his wife is from a middle-class family in a small Texas town. Despite the differences, their standard of living was similar. A woman has a bachelor's degree in psychology and her husband has an MBA — different, yes, but still more or less "equal" in terms of education.

People also tend to hook up with partners whose level of physical attractiveness is similar to theirs. The hunky football hero is more likely to end up with a supermodel lookalike, or an actual supermodel, than with someone more ordinary looking. There are exceptions (apart from the obvious stereotype of the beautiful young woman with the rich but old man), but most couples are pretty close on the "looks" spectrum.

The picture can change, however, when we're talking about personality, interests and personal tastes. We've all heard the expression, "opposites attract". And quite often that's true. There are probably many reasons this is so. Sometimes people are looking for a part of themselves that is "missing". A shy, quiet man might be drawn to an outgoing social butterfly who brings him out of his shell, or a timid woman might be attracted to a daredevil who does many of the things she can't quite work up the courage to do. Sometimes the reason is not that profound. Frequently people are attracted to someone with different interests or tastes simply because they're curious or fascinated, and they want to expand their own horizons. That fascination develops into love.

I can tell you firsthand that a union of opposites can work very well. Take my husband and me, for example. We come from similar backgrounds and have much in common, yet we are opposite in many respects. We both love people of all ages, from the very young to the elderly. We both have friendly, outgoing personalities and we share the same values and goals, but that's where the similarity ends. I can socialize all night; my husband cannot. He likes everything on his pizza; I like mine plain. He puts sweetener and cream in his coffee; I drink mine black. He loves soda; I don't. He can sit still; I have to be busy. His favorite ice cream is rum raisin; I despise it. He loves steak and can't put enough A-1 and Worcestershire Sauce on it; I wouldn't care if I ever ate steak again, but when I do, it's plain. He loves jazz, boxing, horses, swimming in the ocean and…well, I'm just not that enthusiastic about any of those things. The list goes on and on. Yet we have been happily married for over forty years.

Not long ago I heard a couple who had just begun dating say they knew their relationship would be good because they had so much in common. They loved the same food, the same music, even the same movies. Granted, some aspects of a relationship may be easier if the two people have similar tastes and habits. At the very least, deciding what to do on a date will be a no-brainer. The couple I just mentioned did have a good relationship for about six months, but eventually they decided they really had more differences than similarities, and they went their separate ways. Don't fall for the notion that having common tastes is the key to a future successful marriage. On the other hand, don't despair if you don't share a lot of interests with a prospect – it doesn't mean that you're poorly suited to each other. Remember that a relationship is whatever two people agree to, not what two people like or dislike.

Don't automatically give up on a prospect when you see your personality types are different. If, for example, he's an aggressive, hyper Type A personality, and you're a quiet, thoughtful Type B, don't jump to the conclusion that the relationship has no future. If he doesn't force his energy on you, then there isn't a problem. He may enjoy taking charge of everything, and if it doesn't bother you, let him. If it does, simply tell him to back off. I know so many couples who are opposite personality types and they have wonderful marriages.

What if you are a Type A personality and feel you need a man with a similarly strong personality? Don't be so stuck on the idea that another Type A is the best choice for you. If you're worried that you will turn a man into a dish rag, your fears are probably unfounded. Most men won't put up with that, and most people frown on a woman who steps all over a man. Just because you're Type A doesn't mean you need to be with another high-achieving, high-profile personality. A quieter, less aggressive mate could very well be the best balance for your energy.

For better or worse, opposites do attract, but the downside is that sometimes those "opposite" traits that drew people to each other in the first place end up driving them crazy. And some people, though initially attracted to someone who is their polar opposite, spend their marriage trying to transform their spouse into a mirror image of themselves.

---

## Remember...

*pposites do attract, but as time goes by, some of those "opposite" traits that seemed so appealing in your mate early in the relationship can get on your nerves. If your prospective mate is very different from you, you might have reservations at the very beginning. Either way, you need to ask yourself if you can accept him as he is now — without expectations that he will change and become more like you.*

---

So why does it work so well for many other couples who really are "opposites"? I can tell you how my husband and I work it out. Sometimes he remains at parties longer than he'd like to, and sometimes I leave earlier than I'd prefer. We order our pizza half and half. He laughs at me as I run around doing things while he's sitting relaxing. We both love music, so there's plenty to listen to that we both enjoy. We live in a big city with plenty of terrific restaurants where he can get his red meat fix and I can enjoy something lighter. After all these years, we still comment how opposite we are in so many things — but they're all minor, and we know it. We've learned to live with, laugh at and love our differences.

What happens if your partner's formerly charming "opposite" traits, tastes or interests begin to get on your nerves — or vice versa? Talk to each other. I know you've heard that before, but it really is the best way to solve most problems in a relationship. Bring your concerns out in the open. If your mate is a party animal and you're the exact opposite, nego-tiate to spend Saturday night at home once in a while. Plan an especially romantic evening at home, a night you'll both enjoy. Learn to laugh at each other's differences instead of complaining about them. When you get disgruntled, remember how attractive the two of you found each other's dissimilarities in the first place. And if you catch yourself trying to make your partner more like you, remind yourself that if you had wanted some-one just like you, you could have stayed single!

Of course there is more to a successful marriage than just learning to appreciate each other's differences. What you always need to keep in mind is not what you *don't* share, but what you *do* share. The best mar-riages are those in which the two people are opposite in some respects but similar in others. You can have different tastes, and completely oppo-site personalities, but the truly important elements — your values and goals — absolutely have to be similar. If they aren't, you will have a diffi-cult time making your marriage work. If your values are the same, your marriage can survive and thrive despite your other differences. In Chap-ter 19 we take a closer look at values.

Don't automatically give up on someone just because you think he's too different from you. At least give him a chance. If your hearts are in the same place about the things that really matter, it makes no differ-ence if he likes classical music and you like Zydeco, or you love snowboarding and he prefers a quiet evening at home playing chess. You will find a way to work things out. Believe me, I know! ♥

# *19*

# LOOK FOR SOMEONE WHO SHARES YOUR VALUES

Once you have met someone and established that there is a mutual attraction, or at the very least a mutual interest, you have to quickly determine whether or not you share the same values.

A successful relationship requires that a couple share the same values. Over the years I have repeated this often. Before a couple can even think ahead to a permanent relationship, they must share the same values. If you see early on that your values are too dissimilar, that's a signal to run. Too many issues will arise in the course of your relationship (and subsequent marriage) that cannot be resolved. Why set yourself up for heartache and frustration?

You cannot build a house on sand; you have to first dig down to the solid bedrock. That gives the structure strength and stability. Similarly, relationships not built on a solid foundation — a foundation of common values — will tumble. Many unforeseen problems will test the stability of a relationship, and if the foundation isn't strong enough to begin with, it will not weather the many storms of life.

In case you're wondering, this in no way contradicts the assertion that opposites attract. When I speak of opposites, I'm referring to personality traits and personal taste, not basic values. Admittedly, sometimes the two seem to overlap, but there's a big difference between, say, having dissimilar tastes in movies or pizza toppings, and being in vehement disagreement about one's business ethics, or the best way to raise a child.

Nor does my suggestion to look for someone who shares your values contradict my admonition to throw away your "lists" (Chapter 15). Even as most of my residential real estate clients had a few basic requirements on which they were not willing to compromise, there are certain things you have a right to expect of your future mate. It's not asking too much to want a man who shares your values about the important things in life.

Values affect every aspect of your life, from the way you conduct business to all of your family and social interactions. If you consider yourself to have high principles, will you be able to live with someone whose principles are lower than yours? Probably not. You will continually be frustrated and ultimately disgusted by this person, and he may simply think you are self-righteous and will grow to resent you. This is hardly the foundation upon which to build a lifelong relationship.

For instance, let's say your prospect has a shady side. He's a deceptive businessman, and you clearly see that he is less than honest with his clients. Obviously that shows a character flaw, unlike so many people who occasionally may tell a white lie. When deception is constant and ongoing, it isn't a white lie. If you think a prospect does not share your high values, you have to ask yourself if you are lowering your standards by entering into a relationship with him and turning a blind eye to his dealings. Again you must ask yourself, will you be happy living with someone whose standards aren't as high as yours? I don't think so! The one given we have in life is our good name. That is who we are. If you hold yourself in high esteem you will be happiest with someone who also does. You will both know how to give and command respect.

I assume that you have good solid values in life. Even though to some degree "good values" and "high standards" are subjective concepts, there are certain basic principles to which most of us adhere. We try to avoid harming others, to be honest in our dealings with them and generally speaking, to be considerate of our fellow human beings. We expect the same consideration in return. That's what I mean by high standards.

No matter how high you consider your standards to be, however, don't make the mistake of believing that you're better than anyone else. There may be traits about someone that you dislike, but this doesn't necessarily mean that person has lower values than yours. Manners are a perfect example. When most of us were growing up, manners were a part of our upbringing. Everything changes, though, and the rules of etiquette have eased up in many situations. I still think everyone should know proper manners, but manners aren't necessarily the same as values. They do reflect one's feelings of self-worth, but sometimes people are just lazy or they really do not know what is "proper". If you reject a man only because he has "iffy" manners, you could be overlooking a great guy. If everything else is fine, perhaps a few gentle suggestions will help him in the etiquette department. Your guidance may or may not be effective, but if the two of you are attracted to each other and share the same values, you need to give him a chance.

---

### Remember...

*here may be traits about someone that you dislike, but this doesn't necessarily mean that person has lower values than yours. If the two of you are attracted to each other and share the same values, give him a chance.*

---

I am frequently asked for examples of having similar values. One that comes to mind is a couple who definitely seem to share the same values — but in this case, they're just not very high, at least not in my opinion. The husband seems to have problems with everyone who does any work for him. Whether it's work done inside their home, yard work or automobile repair, he always finds a reason to either fire the workers before they've completed the work, or renegotiate the money due after the work is completed. Why? It's probably because he's just cheap. Or he likes to feel that he's come out on top and has received something for nothing. At any rate, he takes advantage of people, and to me, that's inexcusable. Apparently it doesn't bother his wife, because she seems to accept his behavior as just his way of conducting business. I would not want to live with someone who is dishonest or who takes advantage of others. But if it doesn't bother his wife, at least not so much that she can't live with it, then they probably share the same values. As a matter of fact, they appear to have a good working marriage.

If you are dating someone and you see that his values aren't as high as yours are, you can of course give him the benefit of the doubt by asking him why he does whatever it is that is bothering you. In Chapters 43 and 44, we go into more detail about how you can approach a man in such a situation. Remember, you can't change him and shouldn't try, but you can give him a gentle nudge in the right direction. If that doesn't work and you know you cannot live with his behavior, it's probably best to find someone else.

On the other hand, when assessing the relationship and asking yourself if it is worth it, you could still come up with a positive answer. Does he value and respect his family and yours? If so, that's a definite plus. Does he respect the law, is he a good citizen and is he a decent human being? All are indications of a person's character.

---

## Remember...

ifferences in tastes, opinions and even personality traits between two people can make a relationship interesting. But if there is too much difference in core values, the relationship doesn't stand much chance of long-term success.

---

I'm only going to touch on religion, because for many people it is a factor in their choice of a life partner. It is less important today than in the past, especially when you are older and there may not be children involved, but even so, differences in religion can be a problem. Keep in mind there is no right or wrong, and today we are more accepting or tolerant of other religions and mixed marriages than we were perhaps twenty or thirty years ago. My own personal opinion is this: Marriage is difficult, and religion issues do not make it any easier. If religion is important to one person and not to the other, a marriage can work, provided the religious partner isn't set on "converting" the non-religious one. It becomes a problem when one is intolerant or uncomfortable with the other person's religion or lack thereof, and isn't honest with themselves or with their future spouse right from the beginning. It can also become a problem when children are involved, even if you think the religious issues have been resolved before marriage. One spouse could change his or hers mind after the children are born, regarding which religion, if any, to raise them in.

There is no guarantee that mixed religions will pose no problem, even when no children are involved. A couple I know both married for the first time later in life. She was in her late forties, he in his mid-fifties. She was Catholic and converted to his religion, Judaism. A few years into their marriage, she could not live with her conversion and returned to the religion in which she was raised. When I asked her why she ever converted to begin with, she said she just thought it was the right thing to do.

Her converting back to Catholicism wasn't a problem because her husband did not care, but it easily could have been a disaster for their relationship. Holidays and other occasions could have been a constant source of conflict. My friend would have been unhappy had she not been at liberty to practice her religion and might ultimately have grown to resent her husband. Even if you don't have children and don't plan to, couples have to closely look at the ramifications of a mixed marriage.

Years ago I believed that marriage works best if a couple share the same background, including religion and even race. Generally speaking I still believe this, but there are many successful intermarriages today. If you're in a relationship and religion is important to you, resolve your issues beforehand; spell everything out and try to think of all the consequences, with or without children. Yes, intermarriages work, but you must address all the issues before you commit to a permanent relationship. And even then, you still might have doubts and conflicts somewhere down the road, as my friend did. However, if your love for each other is strong, and all of your other values are in sync — if your foundation is solid — your marriage will probably survive these difficulties.

Differences make a marriage interesting. It's no big deal if he likes comedies while you like period pieces, or he likes to dance all night and you prefer getting up early in the morning and going out on long bicycle rides. You can adjust. But if the two of you differ too much in your core values, your chance of having a successful marriage is very slim. Look for someone who shares your values about the things that matter most, and you'll have a good start on a relationship that will last a lifetime. ♥

# *20*

# REMEMBER THAT WHEREVER YOU GO, YOU BRING YOURSELF WITH YOU
## (SO DON'T GIVE UP ON YOUR HOMETOWN JUST YET)

o you know women who decided to move to a larger city when they weren't finding a husband in their hometown? A move doesn't guarantee they'll find a spouse. In fact, more often than not, they could have remained where they were and they would have found a husband. Conversely, many women who move just to find love have no better luck in the big city than they did back home. Why? Because, as I've said before, it isn't about the man, it's about *them.*

When we were growing up in Upstate New York, the single women went either to Manhattan or Boston after college. The trend was to marry younger then, so when a woman who had moved to the big city turned twenty-four or twenty-five and was still unmarried, she frequently returned to her hometown. Believe it or not, within a year or two, those single women all met someone right in their "own backyard"— and before long they married.

Unless the town where you live is so small that there really are no eligible men, you don't need to move. Even then, there may be a city close by where you can align yourself with groups and organizations. Establishing a social life within an hour or so of a large city is not impossible. I live in a large city, and meet people all the time who live an hour or so away — and I'm talking sixty or seventy miles, not an hour of bumper-to-bumper traffic.

If you live near a large city where there really are better opportunities, try making a friend in your town who can share the driving with you. You could even share a hotel room. You might also consider making a friend or two in the larger city who may offer you their apartment on an occasional weekend. (In return, be sure to buy your friend dinner, a house gift, which is always welcomed, or even a gift certificate to a day spa.)

If you're still obsessed with the idea that your problems will be solved if you live in New York, Boston, Chicago, Los Angeles or some other major U.S. city, you could be in for a shock. The competition in these cities can be tough. There is a whole generation of young, beautiful super-achieving women who have, perhaps, an exaggerated sense of their self-worth. The truth is that they can be quite intimidating to men, but nevertheless, they *are* part of the competition. Unless you have very healthy self-esteem and a thick skin, you might really be better off sticking closer to home. In no way does this contradict my advice throughout the book to believe in yourself and not sell yourself short, but if you have as great a chance of meeting someone in or near your hometown, why subject yourself to the rigors of the big city?

There's another point to consider when deciding whether or not a move will increase your chances of meeting "the one". While you ultimately may end up moving to a new city to be with your future mate, you don't actually have to make a major move in order to meet him in the first place. The Internet and other media have truly made our world smaller in many ways, and if you're smart about meeting people online, you could initially meet the love of your life without moving any further than to your computer. Online dating is not without its risks, of course, but for many couples it has been the path to happiness and has even led to marriage. In Chapter 38 we discuss the ins and outs of meeting people on the Internet.

## Remember...

*Y*ou don't have to move to another city to meet your Mr. Right. Chances are you'll find him in your own hometown. But even if he lives across the country, it's still possible to "meet" him via the Internet. You may ultimately move out of town to be with him, but you don't have to make a major permanent move simply to meet somebody.

My point is, don't be so quick to pack up and leave town. No doubt you've heard the saying, "Wherever you go, there you are." That may sound a bit flippant until you think about it. To put it more bluntly, you can't run away to happiness if what you're really trying to do is run away from yourself.

One of the highlights of having sold real estate was all the wonderful people I met. Kathy and Scott were two such people. They had been in their home less than two years when Kathy called to say they had decided to sell and move on to greener pastures. Scott had a good job, and Kathy seemed happy in hers, so I didn't quite understand why they were leaving town. Within two months their house was sold and they were heading to Santa Fe, New Mexico. A couple of years passed before I received a holiday letter from Kathy. They had moved again and were now living in Denver. She included her new phone number, so I called her one day and was shocked when she told me the story behind their moves.

Kathy explained that she and Scott were alcoholics and had been "running away", thinking the change of environment would bring changes in their lives. This is what is known in the recovery community as seeking the "geographical cure". It doesn't work for alcoholism, and it doesn't work for any other problem that stems from within. Fortunately Kathy and Scott had found the help they needed through Alcoholics Anonymous, and were now sober and truly happy for the first time. The last I heard from them, they were thinking of moving back here to their hometown. I hope they do.

If you're convinced the "geographical cure" is the solution to your singleness, maybe you should reconsider. Unless your chief problem is simply that you hate cold winters, moving from Fargo, North Dakota to Los Angeles won't necessarily make you happy. I know you've heard this before, but happiness has to come from within. If you are happy with yourself, you have a much better chance of finding the man of your dreams, perhaps even in your own hometown. If not, there are plenty of other places you can look, without packing up your earthly possessions and moving halfway across the country. ♥

# 21

# NEVER UNDERESTIMATE
# THE POWER OF "NICE"

*I*magine that you've met a man and have had two or three dates with him. Although he didn't set you afire, you did have a good time. At this point, however, you don't know how to describe him other than to say that…well…he is a really *nice* guy. But that's okay — after all, you do want someone nice…right?

The truth is that to some women, "nice" is equivalent to "dull". In fact "nice" is a word that's often used when describing someone about whom you can't think of anything overwhelmingly positive. Sometimes it is even used as a term of derision; we've all heard that "nice guys finish last". Most of us don't really believe that — or do we?

I think "nice" has gotten a bad rap lately. In the movie *Shallow Hal*, Gwyneth Paltrow, wearing a "fat suit", plays a grossly obese woman with whom Jack Black's character, Hal, falls in love. As the movie title implies, Hal is a shallow man who judges women only on appearance. Under normal circumstances, he never would have fallen for a heavy woman, but thanks to a hypnosis session with Tony Robbins, he now sees the "inner person". To his eyes, this overweight woman is a slim and lovely goddess. And as an unbelievable bonus, she is one of the kindest, sweetest people he has ever known. When he describes her sweetness and physical attractiveness to his equally shallow buddy, the buddy is disbelieving. How could a woman be both beautiful and nice? Hal insists she is both, so the buddy concludes that Hal's new girlfriend must have been an ugly duckling when she was younger and was humbled by that experience, so she retained her sweetness even though she grew out of her homeliness. Of course when the buddy meets Hal's gal, he sees her for the overweight woman she is, which only confirms what he believed all along.

Though this is a movie, it illustrates the common perception that "nice" and "attractive" are mutually exclusive. And even though you might not hold that belief yourself, perhaps you have overlooked guys who were "nice" but not overwhelmingly attractive in a conventional sense. Don't be so quick to pass these men up. Sure you want someone to whom you feel attracted, but attraction is not always instantaneous. At the very least, you should give that "nice guy" a chance. Whether he ultimately turns out to be a prospect or not, if he is nice, at least appreciate him for that.

I am not talking about the Casper Milquetoast type. Naturally you want him to have a little bit of fire to him. You certainly want him to have opinions and a will of his own. But there's a huge gray area between a Milquetoast and the Marquis de Sade. If he is kind and considerate and doesn't turn you off, give him a chance.

Of course, you should always make an effort to be nice yourself, which will win you points in anyone's book. I have repeatedly heard men say after an unpleasant experience with a woman, "What a bitch she was...with a little effort she could have been nice." And it's true, if she had wanted to be nice, she would have been. It goes both ways. What is it that's bothered you about so many of the men you've met? They're controlling, they're arrogant, they have unreal expectations — and they sure aren't nice. You're tired of that, aren't you? Well, a lot of men are tired of bitchy women. NICE isn't everything, but believe me, it goes a long way.

## Remember...

*N*ice isn't everything, and of course you don't want a Casper Milquetoast. But there's a huge gray area between a Casper Milquetoast and the Marquis de Sade — so if the man you're dating is kind and considerate and doesn't turn you off, give him a chance. He may turn out to be Mr. Right.

What if you find someone "nice" who fits the bill in many ways, but doesn't make a lot of money? Could you live with that? If you're working and independent, your lifestyle won't change. Without him in your life you're still at square one. So ask yourself, do you like him well enough to spend more time with? Does he make you feel good when you're with him, instead of insecure or stressed out? Does he seem sincerely interested in you? Is he fun, light-hearted and easygoing, and does he have a sense of humor? Do you look forward to his phone calls and to your next date? Is he stable? These are all characteristics of a really good guy, maybe even a great one. If you can answer yes to most of those questions, you may have found your man. You don't need to believe he's your knight in shining armor, though he may well be — you just don't know it yet.

A woman I know married quite young and had her family, and after twenty-something years, her husband left her for his secretary. At the time she was in her late forties. After a few years on the dating scene, she eventually gave up, thinking she was too old and no one wanted a divorcee with two kids. I hadn't seen her for a few years when she suddenly surfaced. She had remarried and apparently was very happy. I was surprised to see her new husband. He was half a head shorter than she and didn't seem to have much personality. We met again soon after and she told me how they met and how her marriage came to be.

They had both attended a divorce support group and she had known him for quite a long time. They began going out after the meetings, first for coffee, then for dinner. He took a personal interest in her and she in him. Their bond became so strong that they realized there was something more there. He wasn't the mad passionate lover she would have liked, but he turned out to be her rock of Gibraltar. Not insignificantly, he is also — you guessed it — *nice*. They have a wonderful marriage and she tells me she couldn't be happier. That is a smart woman!

Another woman I know divorced her husband when she was in her early forties, saying she would be happier alone. She went to work full time and never regretted her decision. About ten years later she met a man she had known when she was in high school. His wife had recently died. They began dating, and six months later they announced their engagement. She said that not only does she have a good marriage, but he's wonderful to her and she's happier than she ever was — including the early years of her first marriage. Her husband is the type of man that many women would overlook. But my friend is absolutely insane about her bald-headed, *nice* guy.

*Myra Kaplan*

A friend tells me of a couple she knew, Natalie and Mark, who were blissfully married for over twenty years, until an illness took Mark's life. My friend says Mark used to tell everyone he met that one of the things he loved most about Natalie, from the moment he first met her, was that she was so *nice*. Sure, there was physical attraction, but he couldn't help noticing from the beginning that she was absolutely one of the nicest people he had ever met. It wasn't a fake nice, either; it was a nice that came from really caring about others. "Hearing him express this just seemed to give a whole new meaning to the word 'nice'," my friend told me. "You really can fall truly and deeply in love with 'nice'."

I am certainly not trying to downplay the importance of physical attraction and any of the other exciting qualities you might wish for in a mate. But don't ever underestimate the power of "nice" — because it really is the foundation for a long and lasting relationship.

# 22

# REMEMBER THAT EDUCATION AND CAREER ARE IMPORTANT
## BUT THEY'RE ONLY PART
## OF "THE WHOLE PACKAGE"

As discussed in other chapters in this section, finding your "keeper" may be closer than you think, if you change your perception of who and what Mr. Right will be like. Of course, if you're a college graduate, you wouldn't consider anyone without a degree — or would you? That is a common attitude, and maybe it's one you take for granted, but perhaps you should reconsider. There are plenty of wonderful people who, for various reasons, don't have a degree, but they may be just as bright and successful as those who do have them.

In past generations, most physicians graduating medical school were males. Many didn't care if their wives were college graduates or not. And I don't think they thought of their wives as beneath them if they didn't have a degree. Today there are many female physicians, and certainly not all are married to other physicians. If you are a physician, an attorney, a CPA or are in any other high-paying professional career, that doesn't mean your husband has to understand microbiology, torts or statistics. He's not your associate in the office — he's your partner in life. You may well be missing some good men if you're looking for an equal on the professional ladder.

Sometimes the problem is not that the woman's expectations of a potential mate are too high, it's that the man is intimidated by accomplished women. If you meet a prospect and he seems a little overwhelmed by your career, put him at ease. It's only a job — no different than his, but yours has a mystique that makes it sound impressive. If you are a man and you're reading this, take heed; you have missed some great women if you're looking for an "equal". The professional woman *is* your equal (and vice versa); you just have different careers.

Consciously or not, many people judge their self-worth by their education level and/or their careers. Even worse, many use the same criteria to evaluate potential mates. This is a mistake on both counts. Certainly there is nothing wrong with being proud of your own accomplishments, or admiring someone else's. Conversely, there's nothing wrong with being dissatisfied with your level of achievement and wanting to improve yourself, nor is there anything wrong with encouraging someone else's efforts towards self-improvement. However, careers and education, just like money and other issues we discuss in this book, need to be placed in proper perspective. Your college degrees, and what you do for a living, are only facets of the person you are. They are not you.

Education at any level and any age is available if one desires it. No matter how old you are, it is never too late to further your education. NEVER! Whether you seek an undergraduate or graduate degree, if you have the desire to get one, go ahead and do it. Yes, the thought of it may be overwhelming and may even seem impossible, but — and I can't be too emphatic here — you can do it. If you graduated high school with only mediocre grades and were not a good student, do you think you can't get a degree? Of course you can. You can begin with your local junior college. Make an appointment to speak to someone in admissions; they will confirm what I'm saying. Young adults, middle-aged adults, seniors, and people of all ages enroll in college all the time.

I have a friend who desperately wanted to be a nurse. She could not pass college biology; she absolutely hated it! But she wanted to be a nurse so badly she stuck with it. She took biology three times. The first time she failed, and the second time she passed with such a low grade the school advisor recommended she repeat the class so she would be better prepared for the following courses. The third time she aced it with an A, and the rest came easily. She never repeated another class, and she graduated one of the top students in her class. You have no idea how much potential you may have once the required courses are completed and you begin to take classes that you like. My friend's dreaded biology class was a means to an end. She wanted nursing badly enough to persevere.

By the way, colleges love older students. They will work with you and help in any way possible — so if you've ever entertained the thought of returning to school, do it. It will be more fun than you can imagine, and you never know who will end up sitting next to you!

You may be thinking to yourself, "Get real, woman, how can you go to school when you work full time?" *You can do it*, even if you begin with one course at a time, two nights a week or on the weekends. These days there are even many options for taking college credit courses on the Internet. If you really have the desire you will find a way.

Even if you just take courses and don't complete the requirements for a degree, you will have gained more knowledge than you had before. It will make you more interesting to everyone, including yourself! If you think college truly isn't for you, it's still important to continue your education on your own, if for no other reason than to broaden your horizons. I cannot say it often enough or strongly enough: *Never stop learning*.

## Remember...

 *on't let your age or your busy schedule deter you from going to college. Colleges love older students and will do what they can to help you. Furthermore, there are many options for taking night classes or Internet courses.*

Education is important, and so is building a career you love. These things are part of who you are. Just learn to put them in perspective, and don't let your entire sense of self-worth be dependent upon the letters after your name, or the title on your business card. Equally as important, never close your mind to a potentially wonderful mate because of his education level or his chosen career. ♥

# 23

# REMEMBER MONEY MATTERS,
## BUT PUT IT IN PERSECTIVE

W hy do some women go after a man who, though appearing on the surface to be a good marital prospect, is all wrong for them? The truth that many people don't want to admit is that there are still women who want to be "taken care of". This may be an old-fashioned concept, but I am not going to pretend the phenomenon doesn't exist. Even though today most women have careers outside the home, there are still some women who would rather stay home, be a full-time mother and run the house. Actually there is nothing wrong with that. It may even be in our hardwiring, or it could just be the result of thousands of years of conditioning, but women are "nesters", and may unconsciously expect a man to be the provider in one sense or another. These days, however, those traditional roles are harder to come by.

It is not just a matter of economics; there are men who make enough to support a wife and family on a single income. Women who want to be stay-at-home wives tend to be attracted to the man who can more easily give them that lifestyle. On the other hand, that man doesn't necessarily need or want *them*. For better or worse, the "feminist revolution" and many other forces have changed things, and if a woman can't stand on her own today, many men aren't interested in her. For some reason, however, these men aren't as interested in what a woman makes as in what she *can* make when and if she works. Present a professional man with two similar choices, and he most likely will choose the woman who has the highest earning capacity. Years of observation and conversations with professional men and couples have led me to this conclusion. Some people say everything in life boils down to money. I hate to admit it, but they have a point. What *isn't* about money? You may argue with this, but unfortunately, it appears to be true.

So what do you do if you're convinced there is no way you're ever going to make a lot of money? You have to compensate with something else — a passion for what you do, and pride in doing it well. My husband always told our children that it doesn't matter what you do in life, just try to be as good at it as you can be. Whether you are a physical therapist, office manager, graphic designer or teacher, you may not be on the higher side of the pay scale — but if you're good at what you do, if you sincerely like your job and your co-workers, that says a lot.

If any man questions you about your income, or makes you feel beneath him or less than adequate, stop him in his tracks. Just tell him you are so lucky because you have the greatest career, and you couldn't be happier. If his heart is set on dating a woman who makes six figures, he may have more issues than just money, and it's a safe bet that no amount of money would make him happy. And if he is on the lower end of the income scale himself that should be pretty obvious — he could be looking for someone to support him. Move on.

Should a man show a lack of respect for you because of what you do for a living, give him the cold shoulder before he gives it to you. He, not you, has the problem. It is far more important to be happy when you get up and go to work every day than to just focus on how much you bring home. Of course everyone wants more, but if you are relatively happy with what you do, you already have a lot more than many people with much higher incomes.

---

## Remember...

ny man who will not date you because you don't make enough money is shortsighted. Enjoying what you do, and being good at it, are more important than a large salary.

---

What about the average working man who simply wants a partner who is more or less equal? What that man is looking for is no different from what an employer seeks. He wants to see someone who is dedicated and hard working. I would be less than honest if I didn't add that most of these men also want someone who can make them money (or at least not cost them too much).

Yet despite its importance, money isn't everything; *stability* is what really counts. You may not have a high-paying job, but if you can show stability, that will suffice for many men. A stable person is one they can depend on. Marriage is a team effort, and these days it is more important than ever to be part of a team that works well together. Whether or not it is a conscious decision, men look for stability, just as much as women do. They need to know they can depend on their wives.

So how does one show the stability I've been talking about? Everything about us advertises it. Elsewhere in this book I discuss at length how to project a "married woman" attitude. What this essentially means is that you project strength and maturity. When you speak to a prospect, try to sound mature. Be light-hearted but not silly, and most importantly, don't talk like a little girl. Many women still think it's cute to sound "little-girlish" or even to talk baby talk. Word to the wise: Baby talk drives men crazy, and not in a good way! Another instant turnoff to men is when women become defensive and announce, "I don't cook, why should I!" or "No man is going to expect me to do this." And finally — and I have heard this many times, even regarding married women — men don't like women who giggle. Save your giggles for your girlfriends, and when in public, remember to tone it down. Nothing is more annoying to men than loud women. (Remember that you never know who's sitting at the next table.)

The bottom line is that men want a woman who is serious when she needs to be. They want a partner. Of course money matters, and whether you plan to be a traditional wife and mother or you're a high-dollar executive, the issue of money will invariably come up as your relationship progresses. But both of you need to learn to put it in perspective. Don't close your eyes to the economic factors that can potentially make or break a relationship, and do not judge your real value, or his, by your respective income levels.

# 24

# CONSIDER THAT THERE MAY BE MORE THAN ONE "SOUL MATE" FOR EVERYONE

The romantic notion of a soul mate — the one person in the universe who is another person's "missing half" — has captivated poets, storytellers and everyday romantics for a long time. We all have married friends who say their spouse is their soul mate. Usually it's the wife. For some reason, more women than men seem to cling to this concept, but of course men are not immune to it.

I don't want to break any bubbles, and I sure don't want to hurt any spouse's feelings, but there probably is more than one Mr. Right for every woman, and more than one Ms. Right for every man. I know that some very happily married women (and maybe a few men), will argue with me, but if you can make one person happy, and vice-versa, why don't you think it could happen a second time? Of course it can!

I make this point for two reasons. First, even if you haven't ever married, you may at one time have had a serious relationship with someone you considered to be your soul mate. For one reason or another, the relationship did not last, and no matter what your head tells you, perhaps somewhere in your heart you feel you will never again be able to experience a love like the one you lost. A belief like this can only hamper your search for Mr. Right, because at some level you are asking yourself, "Why even bother?" If this describes you, and you are certain you want to get married, you absolutely have to cure yourself of the conviction that there is only one Mr. Right to a customer. Notice I didn't say you have to give up the idea of a soul mate; just realize there could be more than one out there for you.

# Remember...

*Y* *ou may find the idea of a "soul mate" romantic, but don't let romantic notions hinder your search for Mr. Right. Even if you thought someone in your past was your soul mate, there is almost certainly another one waiting for you.*

The second reason I make this point is that there are many women who may be considering dating a recent widower, perhaps one who was happily married for many years. Maybe you are one of these women, and if so, you might have doubts about filling his deceased wife's shoes. He may still be wrestling with his own feelings of guilt or ambivalence about dating again. Whether or not he believes in the idea of soul mates, he might believe he is somehow "betraying" his wife's memory by going out with you.

On the other hand, maybe he's eager to get back into the dating world, and that in turn makes you wonder how much he really loved his wife. I wouldn't be too concerned about this, however; it's a well-known fact that many men begin to date quite soon after losing a spouse. (For that matter, women do also. They have sworn they could never find another man like the one they recently lost — and a year or two later you see them out, holding hands with a man they've fallen madly in love with. It happens all the time.)

Women start chasing the new widower, and begin calling even before the wife's funeral. Older women are champions at seizing the opportunity to visit a recently widowed man. This is a phenomenon known as the "casserole brigade". The women call the widower to express tremendous sympathy for his recent loss, and after the most empathetic phone conversation, they mention that if it would be all right with him, they'd like to bring dinner over the next night. Generally he says yes, and before long one of the casserole bearers ends up being his next wife. The reason these men are so eager to see another woman so quickly is, quite simply, that they were happy being married, and they want to be married again.

The soul mate question aside for the moment, there are special problems to consider when dating a widower, whether he's the "guilty, ambivalent" type or the "let's get married this weekend" man. His deceased wife will always have a place in his heart, and you have to be okay with this. You even need to cut him a little slack if he wants to keep some of her pictures out. Even so, widowers often make excellent prospects, especially if they were happily married, because they have the memory of a good marriage to draw upon. As long as it is clear to you that he loves you for yourself, and not because you remind him of his wife, you have a good chance at happiness with this man. He may even be your soul mate!

I'd like to add a note here for women who may be in their fifties and beyond. As implied above, the competition for the older, recently widowed man is as fierce as it gets. I certainly don't recommend that you join the casserole brigade yourself unless you happen to be a close neighbor of the widower in question. There are better, not so obvious ways to win his attention. (Read Chapter 37, the chapter on self-promotion, for some ideas.) In any case, you may have a good chance with this man because the majority of sixty-five to seventy-year-old men, and those even older, will not be looking at women their age. These men want to date a woman in her fifties. You may not be thirty years younger than he is, but chances are, you're considerably younger than his wife. As noted above, these widowed men are usually great marriage candidates, so do not pass them up. They are not scared or commitment-phobic and they can give you more happiness than you ever imagined. Many are not struggling to make a living. Their children are grown, and they may have pensions, savings and other income. Further, many are still working because they *want* to, and the added income allows them to live even better.

I know so many women in their fifties and sixties who were introduced to widowers, and they all have wonderful marriages. Are these couples "soul mates"? Who knows? What matters is that they have found happiness, even romance, at an age when many people would have long since given up on that possibility.

An old girlfriend telephoned me one day to tell me that she had found love for the second time around. Her husband had died almost ten years earlier, when she was in her early forties, and although she had dated in the early years, she hadn't had any dates recently. Her children were still young at the time she became a widow and she felt that eventually she would meet someone and find love again. One day the high-rise office building where she worked had to evacuate for a fire drill. She remained outside talking to a friend who also worked in the building, and while standing there, one of the firemen came up to her, smiled and jokingly told her to get back to work, the drill was over! They visited, or as she says, he flirted a bit, and then he asked if he could escort her back to her office. That's how Lynn met Dave. She was on safe territory, she wasn't afraid to talk to him, she wasn't alone, and let's face it, men in uniforms can be pretty sexy!

As it turned out, Dave had been widowed for nearly as many years as Lynn, though he had no children. Although he was a fireman, this was not his sole source of income; he was also a full-time insurance agent. One of the first things Lynn told me about Dave was that she couldn't figure out why he had waited so long to remarry, since widowed men, particularly attractive ones, so often remarry right away. I found this puzzling as well, and so did many other people. But Dave has always given the same answer, which he repeated recently as they celebrated their fourth wedding anniversary: He had loved his first wife dearly, and had felt she was his one true love. For the longest time he believed he could never have another true love...and then he met Lynn!

I believe unequivocally that there is more than one person for all of us. It doesn't mean we will meet them all, and with luck we won't ever need to. But it's a big world, and there is more than one potential "love of your life" out there. So keep your mind — and your heart — open to all possibilities.

# PART Three

# LIGHTEN UP!

# 25

## ELIMINATE ENVY —
### NO ONE HAS IT ALL!

*D*o you think you know someone who has it all? Trust me, they don't. NO ONE has it all. I know it may appear that some people do. Everything seems to go their way with seemingly little effort on their part. For example, maybe you envy your girlfriend because she's married to a really terrific guy, who earns enough money that she doesn't need to work outside the home. They have two healthy children who attend private schools and go to the most exclusive summer camps, they live in a huge beautiful home, and "dream vacations" are reality for them several times a year. What could be better?

Well, final chapters haven't been written. No one knows what tomorrow holds in store for any of us. We haven't a crystal ball to peer inside, but the one thing we do know is no one's life is perfect, not even close. True, some of your friends may appear to have it all, but you really do not know what goes on behind closed doors or in their personal psyche. Besides, if good fortune could happen to her, it can also happen to you.

You may be saying to yourself, "But it hasn't happened so far. She has everything and I have nothing. It's not fair!" If you find yourself thinking like this, you're wasting precious energy as well as time, and you are almost certainly not getting any closer to finding your "keeper". Envy and jealousy are among the most self-destructive emotions, and they are almost always accompanied by resentment, which can poison every part of your being. These emotions make you unpleasant to be around, because believe me, they show, even if you don't say a word. No one, least of all a prospective Mr. Right, wants to be with someone who is obviously bitter about her own life and resentful of others' good fortune. No doubt about it, envy will consume every bit of joy in your life if you allow it.

Realizing that no one has it all is one of the best ways to get envy under control. Look at the people you see when you go to the malls. You will see some who obviously have the extra burden of health issues, and there are many others who have experienced personal tragedies. This may seem unfortunate, but if you were to ask them, many of those same people would say they are actually fortunate in other ways because they've been blessed with wonderful support from family and friends. And what about those who do seem to have everything going for them? Appearances can be deceiving, especially since we see what we want to see anyway. We look at a beautiful young woman dressed in expensive clothes, fine jewelry and expensive sunglasses, and we envy her. Our envy is based almost solely on her outward appearance. We automatically assume that because she's obviously wealthy, she must have everything. Many people are image-conscious and they take pains to make their lives *look* enviable, whether they are or not, so this only strengthens the illusion. No matter how wonderful this woman's life may appear from the outside, you can be assured that it is far from perfect. Those pricey sunglasses could be disguising eyes that are red and puffy from crying. Who knows?

A woman I know found out firsthand that no one has it all. Years ago, she and her boyfriend were living in one of the "gentrified" areas of her city, but theirs was not quite the affluent lifestyle most of their neighbors enjoyed. Instead, they were renting one of the few smaller, older houses that remained in the area. Though they loved the location because it was close to trendy shopping zones, great restaurants and museums, they felt somewhat out of place living in that little old house, surrounded by all those grandiose new homes. Although they didn't quite fit in with the demographic, they tried their best to be friendly and neighborly, but most of the people were aloof and snobbish.

The couple across the street from them lived in a particularly ostentatious house. These people were the epitome of "conspicuous consumption", as it used to be called. Like most of the neighbors they were a bit standoffish and could barely bring themselves to say hello to my friend and her boyfriend in passing. They were a good-looking couple who appeared to have an ideal marriage and they seemed to live a picture-perfect life. It wasn't unusual to see their names mentioned in the society columns, and two or three times a week the lady of the house regularly had a limousine pick her up to take her shopping. There were servants and caretakers everywhere, virtually all the time. Their children's birthday parties were lavish affairs, complete with clowns, jugglers, carousels and baby elephants, and were more like mini-carnivals or circuses than little kids' parties. One Easter the couple hired a professional photographer to take pictures of them standing and smiling in front of their beautiful mansion with their perfect, pampered children. "I was watching the proceedings from my humble little home," my friend said, "and I felt — I confess — a sharp stab of envy. It happens to the best of us, I guess."

Through one of her professional organizations, my friend happened to meet and become friendly with "Mrs. Mansion's" mother, who was firmly grounded in her middle-class roots and did not approve of many of her daughter's excesses. It was then that my friend became privy to some of the Mansion Family's dirty little family secrets. They were living mostly on the husband's parents' money, and because they had been squandering the money on bad business deals, shady investments and a host of excesses, the parents were on the verge of withdrawing their financial support. Shortly after that glorious Easter family portrait was taken, the wife kicked the husband out of their house because she found out that he had been partying with call girls in lavish hotel suites on his many business trips. That was just the beginning of this rich, beautiful couple's troubles.

Did they have it all? Not by a long shot! My friend acknowledged that this story was pretty small stuff compared to the headline-making scandals involving the rich, famous and beautiful. But that small example did bring the point home to her. Although many people love to "hate the rich", she didn't feel any particular satisfaction in finding out that all was not well in the mansion across the street. Those people may have lived a fantasy life, but their problems were very real. "And I wouldn't be in that woman's designer shoes for anything," my friend tells me. I hear her loud and clear. If given the chance to change things, most people would rather have their own problems than someone else's. Instead of being consumed by envy of the rich, my friend and her boyfriend spent their time and energy working to save money so they could buy a small home in a neighborhood where they would be more comfortable.

Envy can and does hit all of us at one time or another, but if our self-esteem is intact, it will be short-lived. It's only when envy is a chronic problem that it's a matter of concern. If you're inclined to look over your shoulder at everyone, comparing your life to his or hers, you need to remind yourself that no one is better than you are. Sure, they may be richer, or more educated, or perhaps even luckier. Who cares? That's their life, and maybe they did make better choices, but don't be concerned with them. You are as good as anyone else, and you can be as successful and as comfortable with your lot in life as the best of them.

I have never looked over my shoulder at others' lives...well, okay, maybe a quick glance or two, but only out of curiosity and never out of jealousy. Those who know me well know I am not prone to envy or jealousy. My sister was always thin, even skinny. She didn't care about food. I always had to watch my diet. So what? I have never envied her. We have different body types and that's a fact, nothing more.

I was a young married woman when I realized that no matter how they painted the picture, no one had everything. Yet when I began using the expression, "No one has it all", it wasn't in response to singles looking for mates. Some of our married friends had been going through a stage of unrest or dissatisfaction. In some cases it was what used to be called the "Seven-Year Itch". Sometimes a friend was unhappy with her marriage and her life in general, so she'd grumble that this friend or that one had a larger home, or took more vacations, or enjoyed a larger household income, or had perfect kids who never gave the parents any trouble, and the story goes on and on. The details varied but the theme was always the same: "She has it all!" I knew better, but for some reason some of my girlfriends didn't. That used to send me through the roof. My response was always, "No one has it all!" I said that more times than I'd like to remember. And over the years, when hearing of misfortune happening to other people — especially those who had appeared to have it all — I would repeat it again. My family and friends became so used to my saying it that they began to repeat it to me. I'm beginning to think I coined the expression!

---

# Remember...

*No one has it all. If you think your married friends or your girlfriends have it all, they don't. You do not know what goes on behind closed doors.*

---

Sometimes envy and jealousy strike when you least expect it, particularly when someone else gets something (or someone) you think was rightfully "yours". Suppose you are out at a club with one of your girlfriends. She happens to see a prospect before you do, and they hit it off. This is a great time for you to practice stopping envy right in its tracks. Don't waste time thinking about the new prospect; just tell yourself it wasn't meant to be. Even though he may seem like an ideal man for you and you wish you had met him first, there was something that initially brought him and your girlfriend together. Besides, what about all the men who have been attracted to you and not to your girlfriend? Whether your friend and this man remain a couple is yet to be seen, and if it doesn't last, he may very well come back on the single scene — and you could still have a chance. For now, though, don't squander a moment's energy thinking about him or being jealous. Wish them well and move on.

Jealousy and envy can destroy you. They are both a waste of time and energy. At the very least they will get you nowhere in your quest for marriage or anything else you want. So what if the next person has "more" than you do? You may not like it, but, as with all things in life, you accept what you cannot change and go on. If you can't accept it, won't the unacceptable continue regardless? Yes, it will...so get over it! Living without envy is a lot easier than living with it, and you will be much happier and more appealing. Once you've eliminated envy, you might be surprised at how much more space you have in your life for Mr. Right.

# 26

## FACE UP TO YOUR OWN FEARS AND DOUBTS ABOUT THE "M" WORD

*M*any women are convinced they want to marry, but for some reason, perhaps even a subconscious one, they may be afraid. Their fear can become a shield, and until that shield is removed, it will be difficult to have any relationship, let alone the relationship they desire.

There's nothing wrong with having some apprehension, of course. Fear of the unknown is natural, and fear of marriage (particularly if you've never been married before) is perfectly reasonable, to a certain extent. It shows that you view marriage as a serious step and aren't so starry-eyed as to believe that a wedding ring is a guarantee of a happy ending. It is absolutely normal to have doubts before you marry and even afterwards. However, you have to strike a balance somewhere; you can't let your apprehension become a paralyzing fear that keeps you from finding happiness and fulfillment.

Even if you don't think you fall into the "fearful" category, it's still a good idea to read this chapter, because you might uncover some hidden fears and doubts that have kept you from taking steps to bring Mr. Right into your life. If you bring them out in the open and look at them closely, you will see that most of them really are groundless.

The first step in uncovering or confronting your fears is to take a good look at your beliefs about marriage. When you hear the word "marriage", what is the first thought that comes to your mind? *Merriam-Webster's Unabridged Dictionary* defines marriage as "the relation between husband

and wife." Well, that defines the union of marriage, but not the actual relationship, which is really what marriage is all about. The dictionary isn't much help there. In Chapter 33 we take a closer look at what makes a good marriage, but for now I just want you to examine your own beliefs.

## Remember...

 t's not just men who are scared of marriage — many women have fears about it too. These fears are natural and normal. If you face them honestly, however, you'll see that most of them are groundless.

As you know, there are scads of books about marriage, and every married couple has their own take on the subject as well. No matter what the dictionary says, or what other married couples say, or what I say, you have your own thoughts on the matter, based on your life experiences. For example, you may think marriage is easy, and you shouldn't have any problem *being* married — after all, you're easygoing and congenial. It's only a matter of finding the right man, and you just haven't found him yet. On the other hand, perhaps when you hear the word marriage you actually get frightened. We think of men as being the ones who are scared of marriage, but believe me, many women are too. There's all that responsibility and accountability. It's a real commitment, and it's so permanent, so final. It creates such major changes in your life...and how will it affect who you are? What if you were to marry and it didn't work out? Then you'd be faced with a divorce, and who wants to go through that? Worse still, what if your spouse dies and leaves you alone in the world?

Or perhaps the concept of marriage is more abstract to you, and you really don't have an immediate response at all, other than acknowledging that you want to be married (I'm assuming you do, since you're reading this book!). Perhaps you have to really stop and think about what the word "marriage" implies to you. Maybe you can't actually imagine yourself being married.

It's also possible that your thoughts and beliefs about marriage may change from one day to the next. I can almost guarantee that any response you have is natural and normal. Most people have fears or feelings of ambivalence before they marry or make any other serious commitment. I daresay your parents, siblings and best friends have all experienced these things, whether they admit it or not.

The good news is that fears and doubts will become less and less important as your relationship grows and falls into place, reaching what I like to think of as a comfort zone. This is the point at which you begin to lose your fears and settle into a more relaxed mode. At some point it *will* happen. (Don't, however, confuse "comfort zone" with "complacency zone". The latter implies a relationship in which the partners take each other for granted, and all the excitement and romance are gone. That's what you want to avoid... and maybe that's what you fear, but that's for another book.) The point I wish to make is that marriage and commitment are really nothing to fear.

On the other hand, if people tell you marriage is easy, do *not* believe them, it isn't. There is nothing simple about marriage. If it were such a simple matter, the divorce rate wouldn't be so high!

Difficult as it often is, marriage has been the social standard in most cultures for thousands of years. The monogamous bond between man and woman has prevailed for millennia, though naturally it has undergone changes. No doubt life was much simpler in many ways for our more primitive ancestors than it is for us. Back when life was "nasty, brutish and short", survival was the main priority, and people probably didn't spend time obsessing over commitment-phobia or divorce rates. In time, however, humans became "civilized" (some may argue that point), as well as more intelligent (again, some may dispute this) — and with these developments came a host of fears that weren't directly related to survival. We're not battling saber-toothed tigers today, but most of us are at war with our own inner doubts and fears, and in some ways this is more stressful than fighting wild beasts.

In any case, fear is something we all have. Everyone has it, some more than others. It's how we deal with fear on a daily basis that sets some of us apart from others. Fear itself isn't bad; it's only bad if it isn't dealt with, and becomes totally consuming to the point that it hampers your enjoyment of life.

If you have doubts about marriage that you think may be holding you back from moving into a permanent relationship, you need to deal with them, starting now. First you need to ask yourself exactly what it is about marriage and/or men that may be hindering you. What are you afraid of? For example, what will a man expect of you? Will he let you be yourself? What if he's controlling? Will you "lose yourself" in the relationship and have to give up your interests and pursuits? Will he expect you to be perfect? What if he's a Type A personality — an aggressive go-getter — and you are more laid-back and carefree? Or what if you're The Type A and you're afraid he'll be too meek for you? And what about domestic roles — will he expect you to cook, do the laundry and maintain a perfect home, all while working full time? What if he's a divorced man with children, and you can't picture yourself a perfect mom, or even a mother at all? (After all, what do you know about raising kids? Besides, you don't want to be his second wife, knowing he still has to deal with his first wife regarding their mutual children...) And what about sex; what if he's too demanding, or thinks you are? What if you're uncertain of yourself because you haven't had sex in ages? What if, what if, what if?

You can go on and on, projecting every possible scenario that gives you the shudders. Actually, we address every one of these issues in this book, and I will show you that you have nothing to fear. But for now, I just want you to consider your fears so you can begin to confront them, which is the first step in conquering them. Write them down on paper if you find that helpful. Confronting your fears may require a little work on your part, but the answers are all within you.

However, you need to be careful that you don't carry this process too far. Whether you list your fears mentally or write them down, don't spend too much time speculating about what *might* happen, particularly if you don't even have a partner yet. Focusing on hypothetical situations can be a way of avoiding dealing with the reality of your life. Just recognize most of these "what-ifs" for what they are: fears about what *might* happen. They are not reality, and in most cases you have the power to prevent them from becoming reality.

There are also many books and other materials that can help you understand and deal with fear, but if you can't work it out on your own, why not get outside help? Therapists work with people who have fears of all kinds. There have been television programs where the therapist has worked with someone right in front of the camera during a one-hour program, sometimes with remarkable results. People have stepped onto an escalator when they hadn't done that in twenty years. They have taken a ride in an elevator, gone out into large crowds, even ventured outside for longer than a dash to the market and back home. These are dramatic examples but not all that unusual, since people are conquering their fears daily.

Obviously, fear of elevators is not the same thing as anxiety about commitment, and I am certainly not suggesting that your doubts and fears about being married can be swept away in an hour. However, there are many wonderful therapists who are trained to help their patients overcome fear of all kinds as quickly as possible so they can go on with their lives. If you have a fear that's holding you back from doing something that you really want to do — whether it's going to a party and meeting new people, or driving over a bridge to get to work — why not seek professional help? Before too long you might be saying, "I should have done that sooner!"

What if your fears and doubts are not exactly paralyzing, but you still feel they're standing in your way of finding Mr. Right (or committing to him once you've found him)? In that case, you just need to learn to put the whole marriage issue in perspective, adopting a middle ground in your thinking. You don't want to approach the thought of marriage like a carefree teenager ("Okay, sure, why not, let's get married; I'm bored with going to the mall!"). But neither do you want to view marriage as a life sentence or a point of no return ("Abandon all hope, ye who enter here!"). Somewhere between these two extremes is a comfortable reality. You can begin by just being a bit more relaxed than you have been! Granted, marriage is a huge step in one's life. Even if in your heart you believe it will work out, it is a major change. But it is not the end of life as you know it. Rather, it is a beginning and, like life, marriage is what you make of it. If you can reach this happy medium in your perception, you might see a different "you" begin to evolve.

## Remember…

 ut the issue of marriage in perspective by taking a middle ground. Don't approach it casually, but don't think of it as a life sentence or point of no return. It's not the end of life as you know it; rather, it is a new beginning. If you can reach this happy medium in your perspective, you're much less likely to be fearful of marriage.

Earlier I mentioned that virtually everyone has fears about matrimony. Yet most people get married. The reason people are able to go beyond their fear and commit to marriage is that ***their desire for marriage is stronger than any fear they may have***. If they can do it, you can too, if you work to confront your fears one by one. Once you are part of a committed couple, the two of you should confront your fears together. (That's where premarital counseling can help.) With or without the help of a counselor or therapist, successful couples determine what each person expects of the other. They talk about every problem; they handle conflict by negotiating, compromising and moving on.

As you continue to confront your doubts and fears, you will automatically lighten up, and your entire demeanor will change. It may be a subtle change at first, but the results will be more noticeable as time goes by. As we discuss in Chapter 3, a mere change in your perception can have a major effect on how others perceive you. Ridding yourself of your irrational fears will almost certainly make you more attractive to men, and much more open to Mr. Right when you do find him. Best of all, life will be a lot more fun. ♥

# 27

# REMEMBER THAT SINGLE MEN HAVE THEIR FEARS, DOUBTS AND EXPECTATIONS TOO

Even though single women outnumber single men, that doesn't mean the men have it easy. Quite the contrary; they have many of the same doubts and fears as women. Often, however, they're not as straightforward as women are about expressing these fears and doubts.

Some simply use a reverse approach. They may claim they don't want a wife who is a "control freak" and would make them accountable for their every action. In other words, they want their freedom. They want their football games on Sunday afternoons and Monday nights, they want their Saturday morning golf games and their Thursday nights out with the boys, and they aren't giving them up for any woman, ever. A demanding, controlling wife would try to change them, and they're not changing!

Other men claim that women are too materialistic or are only interested in how much money they make. All too often I've heard successful businessmen say, "I'm not interested in her, she just wants me for my money." Give me a break! Many women today are self-sufficient and couldn't care less about a man's money. Granted, gold diggers still exist, but most modern, enlightened women are interested in something besides a man's bank account.

Ironically, many of these men who so vehemently object to "demanding women" create their own worst nightmare. Years ago a very close friend married for the first time. He was well into his fifties when he wed but always had an active social life. Whatever his reasons may have been for delaying matrimony, he was considered one of the most eligible bachelors in town. This man was educated from one of the country's top universities, had a graduate degree in business and owned his own business. The woman who eventually caught his heart was not educated and had worked since high school. The chances of these two marrying were slim, but this man had always dated women who seemed to be less educated than he and were surely less demanding than the many other women who chased after him.

My friend's story is typical of so many others. He had the best of everything his entire life, so of course he couldn't settle for a small diamond ring when he got engaged. He already owned a nice home, but how could he not buy his wife a huge new house? Furthermore, all of his friends had been married for years and had large, beautiful homes. He certainly couldn't have a smaller home than his friends had. He had a lavish wedding and honeymoon, and from the beginning he treated his wife just like the spoiled, "demanding" women he'd been so diligently avoiding all of his life. His wife, like so many others in her position, got so accustomed to such nice things that she became the woman he feared. He could have dated one of the numerous other women who had pursued him, because in the end, his wife turned out to be just like them.

So when you hear a successful man complaining about women making demands on him, take it with a grain of salt, because there's a good chance that he helped create his problem. If this man is someone you're considering as a prospect, you may be faced with the challenge of convincing him that you're not the materialistic gold-digger type yourself — and of course, I'm assuming you're not! I am also assuming that if the relationship becomes serious, you will not let him turn you into that spoiled, demanding woman he's been trying to avoid. Realize, however, that if he truly seems fixated on protecting his assets from your clutches, there's a good chance he has more "issues" than you would desire in a life partner.

Single men have other fears besides the worry that women will infringe on their freedom, or the fear that women are only after them for their money. Some men seem to have a general commitment phobia. It probably won't come as much of a surprise to you that many men fear commitment as much as, or even more than, some women do. There are probably as many reasons for this fear as there are men who have it. Some men are lifelong commitment-phobes but most get over their fears. Ideally it happens when they finally meet the right woman, but some men take the leap when their fear of being alone or not having a family be-comes greater than their fear of committing.

Then there are the men who say they're intimidated by very suc-cessful women. Again, there can be several reasons for this. They may feel they don't make enough money to be a suitable partner for a success-ful woman, or maybe they perceive a woman with money as being too controlling. Or perhaps it's an ego thing. They may be trapped in the old-fashioned notion that a man should make more than a woman or he is somehow "not as much of a man". What adds to the confusion is that many men with income issues don't come out and talk about it directly. Instead, they simply couch it in general terms, saying they feel that women's expectations of them are too great. I think much of that is a cover-up because they aren't on the high end of the pay scale. For most men, money matters can be as sensitive as sex issues.

I don't want to make it appear that I'm implying all of men's fears are in their own heads and that women are blameless. Some women can, in fact, be pretty scary. Their behavior, attitudes and expectations could frighten any good man off. Not long ago I saw an extreme example of this when I watched a report on TV about a phenomenon in New York City. I imagine it exists in other large cities as well, but Manhattan seems to be a magnet for a new generation of attractive, very successful young women — super-achievers who really seem to have it all. Of course, as we dis-cussed in Chapter 25, no one has it all. Although some of the most eli-gible men in the country are drawn to these young women, many are also very intimidated by them. I don't really think these men are scared by the women's stunning looks and achievements as much as by their attitudes. Sure, most of these women have worked hard to get where they are, and they're to be commended. But it's one thing to be an achiever, and quite another to think their status gives them the right to wield it over men. If they don't shed some of that attitude, they may very well end up being the next generation of "chronically single" women in their forties and older.

What about you? You may not be one of these Manhattan supergals, but is there something in your attitude or behavior that might intimidate a man? Needless to say, you should make sure your priorities are in order concerning money, success and achievement. Otherwise you're just con-firming many men's worst fears. If you earn a large income, that's wonder-ful, but it doesn't make you superior in any way. Equally important, if you are only looking for a rich man, you have no doubt missed some very good prospects. Also consider that no one knows what the future holds for anyone. I've seen many people who have been fortunate in business, in the stock market or in their individual careers, but I've seen as many lose everything. And I've seen people who were "under earners" early on, but made more money than they ever dreamed possible later in life. What about the people who have good, stable jobs and a steady income, but haven't made enough money to set the world on fire? Fortunes come and go.

As with most issues involved in dating and marriage, I think both sexes need to lighten up about money and success matters (which we discuss in more detail in Chapter 23). As for the man who says he is intimidated by successful women, I say he needs to take a closer look at the reason behind his fears, and realize that most of them are groundless. (If he's one of the New York men who's been frightened by those over-achieving superwomen, maybe he needs to look elsewhere and find a woman who will love and appreciate him for the man he is.) The woman who is attracted to a man because she perceives him as "successful" needs to re-examine her notions of success, realizing that material wealth is often transitory and is certainly a poor standard by which to judge a future husband.

We've discussed the "she's too demanding" category of excuses, but some men turn the tables on this, hiding their fears and doubts about commitment and marriage with their own list of unrealistic expectations or demands that no woman could possibly fulfill. Of course, this just adds to *women's* doubts and insecurities. It may seem that men want perfect physical beauty or top "performance" from a woman, but for most men that couldn't be further from the truth. However, you wouldn't know that from hearing some men talk.

The truth is that men can be as picky as women, and their comments after a date can often be as ridiculous as women's are. A man may refuse to go out on a second date because he prefers a woman with long hair and hers is too short, or he likes blondes and she's a redhead. Or he may complain that her body's not tight and toned enough. Men can come up with all sorts of excuses. Frequently I want to tell a single man he has it all wrong; he's being too picky, or too critical, or he simply doesn't have realistic expectations. (Naturally, I tell single women this same thing, as you've probably already noticed if you've read this far.)

Sadly, some men go through this routine over and over again. No woman ever measures up to their standards. Women do this too, of course. It's human nature to repeat patterns, and they're difficult to break, but they can be broken (see Chapter 40).

Rick was a good-looking 35-year-old who was in his second year of chef's school, and he had the classic complaint of not being able to meet the right woman. He said he didn't want much — "Just someone who's a runner like I am, and is in good shape, a vegetarian or at least a very healthy eater, and doesn't care much about income." The latter was a sensitive spot with Rick since he knew he had good earning potential once he graduated from chef's school, but for now he held a part-time job and was slightly income-challenged. He drove an older model car and was a little embarrassed about that as well.

In the course of his dating, Rick had actually gone out with many attractive women, some of whom he really liked. However, none of them quite "measured up" to his list of requirements. I encouraged him to try to look at each single woman he met as a bona fide prospect. I asked him to try to find something to admire about every woman, even if she didn't meet all of the items on his checklist. (In Chapter 15 we talk about lists and how they can stand in the way of happiness.) Rick said he would give my suggestion a try.

A couple of weeks after our talk, Rick met an attractive woman at a party. She had a great job, but because of that she put in long hours and had never made working out a priority. She had been promising herself she was going to begin a real exercise regimen; she just hadn't gotten around to it yet. However, she tried to eat well, although she was not a vegetarian.

When Rick met her, the first thing he thought was, "Well, she's cute, but she doesn't have the body of a runner." Even so, he stuck around and talked to her a little while, and found out that she really was making an effort to eat a healthy diet, she walked regularly, and was seriously considering hiring a personal trainer and starting to work out. Rick was impressed by that, and he also couldn't help being impressed by the fact that she made good money and owned her townhouse. What was even nicer was that she was apparently not hung up on lots of other things that had been issues with past dates, such as the kind of car a man drove, or his income level.

Nevertheless, Rick hadn't quite put his "list" away yet, and he had some mixed feelings about his new acquaintance. He spent the better part of the evening running an internal dialogue about the pros and cons of getting to know her better. "Yes, she could lose a few pounds…but she's hardly overweight. Does she run? No, she doesn't even work out. But she did say she's ready and willing to do anything to improve herself."

You might be thinking that these are superficial criteria, and in the big scheme of things maybe they are, but they mattered to Rick. Still, I think he would have been a fool not to give this woman a chance. Fortunately, in the end Rick was able to cast his list aside, and I think you can guess the rest. He and his new friend soon began dating, and are now engaged.

There are many men who, like Rick, have a list of some kind or another. It could be a checklist of what they want in a woman, or it might be a list of excuses about why they haven't found the right woman, or it could be a perfectly rational list of reasons they aren't ready for commitment yet. Just as women do, these men need to revamp their dating agenda and, more importantly, re-examine themselves. Beneath all of their fears or unrealistic expectations, many of them are really terrific men who will make wonderful husbands. They desire the same lifelong commitment to marriage that you are looking for, only they are reluctant to admit it. And some are really good actors, so skilled in denial that they've even convinced themselves they don't want commitment.

So how do you reach them, or better yet, how do you change them? Well, first of all, you have to rid yourself of the notion of changing a man, or changing anyone else besides yourself (there's more on that subject in Chapter 42). I know you've heard this advice before, but have you taken heed? Many women significantly overestimate their ability to change a man, and that's a big mistake! When you try to change a man, you are setting yourself up for frustration, and you risk scaring or angering him. Almost certainly you risk reinforcing all those doubts and fears that he thinks were keeping him from commitment in the first place. You can buy a house as a "fixer-upper", but not another human being.

You can, however, change *yourself*, which is what this book is all about. After that, when it comes to all those fearful, doubtful men out there, you can't change them, but during a one-on-one encounter, what you can do is change their perception of you. When you meet a man and you detect that his attitude may be a cover up for what he feels are his inadequacies, take a minute to reevaluate him. He just might be the kind of person you are looking for. If he is, it's well worth your time and effort to get to know him. Make it a priority to help him examine his own fears and change his perception of women. Most importantly, prove to him that he needn't be afraid of you.

Every opportunity I have to talk to single men, I do. I listen to them carefully, and believe me when I tell you that if you can get beneath a man's misconstrued idea of what kind of a woman he wants, there usually is a good person. You may very well be exactly the kind of woman he wants. It's perfectly okay to work towards convincing him of that!

---

## Remember...

*any single men have problems with relationships and commitment because they have distorted perceptions of women. You cannot change all the single men out there, but you can change the perceptions of those you encounter.*

---

I'm not saying it's simple to change a man's perceptions; it does take some work. I can only talk, but you as a single woman have to show him by example. If he perceives that you are confident but not controlling, and genuinely interested in him but not needy, that will go a long way towards assuaging his fears and putting his "issues" to rest.

Men often express their fears and doubts differently than women, and this can lead to frustration and misunderstanding. Once you get past the surface, however, you will see that underneath, we're all just human. As I've said before, most of us — even chronically "independent" types and commitment-phobes — really do want the same basic things out of life.

# 28

## EMBRACE YOUR INDEPENDENCE,
### BUT DON'T WEAR IT
### LIKE A BANNER

e have all heard the single woman's "declaration of independence". The words may vary, but the message is always clear: "I'm an independent woman. I've worked hard to get where I am. I'm not changing, so you'd better accept me for who I am."

All right, we have the message! It's a given that many women have worked hard to get where they are, and are unwilling to give up their independence, even for marriage. These days, most women want to continue working outside the home after they marry, perhaps taking a leave of absence when they have children, but returning to work shortly thereafter. Men today know this, and many are only too happy to have someone share the financial responsibility. (Some men are only too glad to have a woman assume all of the responsibility, but that's another story altogether!) Female independence is the norm. So exactly what are women trying to say when they're so quick to expound on their independence? Are they arrogant, or simply insecure?

In most instances, I'd say it's the latter. Wearing one's independence like a badge is defensive behavior that perhaps would have been justified in the early days of the women's movement. Back in the late 1960s and early 70s, society for the most part still embraced the idea of the traditional family with the father who went to work and the mother who stayed at home. Never mind the reality that millions of women worked outside the home anyway; the Ozzie-and-Harriet ideal still predominated, and women who chose to step outside that traditional picture met a great deal of resistance (which is putting it mildly). However, two generations have come of age since the early days of "women's lib", and most people in our culture accept that women's roles have expanded. Truthfully, being an independent woman is no longer a big deal!

Why then are so many women still so defensive? No doubt for some women, the defensiveness stems from the fact that they are not, in reality, as self-sufficient as they would like to be, or as they think a twenty-first century woman should be. It is possible that despite their independent façade they still have a financial support system — family members who give them money when they need it or an ex-husband who occasionally helps out. There's nothing wrong with this. Everyone needs a helping hand at times, and besides, plenty of men have "hidden" support systems too. The problem is that our society places such emphasis on self-reliance that some people are embarrassed if they feel they aren't up to the standard. Many women today truly *are* self-supporting, but oddly enough, some of these women have a defensive attitude as well. Perhaps they have this attitude because they've had to struggle for every penny and for various reasons are afraid of losing what they've worked so hard to attain. Or maybe they are proud of their accomplishments and have just let it go to their heads.

We could sit here all day and analyze the reasons for women's defensiveness, but the upshot is that it is self-defeating behavior, and is far more likely to turn off a potential Mr. Right than impress him. If you are "guilty" of this kind of behavior, you need to stop. First, ask yourself why it is so important to announce your independence before you've even decided if a prospect could turn into a serious relationship. Second, consider the consequences of your behavior.

Think of how you come across to a man — he may see you as arrogant or selfish. Indeed, when many "independent" women talk about the man that they're looking for, they never seem to focus on the man's needs. You get the impression that after *their* needs have been met, then maybe they will take a closer look at the man. They are so caught up in what they want, or so fearful of losing themselves by giving too much, that they forget it takes two people to make a relationship. It's another case of that "I…Me…My…" syndrome mentioned elsewhere in this book. A man can easily detect this attitude, and it's not what he's looking for in a future wife. Even if you are not the selfish type, and what you're saying isn't really negative at all, a single man who doesn't know you is likely to see it that way. People hear what they want to or expect to hear.

Your overly independent attitude could end up scaring a good man away, or it could backfire in other ways. In Chapter 27 I discuss super-achieving young New York City women who can be intimidating to many men. Apparently the men who *aren't* intimidated are in paradise, but it's not necessarily a paradise for the women. The single men I know in New York who date many of these women say the "market" is glutted with them. Men are less likely to want to commit to any one of them because there's so much to choose from, and "the next one" may be better than the one they're dating now. Maybe it's not so tough in your town, but let's face it, there is competition everywhere. Achievement and success are wonderful, as is physical beauty, but it takes something deeper to win a man's heart. (And you're looking for a man with a *warm* heart, not a cold-hearted egotist.)

If you're still determined to keep that "independent woman" attitude, consider how you would react if the situation were reversed. Think of how you would like it if a man you'd just met said, "I'm an independent guy. I've worked very hard to get where I am. I have a good job and a busy life. I meet my buddies for dinner on Tuesday nights, and on weekend mornings we golf." Oops, and I almost forgot this one: "I don't cook and I don't do housework." Now tell me, if you heard a prospect say that, what would you think? Either you'd laugh, thinking he was singing your tune, or you'd get defensive, but more than likely you wouldn't be enamored.

Not only is it unnecessary to declare your independence early in a relationship, it also isn't necessary to discuss your life plans — nor is it desirable. On the initial meeting, no one wants to hear anyone else's philosophy on dependence, independence or co-dependence. Besides, we all say one thing at one time, and we all change our minds. That is human nature.

# Remember...

arly in a relationship it is not necessary, nor is it desirable, to go into detail about your life philosophy or future plans. Let the relationship unfold naturally. Besides, people change, and you could very well change your mind about what you want as the relationship progresses. Don't spend a lot of time telling him who you are and what you're about — let him find out for himself!

What if he's the one who brings up the question of "the future" early on in a relationship? Let's say you're out on the second date with a prospect, and the subject of marriage just happens to come up. Mr. Prospect asks you about your plans — do you want to stay home and raise your family, or continue working? Let us also suppose you get the distinct feeling that the answer he wants to hear is, "Oh, I want to be a stay-at-home mom." You like him enough to want to consider a future with him, but you're a little put off by what seems like a loaded question. So what do you do? Does his question give you license to open up and hit him with your "I'm an independent woman" speech?

Not so fast. I'll grant you that a question like this so early on is ridiculous, although many women have told me they are asked that very question. If you really like him, you can forgive this *faux pas*. (If you don't like him all that much, why let the question bother you at all?) The best answer is, "Why do you ask?" or "Who knows what will be then, I don't have to make that decision today." And when you say it, smile — it shows self-confidence, and you're not being defensive. While your answer may sound evasive, it is in truth the most honest answer you can give him, since your priorities really could change as time goes by. If you're sure you want to stay home and raise your family, there's nothing wrong with being truthful about it. However, if you think you're going to want to continue working and hire a nanny, or send the children off to day care, it's better to hedge for the time being. You can even use some gentle humor if you wish. Ask him what *his* plans are; does he expect to take a paternity leave and stay home and take care of his babies? This accomplishes several things. First, it shifts the focus from you to him, which is always a good idea. Second, it will deflect the question. Most importantly, it may lighten him up, and that's what you need to do when he asks such a heavy question.

You do need to be careful not to make a strong statement one way or the other. For one thing, you never know when your words may be used against you later. He may not understand that people change and that everything is negotiable, and he might take your words more seriously than is warranted. He could even spend the rest of the relationship trying to hold you to the declaration you made during that early conversation! You might think that's pretty extreme, but it does happen.

What you have to do is beat him at his own game, and the way to do this is with subtlety and discretion. The man could just be testing you to see what kind of a person you are beneath the surface. No doubt you are the kind, caring person he's looking for — and by being a little circumspect and turning the focus on him instead of you, you're giving him the opportunity to see your wonderful qualities right from the beginning.

This doesn't mean you should be hypocritical or phony just to win him over. Certainly you should not hide who you are. If you do, the truth will come out sooner or later (probably sooner), and you will both be miserable. If his expectations are completely contrary to yours, yet he is adamant about the qualities he wants in a wife and seems unwilling to negotiate, it is probably best to forget him. Even then, you don't have to go into your "independent woman" speech. You will have proven your independence by making the choice to move on.

There is one more point to consider. If your relationship does develop into something serious, you will almost certainly have to adjust your concept of "independence". In relationships you have to think in terms of interdependence rather than independence. Interdependence implies reciprocation; you do things for him, he does things for you, you take turns. In a good relationship, no one's independence is threatened, and no one feels subservient.

It is not necessary to announce to anyone, man or woman, who you are. Your actions speak for themselves. Why identify yourself; why put yourself into any category? Why turn anyone off before they have the opportunity to meet the real you? You are a wonderful woman who would like to find a wonderful man. Leave the "declaration of independence" at home, and go out and face the world confident that your fantastic guy is out there. ♥

# 29

## WHEN IN DOUBT, WORK IT OUT — WITH A THERAPIST

iming is everything in life. If you have issues that need resolving, and they continue to surface or never seem to get resolved, now is the time to work on them. Sometimes we can't get where we want to go until we get over the humps that are in our way, and sometimes we really do need an objective outsider to help us over those humps. Finding a good therapist will probably be harder than resolving your issues, but it's worth the time and money. Ask your friends — you may be surprised how many people have seen therapists, and they may be able to recommend someone to you.

If you don't get any good recommendations through your friends, you can check different agencies or even look in the yellow pages of your phone book. There are many clinics that offer counseling, and in large cities, some clinics have multiple locations for the convenience of their patients. When you call for an appointment, ask if it's possible for you to interview the therapist first; if not, perhaps you could talk to them on the phone before your first appointment. It's very important to feel comfortable with your therapist. You might have to try half a dozen therapists until you settle on one with whom you're comfortable. Even then, sometimes they're only good for a while; you may need someone tougher, someone who really will make you "do your work".

If you're thinking there's no way you can afford a therapist, don't give up too easily. Some insurance plans may cover therapy, so check your policy first. Even if you don't have coverage, there are still options.

When you call a therapist for an appointment, ask about their fees. If it will place a terrible burden on your budget, ask if they are willing to adjust their fee in accordance with your income. Some therapists will work with you. If that's still too costly, check with your local hospitals and various agencies. If you live in a small city, you may have to travel to a larger city that has a medical center, but there are many programs that are open to the public, and some are free if you qualify. Sometimes these programs are announced in the newspaper or on the radio. Remember, don't take no for an answer. Never give up trying. There's always someone out there who will help. It's just a matter of finding that person.

My suggestion to consider therapy is hardly what you'd call revolutionary, but you'd be surprised how many people refuse to avail themselves of this tool, even if they can afford it, and even if they have problems they haven't been able to solve on their own. Some people hesitate because they're scared, some think only "crazy people" go to therapists, and some are simply skeptical about the effectiveness of therapy.

It's natural to be apprehensive about the unknown, but a good therapist will help you get past those fears. The idea that therapy is only for "crazy people" or people who are clinically depressed is…well…crazy. As for its effectiveness, I have seen therapy make a difference in many people's lives. Even therapists get therapy! A close friend of mine who is a therapist was with a man for several years. Whenever they faced a problem they couldn't resolve by themselves, either she alone or she and her boyfriend would speak to a therapist. It was therapy that finally helped her decide this man was not right for her, and it was therapy that helped give her the strength to send him on his way!

---

## *Remember…*

 *on't be afraid to call for outside help if you can't seem to work things out on your own. Almost everyone needs the perspective of a neutral third party at one time or another, and there's nothing shameful about turning to a therapist. Even therapists get therapy.*

---

I know a single man who, though extremely good looking, intelligent and self-confident, was a complete mess when it came to women. None of his relationships lasted, and usually it was the woman who left him. He just couldn't seem to "get" relationships, and in recent years was having trouble even meeting suitable women because of his work schedule. He had resisted therapy for years, but finally decided that since he hadn't been able to figure things out on his own, maybe a good therapist could help him. After only a few weeks of "doing the work", doors began to open for him. "Opportunities I never would have had otherwise came popping up right in front of me," he says. "It was phenomenal." He has now met the woman he strongly believes is his Ms. Right, and I expect an engagement announcement any day now.

Throughout this book we talk about lightening up, and there are of course many ways you can do this on your own. But some problems really are best solved with the help of a neutral third party. A few sessions with a therapist could be the best investment you'll ever make. ♥

PART *Four*

# THE FUTURE IS
# AN OPEN BOOK

# 30

## DARE TO IMAGINE YOURSELF IN DIFFERENT ROLES

*E*ven if you are certain you want to get married, it is possible that you are somewhat uneasy because you fear marriage will require you to make changes you're not prepared to make. Or perhaps you have already made up your mind that there are certain things in your life you're simply not going to change, married or not. If your life is working well in most respects — if you have a great career and home, and you generally like things the way they are — the prospect of changing anything to accommodate a spouse may not sit well with you. Even if you're not all that satisfied with your life, you still may be wary of change; a known quantity is always less intimidating than the unknown. You may doubt your ability to deal with the changes marriage might bring.

As with other fears and doubts, you need to confront this one and put it in perspective. To begin with, it's a waste of time and energy to worry about something that hasn't even happened. It's even more of a waste to fret over the prospect of change. The truth is that people are always changing; it's just a part of life. We're not always aware of exactly when these changes occur, but as along as we're alive, we're always changing our thoughts, attitudes and behavior.

Not long ago I was talking to a girlfriend who had a problem. As we were speaking, I heard my words echoing in my ears and was amazed. I thought to myself, *Did those words come from my mouth? I can't believe I said that!* But I had. My girlfriend had been complaining that her son-in-law had recently become rude to her. She said she couldn't remember ever being rude to him, and she felt she always treated him quite well.

His actions had become so intolerable that she didn't want to spend time around her daughter and son-in-law any longer. My usual response to a situation like that would have been, "Try having a talk with your daughter. Gently tell her how you feel without saying too many negatives about her husband. Ask her what might be bothering him, and ask her to tell you if you did something wrong."

So how was my response different this time? I said to her, "Why not confront your son-in-law? Ask him why this sudden change in behavior and attitude towards you." She argued back that she'd never do such a thing and I responded, "Why not? Instead of making your daughter a go-between, go right to the source!"

That was an unusual response for me. Although I know the direct approach is best, I have always tried a gentler, safer way initially, and that's what I would generally suggest others do if they asked me for advice. This time was different — and not just for me, as it turned out. Although my girlfriend disagreed with my advice when we were talking, apparently she had a change of heart. A few days later she called back to say she had followed my advice, and believe it or not, it worked! Her son-in-law had come right out and told her exactly what was bothering him. He was jealous of his wife's relationship with her, and he felt his wife wanted to spend more time with her mother than with him. He wasn't angry with her at all. He was feeling a bit left out, but his problem was between his wife and himself, not with his mother-in-law.

Perhaps you're thinking that this example is pretty small stuff compared to the potential major changes you're concerned about, but I think it's significant because my attitude change was an example of the ongoing, often unconscious evolution that is common to all of us. Whether we like ourselves or not, our thoughts, beliefs and attitudes are always changing. If I usually took the safer approach to adverse situations, why would I have suddenly suggested that someone try a bolder, more direct approach? I don't have that answer, and I can't tell you why my girlfriend decided to take my advice when it was contrary to her usual practice. But it happened and I'm glad it did. It was a change, and potentially a scary one, but it turned out to be the best course to take.

I learned something else from that conversation with my girlfriend and the aftermath. I was reminded that just because one way has worked for you in previous situations, this doesn't mean there aren't better ways of doing things. That goes for every aspect of life.

Life isn't all about unconscious changes, of course. In fact, most of this book is about the changes that we control and direct. However, for better or worse, the events in our lives often do change us in ways that we may not be aware of initially. Sooner or later these changes reach our conscious awareness, and when we resist them, or stubbornly refuse to acknowledge or accept them, we do nothing but stunt our own growth. If we dig our heels in and refuse to go forward, we only make ourselves, and those around us, miserable. And very often, we still end up changing anyway!

I understand how intimidating the thought of a major lifestyle change such as marriage can be. I also understand how tempting it can be to declare, "I'll never do that!" when imagining yourself in some future situation as a married woman. You really need to keep an open mind, though, and never say "Never!" I cannot tell you how often I have seen women reverse their original roles. It happens so frequently that I just smile and think to myself, "If I had told them they'd be doing that one day, they not only would never have believed me, they would have thought I had gone nuts." I've seen ambitious corporate climbers happily turn into stay-at-home moms. I've seen women who were accustomed to dining in fine restaurants, or bringing home take-out from the gourmet markets, learn to love staying home and preparing dinner themselves.

"Not me!" you may still be saying. After all, you have worked from the day you finished your schooling. You vacationed, took some time off between jobs, and explored various hobbies and activities, all by way of trying to make an interesting life for yourself. But you just never got into the domestic arts such as cooking, decorating and gardening. In fact, you not only don't like the Martha Stewart image, her name sends chills up your spine!

You may not want to think of yourself as the perfect homemaker, but don't close yourself off completely to the possibility of domesticity. If you marry, you may very well become more adept in the kitchen or the garden than you could ever have imagined. Even if you are a "career woman" and plan on never remaining home, you could end up getting into some of the domestic arts, unless you are fortunate enough to employ a full-time nanny and cook. Besides, even career women get bored with the same old routine and have been known to change their attitudes toward running a home. They can't help it; it's part of that unconscious evolution I mentioned earlier. Who says you have to be the consummate Martha Stewart type anyway? Not all men are looking for the "perfect homemaker" qualities in a woman.

I'm not suggesting that you be prepared to become a domestic goddess. Many women really have no interest in cooking, sewing, decorating or gardening, and that's okay. All I am suggesting is that you dare to imagine yourself in different roles and to envision yourself actually enjoying them.

---

## Remember...

 *on't be so stuck on your "life plan" that you are unwilling to consider other possibilities, particularly if you really do want to get married. Having a plan is commendable, but you need to be flexible. People change, and marriage will almost certainly change you, so be open to trying out different roles. Even if you've rarely set foot in a kitchen, you might become very domestic after you get married. You could end up surprising yourself!*

---

Sheila and Rob both had demanding jobs that they loved, and when they became engaged Sheila made it clear that she wanted to continue working, no matter what. There was no way she was going to be a stay-at-home *anything*. In fact, Sheila was ambivalent about domesticity in general and motherhood in particular. The truth was that she had serious doubts about her domestic skills or her parenting abilities, but she was so occupied with her career that she was easily able to disguise her insecurities. Rob thought having a child or two someday would be nice, but it wasn't an overwhelming desire. Furthermore, with their combined salary, they could easily afford to eat out as frequently as they wanted, and hire a maid to help with the household chores. He just wanted Sheila to be happy. (What a great guy!)

Shortly before their second anniversary Sheila and Rob found out they were expecting their first child. It wasn't planned, but they decided to make the best of it, and they actually began looking forward to parenthood. Rob said the decision about whether or not to remain home and care for the baby was totally up to Sheila, since his income was sufficient to support a family. In the beginning, Sheila was still set on remaining in the workforce, but as her pregnancy progressed she began to waver a little. She decided to take a leave of absence, still fully intending to return to work when the baby was three months old.

Towards the end of the leave Sheila found herself applying for an extension. Now she was having serious doubts about when or if she would return to work. She had to face one of two possibilities about herself: Either she was not as dedicated to her career as she had formerly thought, or she had found a new "career" she loved even more. She had to do a lot of soul-searching, and she experienced a great deal of inner conflict, not only because of her domestic qualms but also because so much of her identity had been tied up in her job. Ultimately, however, Sheila decided to remain home indefinitely and care for the baby and possibly the couple's future children. She was now a full time mom — something she'd never dreamt of.

Within a few weeks of formally resigning from her job, Sheila felt as if she were doing that which she was meant to do. She was a full time mother and loving it. She went to the play groups three mornings a week, where she met a slew of new mothers. They had so much to talk about, sharing all the new approaches to parenting, new baby equipment, and the like. Best of all, Sheila ended up with new friends, whose husbands met and liked Rob. Finally Rob and Sheila had a circle of friends in common, which hadn't been the case before.

So what happened? This gal who thought she'd never be the stay-at-home mother, never even cared if she had a family or not because her fears were so strong she didn't think she could "perform", *was* performing. Now that she was staying home, this woman, with all her fears and doubts, had become the woman she had formerly thought she had no desire to be.

What Sheila had to do to reach this happy position was set aside some of her preconceived ideas about her role as a married woman. When she found herself actually changing her views about this role, she had to be open to the changes and accept them. Otherwise she could have experienced years of inner turmoil, and this wouldn't have been good for her, her child or her husband. Sheila had to have the vision to see herself doing something that differed radically from her original plans, and then she had to have the courage to do it.

Sheila also had to set aside some of her notions about what marriage was all about. Her own mother had always worked outside the home, and so had the moms of most of her friends. Sheila had just assumed that she too would remain working full time throughout her marriage, whether or not she would take a leave of absence to have children. As Sheila found out, what a person observes throughout her lifetime is not necessarily what she will bring into her own marriage. (By the way, I am aware that being a one-income family isn't feasible for everyone these days, but with a little planning and budgeting, many couples are able to manage it.)

So be open to different possibilities. Your marriage may become entirely different than your parents', your friends' or whatever you imagined it might be like. When you realize that change is inevitable, but that you do have an amazing degree of control over many of the changes in your life, you won't be so afraid to imagine and try different roles. If you don't like the new role, you can change it and make it into a role you do like. Don't spend too much time dwelling on the future, either with a sense of dread or anticipation — after all, you have things to do today. Do keep an open mind about tomorrow, and most of all, don't close yourself off completely to any possibility, for if you do, you could be missing out on some of the greatest joys of your life.

# 31

## KEEP ROOM IN YOUR LIFE FOR CHILDREN
### (EVEN IF YOU THINK YOU WEREN'T MEANT TO BE A MOM)

*I*f you haven't had children by the time you're in your mid thirties, it's only natural to think that perhaps you weren't "meant" to be a mother. Hopefully you're okay with this. For that matter, it's possible that being around your nieces and nephews or your friends' children, seeing firsthand the many problems that arise, reinforces your conviction that children may not be for you. On the other hand, perhaps at times you think you still might like to have children, but the prospect of motherhood frightens you or at the very least leaves you ambivalent. After all, it is the most important and one of the most difficult "jobs" in the world — will you be up to it? Yet it is one of the most fulfilling roles imaginable, or so you keep hearing. Then again, it does require an enormous amount of time and energy, and you're not twenty-five anymore.

It's normal to vacillate on such an emotional issue as this, but even if you're pretty certain motherhood isn't in the cards for you, don't close yourself off entirely to the idea. Granted, we may be thinking ahead here, especially if you haven't even met Mr. Right yet. But bear with me, this is part of the process of opening yourself to new ideas and possibilities — imagining yourself in different roles, as we discuss in Chapter 30.

If you think being a mom might be an option someday, but it scares the heck out of you, take heart. Motherhood is a developing process. You aren't suddenly thrown into the pit and told to care for a dozen screaming kids. Whether a woman is a mother as a result of adoption or giving birth to a baby, she generally has many months to get used to the idea that her life is about to change. Every new mother is scared in the beginning, but those fears begin to lessen almost immediately. Once a baby is placed in your arms, it is the most natural of instincts to care for it. And there's plenty of help if you fear you won't have that natural instinct (for various reasons, some women really don't — at first). Most hospitals and birthing centers sponsor classes on the care of newborns for parents-to-be.

While you are pregnant, you will gather more literature than you ever dreamed of, and by the time you're finished reading through a quarter of what's on your night table, you may feel like a seasoned mother. Everything you need to do, and how to do it, is described in detail. I'm not suggesting that if you can read you can care for a baby today, but it is much easier to find information and support than it once was. If you still have doubts, you'll probably find that all of your friends who are already parents will be thrilled to help, as will the new grandmothers and aunts. There are parenting classes offered that were unheard of years ago, as well as baby nurses and something you may not be familiar with — a doula — not to mention new-mom support groups that meet in person or on the Internet. All are there to help, if you reach out and ask.

For the benefit of readers who are not familiar with doulas, they are women who remain with a woman through labor and her hospital stay, as well as the early days after her return home with her baby. They are experienced with childbirth, and provide continuous physical and emotional support and information to the new mother and father. They perform many of the functions that a woman's mother often did in times past. Now that families are frequently so scattered, a doula can be a welcome and comforting presence for new parents.

If you are wondering how you will care for a baby and run the house at the same time (and possibly still run your career), don't worry. There are books and classes now that tell you how to schedule your time, right down to what time to take a shower! If your husband doesn't think you are doing enough, or if you think *he's* not doing enough, negotiate with him to stay home more and help out. Actually, most couples today share the responsibilities of caring for the children — a very nice change from the way things were done in the past.

This is not to suggest that motherhood is a picnic in the park. There certainly will be wonderful days, but there also will be sleepless nights, and I don't want to play down the fact that being a mom will change your life in many ways. I'm just asking you to lighten up a little and realize that if you do choose motherhood, there are countless resources to help you.

If you (or your biological clock) have come to the conclusion that having children is simply not an option, you still may not get off that easily. What about the attractive divorced man who just happens to have kids? How about the man whose wife died and left him with young children? Before you say, "Forget about it!" stop and reconsider. I can't tell you how many times I have heard single women say, "I wouldn't marry a man with children!" My answer is always, "Why not?" Why not, indeed. As with all other aspects of your future life, you need to keep an open mind about this issue. If you meet and fall in love with a divorced man or a widower who has young children, chances are you will love those children as your own flesh and blood. It's happened to many women I've known — and yes, many of them are the same ones who had declared they would never consider marrying a man with children.

Another point worth bearing in mind is that your chances of meeting a single man around your age without children is getting slimmer by the day. Of course there are always younger men, but if you're set on someone in your age group, you need to be a little more flexible. Rather than closing your mind to a divorced man with children, why not reconsider? Just change your thinking, because as time passes, it will change anyway. This doesn't mean it's impossible to find a great guy without children; it just means your chances of meeting someone *with* children is increasing, so why not get the best pick while you're younger, rather than waiting another few years? Remember, you want to increase your chances of meeting that wonderful man, and you don't want to waste any more precious time.

## Remember...

 ven if you have no intention of having children of your own, there's a very good possibility that many of the men you'll be dating will have kids. Don't close yourself off to the idea of being a step-mom, and don't automatically dismiss a potentially great guy just because he has children.

Granted, the idea of a ready-made family can be overwhelming, particularly if the man is divorced (as opposed to widowed). The prospect of caring for someone else's children *and* having to deal with the first wife is pretty intimidating. First let's talk about the ex. The first thing to keep in mind is that if your relationship leads to marriage, *you* will be the Mrs., not she (no matter whose name she has). If you and your husband have children, he will be living with *your* children, not theirs, unless he has custody. You will never be put in second place, because you will not let it happen. You will always insist that because you are his wife, you go wherever he goes (well, within reason). Most problems he and his ex have can be resolved over the telephone. At the same time, you will try to be understanding and not be jealous, reminding yourself that he loves *you* and that's why he's committed himself to you. Again, you shouldn't spend too much time speculating about things that haven't happened yet. However, if you are truly worried about the problems that could arise when dating a divorced man with kids, it really does help to remind yourself that you have the power to prevent your fears from becoming realities.

Perhaps you're concerned about how you and his children will get along. Many women I know have great relationships with their husband's kids from a previous marriage. (For that matter, some are even friendly with the ex-wives. Yes, it does happen!) If your Mr. Prospect has children from a previous marriage, it doesn't have to be a negative at all. Look at the man for himself first, and give him a chance. He may very well make you a happy woman. Try not to close any doors. You might be losing out by deciding you are not interested in dating a divorced man with children.

By the way, if you are a member of an online dating service, why not say right in your profile that you would welcome a man with children? You might even go so far as to say that you love kids, if that's true. It's a positive feature that could really make a recently divorced man or a widower with kids take notice, especially since many single women wouldn't even think to list this until they are much older. Try it, you'll stand out from the rest.

What if the shoe is on the other foot, and you're the one who has a child or children from a previous relationship? Well, if you've been out in the dating world at all, you already know the challenges a single parent can face. Many men will not consider marrying or even dating a woman with children. In fact, I'd be willing to bet that more men than women are put off by the prospect of a ready-made family. If you meet someone and those are his feelings, don't waste too much time trying to change them. Move on, because there are some great men out there who are more than willing to be family men.

Even if you never have children by birth, marriage or adoption, I hope you will stay open to having kids in your life. They will make it so much richer. Certainly you have love to share with nieces and nephews, or the children of friends, and those relationships can be among the most rewarding you can have. Between my husband and me, we had three sets of aunts and uncles who never had children, but we *were* their children nonetheless, and to those still living, we are "theirs" to this day. We couldn't be any closer if they were our own parents.

Most people don't want to be alone. If you find someone with children who's basically a pleasant person, who wants to please you and enjoys being pleased by you — and doesn't carry too much emotional baggage — give the relationship a chance. You have nothing to lose, and who knows, it just might work. You may yet end up driving a carpool, wiping runny noses, and sticking priceless works of art on your refrigerator door!

# 32

# BE FLEXIBLE —
# EVERYTHING IS NEGOTIABLE!

*A*re you ready for marriage? Is marriage for you? Do you really want to be married? Before you say, "Of course!", think about it honestly. If your answer is an unconditional "Yes!", good for you. (You should still read this chapter, though.) On the other hand, if you reply, "Yes, I'm ready for marriage, but on my terms," you *really* should read this chapter, because you need to reexamine your goals. You may think you want to be married, but your mindset is still centered on yourself.

When a man hears a "yes, but" in any form, it's usually a real turn-off. That's not so surprising. Most women feel the same way when listening to a man spell out what he expects of his future wife. It is patently absurd to make such demands, yet single people of both sexes talk this way all the time.

Of course you have preferences and desires, and there's nothing wrong with that, but insisting that a relationship be on your terms is another matter. This is usually defensive behavior, an attempt to cover up your fears. Unfortunately, it puts up a wall between you and your prospect. You avoid facing your fears, but you also avoid ever having a real relationship that could lead to marriage. With effort, however, you can stop this destructive behavior. The best way is to simply try putting yourself in the other person's place. Every time you find yourself talking about what you want or don't want in a relationship, just turn it around and imagine hearing a man speaking the same way to you. If you were to hear him say, "Sure, I'm ready for marriage, when I can find a woman who has an advanced degree, makes a lot of money and doesn't ask questions when I stay out late," I doubt you'd hang around long enough for him to defend himself. Maybe you're not that blatant, but you still may be communicating that you're used to having things your way.

Pay attention to yourself when you're talking. Even if you are on the phone speaking to a prospective blind date, or you're responding to someone's e-mail to you, stop in your tracks and listen to what you are saying, or read what you're typing, as the case may be. If you would be turned off by a man who responded that way, change your response!

Curbing your defensive responses in conversation is important, but you also need to figure out the "issues" that gave rise to those responses in the first place. Why are you so defensive? What is it that keeps you from saying, "Yes, of course I'm ready for marriage!" — and feeling happy at the thought? There are several chapters in this book on fears and doubts about marriage, and I hope you'll read those too. At the very least, read Chapter 26, "Face Up To Your Own Fears And Doubts About The 'M' Word", and Chapter 30, "Dare To Imagine Yourself In Different Roles".

Perhaps your problem is that you have a general tendency to be inflexible. This trait, by its very nature, is often difficult to detect in oneself, but be assured that others can see it quite clearly. Therefore, a little honest self-examination can be helpful. If you're the kind of person who always has to do things the same way, and can't tolerate even a minor change in your routine, you might qualify for the term "inflexible". Carried to extremes, inflexibility can be a sign of a personality disorder, but of course that is beyond the scope of this book. Even in the less extreme degrees to which we're referring here, being inflexible can keep you from ever finding a husband. Maybe you need to loosen up a little. Once again, reverse the situation and ask yourself how you would view that same trait in a potential boyfriend. You probably wouldn't like it much at all.

I've known women who thought their men were too inflexible, and they were able to argue their point until they broke the guy down. In many cases these women were the inflexible ones, but they had the ability to manipulate the man to such a degree that he couldn't see it. In one case the tables turned and a man told one of these women that *she* was inflexible, but she absolutely refused to believe it. As noted in Chapter 1, very often the negative traits we perceive in others are those we dislike in ourselves but aren't willing to face.

Inflexibility does not work in any relationship, whether it's between a husband and wife, parents and children, two friends, or co-workers. Flexibility, on the other hand, is essential in all relationships. Being flexible and open to possibilities will increase your happiness and decrease your disappointments. It sometimes takes courage to imagine a future completely dissimilar to the one you have mapped out for yourself. Furthermore, being flexible may go against your grain. It's all a lot easier, however, if you remember that *just about everything in life is negotiable* — and this applies to personal relationships as much as it does to business. If you try something and don't like it, the two of you can create something that works better for both of you. Within reason, two people with similar goals can reach them together if both stay flexible and learn to negotiate instead of argue. If you find yourself being overly rigid about an issue, ask yourself how you will feel about it a week from now, a month from now, even a year from now. Will it make a difference then? Chances are you can let it slide.

Merely harboring the thought that marriage or any relationship has to be on your terms creates a problem before there is one. When you let a man know that something has to be your way or no way, you are shutting a door in his face, and no one likes that. It's final, it's hurtful, and it sends a message that you care primarily about yourself. It is normal to have doubts and insecurities, but if you stay flexible and learn to negotiate, you can handle them. And when you do enter into a healthy relationship, you'll find all those issues that compelled you to say, "On my terms only" really aren't that big a deal after all. ♥

---

## Remember...

 *verything in life is negotiable — and that goes double for relationships!*

---

# 33

# GIVE SERIOUS THOUGHT
# TO WHAT MAKES
# A GOOD MARRIAGE

*I*n the chapter discussing women's fears and doubts about matrimony, I quoted a dictionary definition of marriage. As you know, however, the dictionary can only define words. It can tell you what the word "marriage" means, but it can't tell you what marriage really is, and it certainly can't tell you what makes a *good* marriage.

So what does make a good marriage? If you've decided you truly want to get married, that's a question you should consider, and the sooner the better. Even if you haven't met Mr. Right yet, you need to think ahead so you can clarify your own definition of a successful marriage. Notice that this is not at all the same as making a "list" of what you want in a spouse. As I've said before, that just doesn't work! On the other hand, I am strongly in favor of any exercise that will help you understand the institution of marriage a little better.

Marriage is the union of two entirely different people agreeing to live together — in harmony, or so one would hope. When you stop to think about it though, it's a miracle that any marriage survives! Two distinct individuals choosing to spend the rest of their lives together hardly sounds like a formula for harmony, and often isn't. Don't worry; I am not trying to rekindle those fears and doubts we talked about in Chapter 26. Nor am I attempting to take the romance away. I am simply trying to present a realistic picture.

It's true that many marriages fall by the wayside, but many survive. That survival is no accident. These unions endure because the couples' commitment to marriage is *stronger than anything else.* Either consciously or subconsciously, couples whose marriages last have decided they want to have a successful marriage.

Beyond that general commitment, what makes a marriage work? Is having everything in common the key? Not necessarily. As discussed in Chapter 18, many couples say they actually have very little in common, yet they still have good marriages. On the flip side, many couples have a lot in common but are not happy. No, marrying someone who is your mirror image is not the secret.

Having a union free of "issues" isn't the key either. Often some tension in a relationship leads to growth. Most couples have problems — money, sex, children, household responsibilities, in-laws, etc. Financial issues are especially common these days, and they are not confined to those on the lower end of the income scale. Those with larger incomes generally have larger expenses, higher taxes and a host of other headaches. However, when therapists counsel couples who are having a difficult time in their marriage, it isn't the issues themselves that are the problem — it is how the issues are (or are not) approached and resolved. Money, sex, family problems and other conflicts are merely situations. They may be serious situations but are not the essence of the marriage. Virtually all of these problems can be resolved if both people are committed to their marriage. With that basic commitment, they can overcome even the toughest challenges, and without it, the union won't last even in the total absence of major "issues".

Some couples instinctively know how to handle their problems and differences, and others have to learn, sometimes the hard way. I'll bet many women who were married before — those who I said would be the first to remarry — will be the ones who have good marriages. They may have been in bad marriages, but they learned what works and what doesn't in a marriage.

The best marriages are the ones where the couples learn to communicate their feelings to their spouse without letting their ego get in the way. They don't try to manipulate or control the other person. Instead they give each other the space to grow and move, both independently and as a couple.

Not being afraid to admit one is wrong is also essential to a great marriage. It's only natural to defend our actions when someone confronts us, much like the proverbial kid getting caught with his hand in the cookie jar. However, if you and your Mr. Right are discussing issues and one or both of you tend to be stubborn and defensive, you will get nowhere. You both have to back down and say to yourselves, "Maybe I'm not right." It's humbling, but it makes for a much better marriage. Admit your faults, help your future spouse to admit his, and let him help you admit yours. Only then can you move on from there. Without this admission, those "faults" will be a constant thorn.

As discussed in Chapter 7, the ability to laugh at yourself is also an asset, and ideally both of you will have this skill. In my opinion, too many people seem to have been born without a sense of humor. They are completely unable to step out of their own shoes and see how ridiculous they sometimes look. And that's too bad, because seeing how funny we are makes us more fun! More to the point for couples in conflict, finding the humor in one's own mistakes or shortcomings can help defuse even the most heated argument. This doesn't mean you laugh off real problems, it just means you recognize that so many of the situations you find yourselves in do have a humorous side. Some of the arguments couples get into are truly absurd, which is why these conflicts are such a rich source of inspiration for sitcom writers. The best comedy writers base their scripts on the arguments and conflicts they've had with their own intimate partners.

---

## Remember...

*ot being afraid to admit being wrong is essential to a good marriage. So is the ability to laugh at oneself.*

---

Even if a couple rarely argues, it doesn't mean their marriage isn't festering with problems that haven't been confronted. If you feel strongly about something, don't hold it in and bring up the problems a week later. Discuss today's problem today, resolve it and move on. The worst thing you can do is bring up old issues. Bury them. Therapists, and just about any article or book you read, agree on this point. If you  bring up old issues, it's probably a sign of one of two things. Either the two of you never resolved the problem, or you didn't feel satisfied with his response. If you habitually dig up old issues, that may be a sign of a deeper problem, so consider counseling. On the other hand, if you are merely stubborn and spoiled, and have a tendency to argue relentlessly until you get your way, sooner or later he'll see through your manipulation. Do you want a good marriage, or do you just want your way?

It is not difficult to learn how to please each other if you listen and try to keep an open mind. Fortunately, many resources are available, such as books, classes and, of course, counseling. (If you're engaged and see potential problems, premarital counseling can save both of you years of grief.) Often, however, just sitting down and talking to each other should help. If you're both committed to your marriage, you will find a way to work through your problems.

There is a profound difference between saying, "I want to get married" and saying, "I want to have a *good* marriage." If you understand the importance of the basic commitment discussed in this chapter, you have already laid the foundation for a good marriage. ♥

---

## Remember...

*ow two people handle their problems and differences will determine whether their marriage will be successful or not.*

---

PART Five

# USE EVERY TOOL
# YOU HAVE

# 34

# SURROUND YOURSELF WITH POSITIVE, UPBEAT PEOPLE

cannot overstate how important it is to surround yourself with positive people. It doesn't matter whether they're married or single; ideally your circle of friends will contain a good mixture of both. In Chapter 13 we discuss how important it is to adopt a "married woman" attitude, so of course you should befriend some married women. You can even pick up some success tips from women who have been married several times. This chapter, however, focuses on your general circle of friends. Whether you're still looking for Mr. Right or have found him, you absolutely need to have upbeat, cheerful, emotionally healthy people in your life. Why? It's simple: in many ways we become part of the people with whom we associate. If you want to have an enjoyable life, associate with people who enjoy *their* lives. The same goes if you want to be successful at anything — try spending time around similarly successful people.

Haven't you noticed how good you feel after you've spoken to a positive person? I'm not talking about hyper people, who can quickly wear you out. I'm talking about buoyant people who enjoy life. Put down the phone after talking to someone like that and you suddenly feel energized — it's contagious!

On the other hand, surround yourself with depressed people and you feel the same. Hang up the phone after speaking to a depressed friend, and you feel ten pounds heavier. I don't mean to sound indifferent, but if you regularly associate with depressed people, sooner or later you're going to pick up on their attitude, no matter how upbeat you naturally are. A man I know has a friend whom he describes as a "black hole of human need". "This guy is such a sad sack," my friend told me. "He has nothing but bad luck with money, relationships, and everything else you can imagine. He's been to one therapist after another for over twenty years now, has taken every antidepressant on the market, has had disastrous relationships with women…it's always something. I try to be a good friend to him, but really found that for my own happiness and peace of mind I have to limit contact with him."

I often wonder how therapists can leave the office without a heavy heart. If they listen to people's problems all day long, it has to weigh heavily on their shoulders. I am sure their training teaches them how to divorce themselves from their patients' problems, but it cannot be easy.

Fortunately, you aren't your friends' therapist, or you shouldn't be, anyway. If you have negative-minded friends, you don't need to cut them out of your life entirely, but you do need to limit your contact with them. Just shorten your conversations by telling them you understand and hope things will get better for them. (Naturally, if you have a friend who seems to be suffering from clinical depression, encourage her or him to get professional help.) If these are people you truly care for, then of course you want to keep in touch with them. However, you need to have an easy out whenever you call them — let them know at the beginning of the conversation that you're ready to walk out of the office or are leaving to meet someone for dinner — anything that gives you a quick exit. Listen attentively to them, be encouraging if possible (but don't give advice unless specifically asked), and then excuse yourself. If you aren't all that close to your negative acquaintances, it should be easy to dissociate yourself from them. There was an old song, "Accentuate The Positive, Eliminate The Negative". Again, I don't mean to sound cold, but this principle applies to the negative people in your life as much as it does to negative attitudes or situations.

Ultimately, your own state of happiness and emotional health is mirrored in your friends, whether you realize it or not. Quite often, people who surround themselves with negative-minded or emotionally unhealthy friends and acquaintances have many similar traits themselves. Or perhaps they are co-dependent. I'm sure much of this is unconscious, for few people deliberately choose friends for their negative traits. The point is that your friends mirror you, and the reverse is true. However, whether your own negativity is a cause or effect of the company you're keeping, what's important is that you have the power to break out of the cycle of negativity.

# Remember...

*our own state of happiness and emotional health is mirrored in your friends, and the reverse is true as well. We become part of the people with whom we associate, and vice-versa. If you want to be happy, associate with cheerful, optimistic people instead of negative ones.*

What if some of those "negative people" are family members? Suppose you have a sister who seems to have nothing but bad luck and trouble, and she calls you every evening to give you the rundown on the latest disaster in her life. Or your cousin phones you every other day, not to share good news or ask how you're doing, but to complain about her mother, neighbor, her co-worker, and all the other people who are aggravating her. This can be touchy. Of course you love your family and often you can't as easily dissociate from them as you can your friends and acquaintances. Further, family members sometimes have a way of making you feel guilty because they don't think you're being supportive enough. (Friends can do this too, but family members are particularly skilled in this "art".) You may even feel guilty because your own life is going more smoothly than theirs is. Perhaps at some level you think you don't "deserve" to be happy when someone in your family is so unhappy.

I know this is more difficult than dealing with negative friends, but you have to be firm. Be as loving and supportive as you can, but find a way to end the conversations as quickly as possible, or deflect the negativity with something upbeat. You don't want to sound falsely cheery or uncaring, but surely there are ways you can redirect the discussion. If you have an honest and open relationship with your family member, at some point you can sit down with her and tell her how her chronic negativity is making you feel. Tell her you truly wish she were happier and ask if there is anything you can do to help her. But don't get sucked into "the black hole" yourself. Remember, you are not her therapist. And if you are feeling guilty for being happy you need to stop that. To a large degree, happiness, or lack thereof, is a result of choices we make. Is it possible that you have made better life choices than your sister or your whiny cousin? How could you possibly feel guilty about that?

There are many negative people in this world, but positive people are all around you too. The more of them you bring into your life, the happier you'll be. Not only are their cheerful, optimistic attitudes catching, but positive people are also apt to be much better friends than the negative types. They are far more likely to give you support and encouragement when you need it. And people who are happy with their lives want to spread that happiness and help others. You want to stay positive yourself in order to add as much to their lives as they do to yours. Surround yourself with happy people, and Mr. Right will be much more likely to find you.

## Remember...

y surrounding yourself with positive people, you're making it a lot easier for Mr. Right to find you.

# 35

# INCREASE YOUR
# CIRCLE OF FRIENDS —
## (YOU CAN NEVER HAVE TOO MANY!)

Throughout this book I've said change is both good and healthy. Well, friends can be one of your most important building blocks for change. If you don't have a broad circle of friends and acquaintances, now is the time to change that.

First of all, your friends can be your most powerful allies in your quest for Mr. Right. These days there are all kinds of new ways to meet people, but one of your best chances for meeting "the one" is still through mutual friends. For both men and women, there is no better way to meet someone than through an introduction. You both already have at least one friend in common, so you already have something to talk about at the outset. And your mutual friend will be able to give you some insight about the man you've been introduced to. There's no guarantee he'll be a decent person, but chances are he probably will be. (We talk about this more in the chapter on "fix-ups" (Chapter 36). The more people you know and associate with, the greater your chances are for future introductions. Your new associations and friendships may very well lead you to the love of your life, but that is only one of the many benefits of being a "friend collector".

The term "friend collector" may sound a little odd to you. Friendship is something precious that must be nurtured carefully over a period of time, so how can one possibly "collect" friends? How can one person have the emotional time and energy for dozens of close friendships? The fact is that being a friend collector is quite easy if you genuinely like people. I'm not suggesting that every friend you make will be a "best friend", or that every friendship will be a profound, emotionally intimate relationship. That would be a contradiction in terms. However, with a little practice you can cultivate genuine friendships — relationships that go beyond mere "acquaintance-ships" — with a large number of people. In this chapter I'm going to give you suggestions on how to do that.

Naturally, being a friend collector is a wonderful idea even if you aren't looking for a husband. Having a lot of friendships with a variety of people — positive, upbeat people, of course — is healthy. And making new friends can be extraordinarily refreshing. Of course, in order to make friends, you have to go out and look for them. No person, female or male, can meet you if you don't leave the confines of your own four walls. They are not going to break your door down if they don't know you're inside. Don't say they're not out there. Just as there are still plenty of good men to date, there are plenty of potential friends to make. We've spoken about classes and outside interests, which are essential for knowledge and fun, as well as for self-confidence and even for your ego. These are great places to meet friends. I have not forgotten that the majority of you reading this work full time. However, some organizations offer evening meetings, and there is always an evening class or weekend workshop to develop a new interest. There are plenty of things to do on the weekends; use your imagination, because you can find new friends just about anywhere.

Now let's look more closely at what we can learn from the true "friend collectors". These are women who have it down to a science. They make a concentrated, ongoing effort to increase their number of friends. It's like a full time job, only they don't have to work at it because they've done it for so many years that it just comes naturally. I call these women The Collectors because they really are full time collectors — of friends, that is! I'm sure you know some already, but if you're not familiar with them or their technique, this is how they operate.

Ms. Collector starts with a new female acquaintance. They meet at the gym, a party, a conference , etc., and exchange names and telephone numbers. Before they say goodbye, Ms. Collector says, "I'll call you so we can go to lunch one day." People say things like this all the time, but Ms. Collector actually means it. She doesn't wait more than a day or two to follow up with a phone call. "Hi, do you remember me? We met at the party Tuesday night!" After some small talk, she immediately says, "Are you busy next Monday? It would be nice to see you again. How about going to lunch?"

And that's how the friendship begins. The two go to lunch, and Ms. Collector follows up with a phone call the next day, telling her new friend how lovely it was having lunch with her the day before, and she really hopes to see her again very soon. She may follow up again a few days later with a quick, "Hi, just wanted to say hello and see how your week is going." Then a couple of days later she calls again, this time to ask her new friend to join her for a wonderful movie that just opened, or a play or concert to which she has an extra ticket, or dinner with friends on the following weekend. Whatever it takes to connect with this new contact, Ms. Collector has thought of. And that's how the game is played — she has added another name to her phone book, and the numbers continue to grow.

Understand that Ms. Collector never comes across as being needy or desperate for friends. She's the last person you'd ever think of as desperate, for she has so many friends that her social calendar has little room. Nor does she ever try to force a friendship with anyone who's obviously not interested — there are too many people who welcome her friendly overtures for her to waste time on the indifferent ones. Ms. Collector simply loves people, and she loves to make new friends — and most people are flattered when someone new shows interest in them.

---

## Remember...

he equation is pretty simple: *The more people you know, the greater your chances are for introductions.*

---

Remember that although you want some single friends, since their lifestyle is similar to yours, you don't want all of them to be single. Married women who aren't threatened by a single woman can add another dimension to your life, and, as discussed in Chapters 12 and 13, you can learn a lot from them. Also, don't forget women who are divorced or widowed. The more people you know, the more places you'll be invited to, and the greater your chances are of meeting someone. It's a pretty easy formula, and it sure beats staying home and doing the same old things that haven't worked.

Occasionally I've heard some women say they have enough friends and don't have time for the ones they have now! I'm mentioning that only because there's a slim chance you may meet someone with whom you'd really like to become friends, and you can't get the friendship established. If you think that's the case, and she seems to be worth the effort, don't give up too easily. She could very well be one of those busy women who simply thinks she may not have time for another friendship, so don't take it personally. There's a good possibility that she will eventually see something in you that will make her want to know you better. Of course, don't call her too frequently, as you don't want to appear to be overbearing. If you hang in there, and you're friendly and upbeat when you speak to her, she might come around.

Before I became licensed to sell real estate, everyone emphasized the importance of new Realtors meeting people and making new friends. They suggested we join organizations, including networking groups, and that we become active in our churches or synagogues or in volunteering. They understood that increasing the number of people we knew would expand our potential client base.

After I became a Realtor, I wondered where my first sale was going to come from. I worked, I advertised and most importantly, I met as many people as possible. When I could, I tried to connect with someone different once or twice a week for lunch, and I always tried to remember the importance of keeping in touch. I knew from the beginning that it wasn't the first or second sale that was important — I was building my base. The more people I knew, the more contacts I made, the greater my chances were that one day they would call and ask me to help them. If you throw enough coals into the fire, some of them have to catch!

Building your base of friendships is no different than increasing your contacts in sales. Making more friends and becoming more sociable isn't terribly difficult, it just takes some direction and focus. Make a game of it. For example, look at your personal phone book. When was the last time you added a name and phone number to your book? I bet that if you tried, you could add one name a month; you just have to be a little aggressive about it. Not everyone you meet will become your new best friend, but what do you have to lose? And if you only make one new friend in two months, by year's end you will have six good friends you didn't have the year before!

Barbra Streisand's most famous song, "People", asserts that those needing people are the luckiest people in the world. How true that is; we all need people. I believe what the song was really saying is that people who *recognize* their need for others are the luckiest people. Unless one's desire is to be a total recluse, everyone needs friends. The sooner you recognize this need, and the sooner you act upon it, the happier you will be. It's as simple as that.

When searching for friends, keep in mind that you don't have to like everything about someone in order to strike up a friendship. The two of you don't necessarily have to have very much in common, but it does help if you share the same core values. For example, if you are hoping to marry someone who shares your religion, a girlfriend does not necessarily have to be of that religion. I know couples of the same faith who married but were introduced by someone of a different faith. The population is so diverse today, and we all know many different people. Don't sell anyone short.

---

## Remember...

*ou don't have to love or even like everything about everyone. If you find it difficult to increase your friendships, try to overlook the small things that may bother you. Beyond those idiosyncrasies may be the most wonderful person. Everyone is different — give people a chance.*

---

If you're unsure about someone and you get a negative vibe or two, don't write them off too quickly. Just like body types, personalities also have extremes. You certainly should not let a few little negatives turn you away from a potentially rewarding relationship. Within days after I began selling real estate, I met another saleswoman in my office. There was something about Suzanne that I immediately liked, and I thought she was someone I wanted to get to know better. One morning not too long after we met, I walked into the office and this is how she greeted me: "Myra, did I see you playing tennis at the tennis center yesterday?" I answered, "Yes, I was there." Her response was, "You really ought to take some lessons!" I could have been insulted by her remark, but I wasn't. She may have been outspoken, but she was honest and was indeed correct — I absolutely did need lessons. That was nearly thirty years ago. I never did take another lesson, and gave up the game because I really was a terrible player. But before long, Suzanne and I were the closest of friends.

She still makes me laugh when she's so honest, but that's one of the things I love about her, and she's usually right!

What would I have gained at the very beginning by being insulted by Suzanne's remark? Probably nothing, and I would have lost a chance at a wonderful friendship. Someone else may have been so hurt by such a comment that they would have immediately decided this woman wasn't someone they would want for a friend. But you really can't be so thin-skinned that hearing the truth hurts. When faced with a similar situation, try saying to yourself, "She might be right." In cases such as this, the person usually *is* right, and you could even find yourself thanking her for her advice, believe it or not! If I had been overly sensitive, I would have lost out on knowing a wonderful, bright, talented woman who remains one of my dearest friends.

---

## Remember...

 eople come in all shapes and sizes, with all kinds of *personalities. Just as opposites attract when people are looking for a spouse, so you can be attracted to a different type of girlfriend. They don't all need to be like you. Someone different will add a unique dimension to your life — and you to theirs.*

---

Collecting a variety of friends and acquaintances is wonderful, but once in a while you'll come across a real gem, such as Suzanne. Many years ago my mother-in-law told me, "If you make one very good friend in your lifetime, you've accomplished more than many other people have." She was right. If you don't have one *very* good friend today don't worry, because when you least expect it, one will walk into your life. (Much like meeting Mr. Right, you know!) But remember, you have to step forward and do something. Friends can't come out of thin air — you still have to get out and make the kind of changes to your life that will increase your opportunities.

Good friends really do have a way of walking into your life when least expected. I had been selling real estate for two years when a client called on a Friday evening. I had just finished negotiating a contract for her and her husband to build a new home, and I had their present home listed for sale. She asked me if I could come over to her house. She had just met a new couple who was renting in the neighborhood and they might be interested in buying her home. I asked two questions about these new neighbors, and I knew immediately that they would not be buying her home. I easily could have qualified this prospect on the phone and told my client that her home wasn't for these new neighbors after all. But she was excited, and I didn't want to disappoint her. On the other hand, my family and I had only just sat down to dinner, and I was very tempted to say no to my client. Yet I had a hunch it was important to go see her. I walked into her home, met her new neighbor — and an hour and a half later we were exchanging phone numbers. I knew I had made a new friend. That was Sherrie. We met almost thirty years ago, and we've been the dearest of friends ever since.

---

# Remember...

 ncrease your acquaintances, because you never know where you will meet your next friend.

---

I can't say enough about the ways in which increasing your friendships will enrich your life. Girlfriends are wonderful, and we cannot and should not live without them. Of course my husband is my best friend, but so are my girlfriends. My friends are all different, each and every one. Each one adds a different dimension to my life, as I hope I do to theirs.

Although women have always enjoyed powerful friendships with each other, in the past, women in general were more competitive with, and distrustful of other women. It's different today, thank goodness! Many more of us openly acknowledge the importance of having women friends, and this awareness is reflected everywhere in our culture — in movies, novels, TV shows and in real life. Let's face it: Men and women are different, and we need female friends because they understand what we're going through better than any man ever could. It's so much healthier to vent with a girlfriend than to stew in anger at men for not being more like us.

Sadly enough, though, even in these modern times some women undervalue their female friendships. When Mr. Right appears in their lives, these women turn away from their girlfriends and focus their attention completely on their man, looking to him to fulfill all of their social and emotional needs. Most men cannot tolerate this kind of neediness (which we discuss in the chapter on "Baggage" (Chapter 7), and they almost always leave. When the woman turns back to her girlfriends for solace, she finds she has completely alienated them. They're resentful, and who can blame them?

Never underestimate the value of having friends of your own sex. Nurture those friendships, and you'll find that your girlfriends will be there for you long after Mr. Not-So-Right has left. Best of all, they'll also be there to share your joy when you do meet Mr. Right.

Of course to have a friend, you must *be* one; you must do your part to care for the relationship in order for it to grow.

Do you think you're too busy to concentrate wholeheartedly on making new friends? Think again. While working full time, it's difficult but not impossible. Everyone you meet is a potential friend. You have to make the time. Remember that this isn't just about increasing your number of friendships, it's about enlarging your circle of friends in order to bring some change into your life. And change is what this is all about. Keep your old friends, of course, but it's time to make some new ones!

## Remember...

ever underestimate the value of having friends of your own sex. You need female friends, because they understand what you're going through much better than even the closest male friend.

Since we're on the topic of "old friends", what happens to your friendships when most of your girlfriends are married and you are not? If you are in your forties or fifties, you have probably long since come to terms with this situation. More than likely you've remained close to some of these friends over the years. Maybe the friendships changed when your friends started becoming mothers, because although they had a baby, husband and household to think of, you were still working full time and had few free hours in the week. Some of your girlfriends may not have understood that. Maybe they justified their distance by telling themselves your lives had just taken different directions now and you had little in common.

If you were wise, however, you made every effort to preserve the friendships you truly valued. You realized that if there was something you really liked about these women before they became mothers, it was probably still there. You understood that they were overwhelmed by their new responsibilities. Perhaps you met them halfway, knowing that a new mother likes nothing more than talking about her baby. You showed interest, asked questions, and stopped by for short visits when you could. If you brought a little something for the baby, it was always welcomed. Once the initial newness of motherhood wore off, your true friends came around again, and even began to show interest in your social life. But it was you who had to work hard to keep the friendship going.

It's possible that now some of your friends are becoming grandmothers for the first time...and that's a whole new experience for them, and for you. For a while they may be as distracted as they were when they first became moms. Perhaps some of your other friends are getting divorced and remarried, and maybe with everything that's going on in their lives they don't have much time for you anymore. No matter how your respective circumstances may change, you should always try to maintain established friendships because they are generally worth the effort. Besides, keep in mind that when a friend of yours gets married or remarried, she will probably know new people through her husband — thus affording you a chance to increase your own circle of friends and acquaintances. If you're out of sight, you're out of mind — so don't let your friends forget about you!

Once in a while a big problem arises out of old friendships, and this can happen no matter what your age or how long you've known your friend. If one of your girlfriends sees you as a threat because you're still single, she may actively discourage your friendship. She isn't saying she's too busy to have any interest in your life at the moment. She is saying she's insecure and views you as a threat to her marriage. In this case there is little you can do except to write her off for the time being. She is not worth your time or energy. If she wants to come around again one day that's fine, but don't chase after her. There are too many new friends to be made. In fact, the best way to get over the loss of an old friend is to bring new friends into your life.

Friend collecting comes more easily to some people than to others, but like everything else we talk about in this book, it can be learned. Even if you're shy, you can become a friend collector. Take it from the "pros" — it works! ♥

# 36

## DON'T SHY AWAY FROM "FIX-UPS"

lind dates or "fix-ups" have gotten a bad reputation over the years, and as a result many people shy away from them. In your early to mid-thirties you probably had quite a few fix-ups, but after that there were less and less. Given your choice, you'd probably never go out on a blind date again — but don't argue with statistics. The fact is that many people of all ages have met their husbands and wives as a result of a fix-up.

This doesn't mean that blind dates are without their perils and pitfalls. You and I both know better. Even if you don't necessarily have a disastrous date experience, when fix-ups don't work they can cause tension in your friendships. Friends have a tendency to become defensive when they introduce you to someone and nothing materializes, especially if it has happened a lot. Perhaps your friends have accused you of being too fussy. Well, I don't agree with that. Just because you haven't had successful fix-ups, it doesn't mean you're being too picky. Sometimes the guys your friends introduce you to really are jerks. Or there simply aren't any sparks and you can tell there never will be.

That said, I still can't say enough good things about fix-ups. Sure, not all of them will be successful, but you are overlooking potentially wonderful opportunities if you rule them out entirely. Remember, you can't meet too many people. If someone wants to introduce you to someone, say "Yes!" without any hesitation. What do you have to lose? Within five minutes on the phone you can probably tell if he might be worth meeting or not. If you do agree to meet and nothing comes of it...so you spent thirty or forty minutes at a Starbucks. It's not a big deal.

If you get bad vibes on the phone, go with your gut feeling. Tell him he seems like a nice person, but you can see you are worlds apart. Or acknowledge that it was nice of your mutual friend to want to fix you up, but you can see it wouldn't work, so why waste each other's time. Whatever you can say to gently end the conversation without hurting his feelings will be just fine. But always follow up with a phone call the next day to the person responsible for the introduction, whether it was successful or not. Your friend may or may not ask for details, and what you offer is up to you. You don't have to defend your decision to your friend but do make it clear that you could tell he wasn't for you. In any case, whether you liked the person or not, be sure to thank your friend for thinking of you, and ask them to please keep you in mind in the future.

What if you think you might like to go out with this person, but you're still not quite certain? Well, just because they call them "blind dates", it doesn't mean you should go into them totally "blind". If you can find someone else who knows this man, by all means ask their opinion. However, keep in mind that for a variety of reasons, they may not give you a clear picture. Try not to be too influenced by others — you have to make up your own mind. Unless you are told he has some major character flaw or is an alcoholic or heavy drug user, at least meet the man. If there is a problem, you'll find out soon enough.

Let's say someone calls and wants to fix you up with someone you met many years ago — but all you can remember about this man was that he was a dud. He wasn't a talker, or didn't seem terribly bright, or didn't seem to have much of a personality. Why in the world would you waste your time meeting him again? I'll tell you why: Because once in a while, people change. If it's been more than a few years, treat it as though you never met him. Give him a chance. You will make your friend happy, and even if it doesn't work out, that friend will be much more likely to keep you in mind when someone else surfaces.

If you are open to seeing this man again but are not sure you're ready for a one-on-one date, let your friend know. Tell her that if she wants to ask a few people over to her house, with this man included, you'd be happy to come. That way you're with others, so if this guy still doesn't have much to offer, or if you really dislike him, there will be others to talk with. At least you are trying, and you're being sociable. Remember, it's only a couple of hours out of your week — and there's always a chance you might find him less of a dud than you did five years ago.

Todd moved to my city when he was in his mid-twenties. He made a few friends who were part of a large social group, and within a few weeks he was going to their parties and dating, though not very successfully. He seemed to have a chip on his shoulder, and the word spread among the single women that he wasn't very nice. A few years passed, and I happened to meet him one day. He still seemed to have that chip, but beyond that, he seemed like a genuinely nice guy. I figured that he was still young and maybe he'd outgrow it. Years later I met up with him again, and guess what? He had indeed matured, lost that defensive chip and developed into a great guy. He is a perfect example of how people can change. Abby was a law school graduate who moved here for an internship with one of the Justices, and Todd, now almost forty, was fixed up with her. She'd met some of his old acquaintances and heard all about his reputation, so was a little reluctant to meet him. But she put her apprehension aside and decided to give him a try. They married a year ago!

Todd's tale is not only a successful "fix-up" story, but it's also an excellent example of how people can change. If you happen to meet someone with whom you were friendly years ago, or perhaps you have become reacquainted with someone you have known only slightly, give him another chance, even if sparks didn't fly the first time. Almost certainly, he has changed some. Think back to yourself when you were younger. Wouldn't you hate to think you were the same person? We all change, and often for the better. We grow, mature, and become more worldly. Life's experiences help to shape the person we are today. Meeting someone from your past gives you something to talk about and that's a great icebreaker. He may not be Mr. Right, but at least you'll have a pleasant time together — and you never know who *he* might know.

I have so many great "fix-up" stories that I could easily fill another book. Michelle's and Larry's story is one of my favorites. They went out on a blind date and really hit it off. They definitely wanted to go out again, but a second date never came to be. Larry's father suddenly became ill and died, and he moved back to his hometown to take care of his ailing mother. He ended up staying five years, and during that time Michelle had a short first marriage that resulted in her having a child, of whom she had full custody. When Larry moved back after his mother passed away, the same friend who had fixed him up with Michelle the first time suggested they go out again.

Looking at their backgrounds, few people would ever have put Larry and Michelle together in the first place. Michelle was well educated, had a double major in college and two master's degrees. Larry had a bachelor's degree in psychology but no advanced degrees. Michelle had grown up in a wealthy family and Larry's was very much a middle-class background. Either one of them could have turned away from the fix-up, saying their backgrounds were too dissimilar. Yet upon seeing the two of them to-gether, it was obvious how well suited they were for each other. When they met again, the attraction was definitely still there, and they quickly found out they were a good balance for each other. Before long they mar-ried and Michelle became the breadwinner. Larry was able to adopt her daughter, and soon she was calling him "Daddy". He stayed home after the birth of their first child together and they have, by all indications, a wonderful marriage. The mutual friend who suggested they meet again must have seen something in their personalities that she thought would click. Smart girlfriend, smart couple! Once again, keep an open mind and try not to shut any doors.

---

## Remember...

*efore you say "no thanks", give him a chance. Even if he's someone you tried to date years ago and it didn't work out, give him a second chance! People change.*

---

It was a Sunday afternoon when Jenny, a girlfriend of mine, was at home, having just finished painting her bedroom. Another girlfriend called, telling Jenny she just *had* to meet her at a nearby restaurant. The friend had just run into a guy she hadn't seen since high school. Without going into too much detail, she told Jenny to put on some lipstick and hurry, because she thought the two of them might hit it off. Jenny had two choices: She could either go or stay home. She came very close to saying no, as she still had to clean up the mess and move her furniture back. But she did go, even though it was the last thing she wanted to do. She pulled her hair back, didn't bother to change her jeans, grabbed her lipstick and was out the door. She was annoyed that her friend had called, and annoyed with herself that she'd agreed to meet them. She grumbled all the way over there. I think you know the rest. There was an instant attraction from the minute her friend introduced her to Steve. They are married and have one child, and they love to tell their story to singles.

Not all introductions are as easy as that, of course. But as I've said, at the very least, maybe the person to whom you're being introduced has a brother-in-law, cousin, friend or someone else they can introduce to you. Even if the fix-up turns out to be a failure, if you were nice to him you have a greater chance of having him say something nice about you. You can even go one step further and say to him, "Look, I'll keep you in mind, I know many single women." Voila, he walks away feeling good about himself and…well, one never knows. You could fix him up with someone from your office, or someone you work out with.

There are hundreds of stories like the ones in this chapter. I just mentioned a few to get you thinking in a new vein. I'm sure that if you think about it you'll have just as many stories, maybe even more. Consider your married friends. How did they meet, especially the ones who met later on when they were already in their late thirties and forties? If you don't know their "how we met" stories, by all means ask them! If they say it was a fix-up or introduction, ask them if they know of anyone to fix *you* up with. And ask them to pass the word to the person who fixed them up — after all, if that person did it once, she or he might like to do it again! (Be sure to read Chapter 37 on the art of self-promotion, too.)

It's never too late to meet someone — it's just a matter of being at the right place at the right time. Sometimes it really does take a little help from your friends. So don't say "No thanks" to fix-ups. Even if the man you're being fixed up with is a head shorter, meet him anyway.

Don't ever forget that you can't meet too many people — and if you keep up your efforts to meet more, sooner or later you are going to find your "keeper".

# 37

# BE YOUR OWN PROMOTER —
## IT'S EASIER THAN YOU THINK

*I*f you are really serious about getting married, you absolutely must become your own promoter. This doesn't mean that you're going to put up billboards along the freeway (though some single men have done that, with varying degrees of success). Billboards aren't necessary when word-of-mouth "advertising" can be so effective. What you need to do is tell *everyone* in your life about your search — and more than that, tell them exactly what you want them to say about you to a prospect.

If you're already participating in online dating, which is discussed in Chapter 38, your next best opportunity for meeting someone is to be introduced through a mutual friend or associate. That's been the case forever. If singles don't meet their mate in college or soon after, they are most likely to meet them through a fix-up or an introduction. However, you can't assume that the people who know you will automatically think of you when they run across an eligible man. You first have to tell them you want to be introduced to someone. Although it may seem strange to you, even your closest and dearest friends — not to mention your acquaintances, associates and relatives — all need to be reminded that you want to be fixed up.

In the chapter on "fix-ups" we discuss the reasons you should not shy away from introductions. Not only should you not shy away from them, you should actively encourage them, and that's what this chapter is about. If your friends have never tried to "fix you up", or it's been a while since they did, this chapter is especially important.

Your close circle of friends and relatives all know you're single, but when was the last time you told them you were actively searching for a mate? I don't mean complaining to them that you haven't met anyone. When was the last time you asked if they knew anyone to introduce you to? When was the last time you asked them to ask their other family members, friends or co-workers if they knew of someone to introduce you to? *Even the people closest to you need to hear it from you again.*

Tell them that you would like to be introduced, and ask them if they know of any men around your age who are single, recently divorced or widowed. You want to jar their memories. Perhaps they have just heard some news about someone, but you weren't on their mind at the time. It's important that you continue to remind them — remember, out of sight, out of mind. Even if you talk to your friends on the phone fairly often, everyone goes on about their business once they end the conversation.

Promoting yourself is not a sign of desperation. It is simply a way of telling people what you want. It sends the message that you like yourself, and it shows self-confidence. Most men today like self-confident women. If you don't make an effort to show that self-confidence, what will the people who know you think about you (if they think about you at all)? *Oh, she's single — quiet, nice gal, not much personality.* But get out there, speak with confidence when you promote yourself, and their opinion immediately changes. *She's terrific — friendly, outgoing, easy to talk to; you'll really like her!*

After contacting your immediate circle of family and friends, go through all the names in your personal phone book. Think of the people in the clubs, organizations and professional associations to which you belong. Are you taking evening classes? Do you regularly go to the gym? What about your bicycling group that meets in the park every Sunday morning? The people at all of these places can help you in your search. Even the service people at the stores you regularly patronize can be allies. Don't forget your doctors and dentist — many people walk through their doors. Remind them that you're single, and tell them to keep you in mind if they know of any single men. You can probably come up with a long list of people to aid you in your quest.

The next step is deciding exactly what you want to tell them. It's not enough to say, "Keep me in mind when you run across a single man about my age." You need to give them something that will stick in their minds and that they will repeat when they talk about you to a prospect.

This may require a bit of thought and you might not know where to begin. It helps if you try to look at yourself through the eyes of the people who know you.

Long ago you created the person you are. You established your reputation by your actions. While in school, your classmates knew what kind of a student you were. After you entered the work force, your co-workers observed you and your work ethic. Your actions, or lack thereof, have helped establish your reputation. Most people who know you, and maybe even some who don't really know you, have formed an opinion of you. But that doesn't mean you can't alter that opinion — you absolutely can.

People repeat what they hear; it's human nature. Politicians and actors exploit this principle daily, as do public relations firms that are paid top dollar to create, enhance or in some cases repair their clients' reputations. This is a form of third party selling. You, however, don't need to hire an ad agency to enhance anyone's established opinion of you. All you need to do is give them some additional information, and you can do that by simply saying what you want people to know about you. Then your friends and associates will become your personal "PR firm".

---

## Remember...

 ell everyone you know about your search, but don't just tell people to keep you in mind when they come across an eligible man. Tell them what you want them to say about you. Then they will become your very own "PR firm".

---

We all have attributes that we're proud of. It may take a few minutes, but think of a few nice things that you would like others to say about you. In the chapter about online dating we talk about writing your profile, which describes you. The same general principles apply here. Think about some of your best qualities, and write them down. Are you more than a good listener — are you empathetic? Are you in good shape, do you regularly work out, are you into mind/body healing or yoga? How about your great sense of humor? Are you well-read, laid-back, easy to be with? All of these are wonderful attributes. Decide what a few of yours are, and when you speak to your friends and acquaintances casually mention those nice qualities about yourself. It's easier than you think. Let's look at a few examples.

You are out to lunch with one of your co-workers, and you happen to mention you cooked the best dinner last night for two of your girl-friends. She asks what you made. You had a beautiful salad, grilled salmon served over a bed of wild rice, grilled Portobello mushrooms and steamed veggies. For dessert you made homemade sorbet that you served with your to-die-for brownies. Chances are your co-worker will be impressed. Maybe she didn't even know you knew how to cook. Even if she doesn't respond, just continue talking. Casually mention that you love cooking, you make lots of fancy dishes, and it's easy.

All right, so you're not into cooking. No problem. You're speaking to a friend on the phone, and you're telling her an amusing story. Some-one stopped into your office to see you and couldn't remember your name, but tried describing you to one of your co-workers. He asked for the short blonde with that beautiful smile that could make one melt. ("How em-barrassing!" you add modestly.) Or you receive a phone call from an old friend who mentions she'd like to introduce you to someone. While speak-ing to her, you just happen to mention that you have completed your first marathon. You've been running for years but this was your first attempt at long distance running, and you finished in the top half of your age group. Just having *finished* is a great accomplishment itself!

And so on. Whatever you say, people will repeat; it's as simple as that. So tell them what you want them to say. When they talk about you to others, they will be promoting you — that's third party selling.

Create every opportunity to talk about yourself, but be prepared so it will sound natural. That is not a contradiction in terms; you need to learn how to work the subject into conversations effortlessly, without sounding boastful or appearing self-centered. You're not patting yourself on the back, you are just subtly describing yourself. And you're doing your friends a favor because they don't have to think about how they're going to describe you. You've done it for them and they won't even realize it! Try it on those closest to you at first, and then those you don't know quite as well. Practice it until it becomes second nature. Soon you will have created your own reputation, one that you know you'll be proud of.

Are you still not convinced? Then read on. Steve, a single man in his early forties, received phone calls from two different friends who wished to fix him up. The first friend wanted to introduce him to Allison, who happens to be a very attractive, intelligent woman. But the friend didn't know her very well, and he hadn't seen her in ages, so all he said was,

"Hey, Steve, I know this woman…she seems nice, I think she's smart, don't know much about her but give her a call." Steve had experienced his share of unsuccessful fix-ups and decided to pass. Allison just didn't sound very interesting, and the lack of detail made him even more wary. His friend might as well have said, "She's got a great personality." A couple of weeks later a second friend called and said to him, "Steve, I have a great girl to introduce you to. She's easy to talk to, smart and in great shape! She's kind of laid-back and has a great sense of humor, but really seems to have her feet on the ground. She just might be the one!"

As it happened, the second friend was describing Allison too. But this call piqued Steve's interest. Why? Allison had promoted herself ever so slightly to the second caller. To the first, she'd just said she would like to be introduced to a nice man and would appreciate being kept in mind. To the second caller, she added a few things that were passed along to Steve. She mentioned she had just returned from working out. She kept the conversation light and made a humorous remark that made them both chuckle. And before she ended the call, she said she was about to meet a friend for lunch; they were both taking an evening course in investments. Same woman, different results. After he received that second call, Steve called Allison and they went out. They have been dating for several months now, and wedding bells are definitely in the near future. Is it worth taking those few minutes to think about how to promote yourself? No doubt about it. Just ask Allison!

A man I know recently lost his wife. They had two children under the age of ten. I told him he'd be remarried in no time, and he was. Carly, a single woman, knew a close friend of the deceased woman's and called her up to say she wanted to be introduced to the widower. Carly made it clear that this was not a date; she just wanted to know if she could call and talk to him. In that same conversation, Carly just happened to drop a few hints about herself. A male associate at work had recently commented to her that she had to be the best catch in the city and he couldn't understand how it was that single men couldn't see how wonderful she was. Before long, her girlfriend called back to say the widower would welcome Carly's phone call…and I think you know the rest. The other women never had a chance. Carly seized the opportunity; in her case, a little self-promotion went a long way. It can work for you too.

If you want something badly enough, you have to do *everything* you can to get it. If you're not willing to put forth the effort, you're not committed to marriage, and you need to figure out just what is holding you back. Maybe you need to go back and read the chapters on fears and doubts. If you think helping promote yourself is too difficult, then ask yourself if you are happy alone. Would you rather be single than be in a wonderful, loving relationship? Isn't it worth the effort to say those few nice things about yourself, which are true? There's no question in my mind that if I were a single woman today, I would tell every person I came in contact with that I was looking to be introduced to someone. I'd also be telling them some terrific things about myself that I wanted a prospect to hear. The more frequently you do this, the closer you are to finding Mr. Right. So get on with your self-promotion program now — don't wait another day! ♥

# 38

# SOAR INTO CYBERSPACE —
## ONLINE DATING IS A MUST

Online dating is without a doubt a major source of meeting people today. Everyone is busy, and, as discussed in other chapters, the older you get, the fewer new faces there are on the singles scene. But cyberspace is a huge "place" and can offer so many more opportunities than you would otherwise have. There are no guarantees you will meet your future husband on the Internet, but where else will you find more men than women without ever having to leave your home?

You might say online dating is the high-tech, enhanced version of the "personals" ads that were popular for so many years. Newspapers and magazines all over the country ran these "classifieds", affording singles another option for meeting besides personal introductions or singles bars. While these print ads are by no means obsolete, the Internet has become the matchmaking tool of choice now. However, successful matches have been made and continue to be made through the "personals", so don't overlook this tool as a supplement to your other efforts. Just remember that all the rules about honesty, etiquette and most of all, caution apply to the "personals" as well as to cyber-dating or "face-to-face" dating.

So let's take a closer look at the world of cyberdating. We know that optimally, the very best way to meet someone is through an introduction or fix-up, and we talk about increasing those opportunities in Chapter 36. Even if you know a lot of people and have many opportunities to be introduced to someone new, online dating is still well worth looking into, simply because it will provide you with so many *more* opportunities! Online dating may not be for everyone and there are certain disadvantages, but if you approach it with the attitude that you'll give it your best and try not to take it too seriously, you can make it work for you. It is important, however, to keep it in perspective; I know women who became so obsessed with it that after a few months or a year (or even longer) they had to walk away from it. It was literally making them ill. That is hardly the way to approach Internet dating. Other women have been participating in online dating for years, and although they weren't always successful, they stayed with it. Before you begin, tell yourself it may not work, but you have nothing to lose so why not give it a try!

Years ago, people said online dating was for the socially inept (they said the same thing about "personals", for that matter), but today if you're unwilling to consider cyberdating, you aren't serious about finding a husband. Single people of all ages, including widows, widowers, divorcees and those who have never been married, are taking advantage of this phenomenon. Website memberships have grown rapidly, their members ranging in age from the mid-twenties to mid-eighties — and by all reports there are countless happy endings. Your chances of meeting your husband online are increasing daily.

In fact, I can't think of a good reason for *any* single person not to join the cyber-dating scene. If you haven't because you don't own a computer, you'll be surprised at how inexpensive they are. If you absolutely cannot make the purchase, ask to use a friend's computer, or go to the library or a cyber-café. Many of the popular chain coffee shops now offer wireless Internet access. If you think you don't know enough about computers, don't let that stop you. You don't need to be a computer genius to register; these sites are designed to easily "walk" you through the steps. If you've tried Internet dating before and had no success, or perhaps had a few bad experiences, then you may have done something wrong. Give it another chance. You *must* become part of online dating — it's definitely where the action is!

This chapter is not intended to be a condensed version of a handbook for online dating; there are books written specifically for that purpose. However, I have spent countless hours studying various dating websites, and have spoken to many people who tried cyber-dating. In the process I picked up a lot of good information that I want to share with you. Of course, if you're already experienced in Internet dating, you may not need this chapter. But if you've tried it and haven't had much luck, perhaps you can benefit from some of the advice. I will be focusing on areas where people do have problems, and I'll offer suggestions for minor changes that should bring better results.

To begin with, if you aren't a part of the cyber-dating scene, decide you're going to do it and then *do it!* Tell yourself this is the weekend you will do it. You do need to do some preparation beforehand, though. First decide which websites you want to register with. Select one of the biggest and busiest; after all, you want as much exposure as possible. There are some smaller "boutique" sites, but for the most part they're really too exclusive, so if you use them, do so as a supplement to one of the more popular sites.

Before you begin, you need to have your photo selected and have your information all written out, so that when you decide on your website(s), you'll be ready. Finding Mr. Right is like finding a job, and registering on web sites is just part of the process. It's like filling out a job application and attaching a resume, only you can be clever and creative, and you can definitely have fun with it. But just because it's fun doesn't mean you shouldn't give it your all — otherwise, you most likely won't get the results you want. You cannot do it quickly, with little thought. It's easy to be lazy about it — to just write what comes to mind, scan in an old photo and hope for the best. But it's no different than anything else — you get out of it what you put into it! When you're looking for a job, you work hard to get your resume up-to-date and you make sure you have the right clothes. You prepare for interviews so you'll be able to ask the right questions and give the perfect answers. Then you send your resumes out to carefully selected companies. You have to treat your search for Mr. Right at least as seriously as you do your search for a job.

A friend told me her daughter was registered on a few websites but was getting little, if any, responses. This girl is pretty and slender and she loves life. I couldn't imagine why she had so few responses. Then one day my friend mentioned that her daughter had never posted a picture. *A picture is an absolute must!* If you don't post a picture, don't register. If you were looking at two equal profiles and only one had a picture, which one would you consider first? You have to maximize every opportunity to catch their attention. (Besides, if you don't post a picture, you know they'll automatically assume it's because you think your picture would not be a selling point.)

If you don't have a recent photo, get one. Don't use one that's ten years old. Have a friend take some pictures of you. Select at least two, one that can be used for a head and shoulder shot and another that's a three-quarters body shot. Everything you say and do, including a picture, sends a message, so think first what it is you want to "say". Forget plunging necklines and suggestive poses. I'd also recommend that you not include pets or children. Some people believe if you have a pet in the picture you may eliminate prospects who really aren't pet lovers. The same goes for having your nieces or nephews in your pictures. There probably are some people who would be turned off by those photos, but once they meet you they may fall in love with you and your loved ones! Your goal is to increase interest, not decrease it, so you consider using another photo.

Some women in their early forties to mid fifties tend to use photos that someone may have taken at work. An office background is cold and less inviting — remember everything sends a message! If you say in your profiles that you're looking for someone warm, kind and loving, a cold office setting doesn't go hand in hand with your message. A photo taken in a home or a home-like atmosphere sends a warmer message. You're not looking for a business contact; you're trying to make a personal connection. A suit or blazer may look nice, but it's a bit too rigid looking. A softer look is more appealing. If you're busty, a shirt or blouse that's open at the neck looks better than a sweater or turtleneck. Also remember that it doesn't take ruffles and bows to be feminine.

As for getting your picture online, if you don't know how to do it, ask someone. If that's not a possibility, many of the websites accept mail-in photos. Also keep in mind that you can change your picture or information any time you want to, so consider having new photos taken if you've changed your hair style and no longer look like the photo that's posted.

All websites ask for a personal profile and a description of what you're looking for in a man. Read through both the women's and men's ads to see what they say. Take notes and then begin to write yours. Don't be afraid of using someone else's words; no one owns words, and chances are that the people whose profiles catch your eye have borrowed from someone else's profile. On some websites, you'll notice that only the first line or so of the profile comes up in the first window. Make the most of those first words so the reader will want to read more. After you've written it, you can't read it too many times. Try it from a man's viewpoint — you may want to run it by one of your male friends. Remember, you want to say something that will catch their attention.

If you like sports, you can say, "I really do like sports!" — if in fact you do. *But don't lie.* Or say, "I really do love staying home, cooking dinner and sitting by the fireplace!" if that's what you like. If you're writing something about a personal attribute, add, "That's what I've been told." You can be serious, light-hearted and fun all in the same few lines, but make sure there's a hint of self-confidence without sounding smug. While it's perfectly okay to "borrow" ideas, do take your time to write out something that doesn't sound like everyone else's.

If you're already online and your responses have been nil, take a break. Remove your name and begin the process again with a fresh start. A few changes can bring better results. If you haven't been using your first name for your screen name, for example, you might want to try that. It may not be flirty or creative, but it's sincere and that translates into warmth. You could consider updating your hair style and make-up and then having some new photos taken. If you're sure your hair and make-up don't need updating, it couldn't hurt to change your photos when you register again. If you've been a member of a website for a few years, you need to change your pictures. No one stays the same and you may be recognized as an "old" member just by your photo.

As I mentioned above, and throughout this book, everything you say or do is a reflection of what you really are like. The profiles on the dating sites reveal a lot about the person. Scanning through hundreds of profiles, I often wonder why some women say what they do and submit the photos they do. Either they're too lazy or they just don't care, but either way, that sends a very direct message. If necessary, reevaluate your profile. Find a better way to describe yourself. Whatever you said previously, try another angle, and remember, always read it back from the man's point of view. Unfortunately, what works best is telling the men what they want to hear. That does not mean lying — it just means putting a "spin" on your profile.

In fact, you absolutely should never lie about anything. There is so much deception on the Internet; don't be a part of it. If you had a birthday last month, change your age *now*. Don't wait. I know women who have lied about their age and will give every reason why. They say they look five years younger than their age, or that men won't look at a woman past thirty-five, or they ask why shouldn't they lie, since the men always do. Once these women connect with a prospect, they immediately tell their true age so they feel no harm was done. That's wrong! If you lied, you are saying it's okay for him to lie to you, and immediately he'll wonder what else you lied about. Even though the temptation is there, don't do it. You cannot change the rules of life; lying, like cheating, is *unacceptable*. If you do it, expect it in return. Remember, if you're looking for a first-class man, you must be a first-class woman.

Be open-minded, upbeat and positive. If the questionnaire asks, "Are you willing to relocate?", don't automatically say, "No." Ask yourself why you wouldn't move if the most wonderful man came into your life and lived elsewhere. Never say "never", because we never know what life has in store for us. As we've discussed elsewhere, everything is always open for consideration, discussion or negotiation. If you categorically say "no" to relocation, you may be passing up the greatest man in the world — and who knows, you could end up moving one day anyway.

---

## Remember...

*hen filling out your profile for a website, don't lie about anything — including your age. Lying, like cheating, is unacceptable online, as well as in the "real" world. If you do it, expect it in return. If you're looking for a first-class man, you must be a first-class woman.*

---

Part of being upbeat and positive is being discreet about your past disappointments. Remember, your history is just that — history. It's difficult not to wear some of your past hurts, but the person reading your ad doesn't have to know them before he's ever emailed you. When the questionnaire asks, "What have you learned from past relationships?", it isn't necessary to tell your whole life story. You'll have plenty of opportunities to tell it after you've made a "connection". A better response might be a simple statement such as, "If you don't share the same values, move on."

The questionnaires ask for your preferred age range for your partner. If you broaden your desirable age range by three to five years, you may be surprised at how many more responses you will receive, and they won't all be too old (or too young). Your knight in shining armor may be five years older than you expected him to be, but he may look younger, be in excellent health and be exactly, if not more than, what you've been waiting for. Or he may be younger; in Chapter 17 we talk about the potentials of a relationship with a younger man. In cyber-dating as in traditional dating, you need to keep an open mind, and broaden your scope whenever possible. And remember that you can always choose not to answer any emails that don't interest you.

While scanning through different websites, I noticed that some sites bring up profiles according to how recently they were logged onto, or when they were last updated. If you go into your profile and just change a word or two, it will show "last updated", but more importantly, when someone is doing a search, your listing will come up more quickly in his search if it has been logged onto or updated recently.

When you're reviewing your responses, and you should get quite a few if you do it correctly, don't be too quick to delete those that don't interest you at first. Someone saw something about you that piqued his interest, so give him the benefit by doing more than taking a quick glance and moving on. The "tall slender dark-haired man" you envisioned may in fact be there, but maybe he has sandy blonde hair, isn't quite as tall as you would have liked, and is a few pounds heavier. Stop, reread his profile, and try to find out what he's all about. Otherwise, you could be passing up a perfectly wonderful man. Try to keep your options open a little bit more.

Just because you aren't face to face with someone, or ear to ear, this doesn't mean that you can throw out all the old guidelines about being careful. There are a few new guidelines as well, and unless you want to attract the wrong type of man, keep within those parameters. Not unlike regular dating, online dating follows certain rules. It is best to let the men contact you first, lest it seem that you're desperate. It doesn't matter how old you are; that's the wrong message to send, and the chances of a second or third actual date are poor. You're there online for him to see, so let him do the pursuing. If you don't, the relationship could start off on the wrong foot. This may seem like old-fashioned advice, but some things never change. Have there been exceptions? Absolutely, and I know a few, but generally speaking, in person or online, let the man pursue *you*.

Once a man contacts you, it probably doesn't do any harm to wait a day before you respond; the old truisms still hold. A little bit of "hard-to-get", a little bit of aloofness, goes a long way. People want what they can't have. These may be pretty simple actions, but they still work. Answering the same day can also say you're desperate, and again, that's definitely the wrong message.

When responding to a first email, keep your message light and friendly. You can say something that refers to his profile, ask a question, and say something about yourself. An example could be, "I see you were born in Iowa. How old were you when you moved away?" If he's not from your city but lives there now, ask when he moved there. Follow that by a sentence stating where you're originally from and when you moved from there. Just three or four sentences are enough. Keep the discussion on a superficial level for now, and don't say anything that could possibly indicate you've carefully read his profile and know it word for word.

As a rule of thumb, after three or four emails or phone calls, it's all right if he asks to meet you. But there is no sense in going on and on if there won't be any real interest, so it's better to find out earlier rather than later. Always use discretion, whether it's giving out your phone number or your name. If you get weird vibes in the beginning, listen to your gut. The signs are the same as when you meet someone face to face. Is he controlling, or does he come on too strong and too quickly? Does he lose his temper, is he rude in any way, does he show disrespect — perhaps not to you, but when he speaks of others? Does he continually put other people down? If you have any doubts, do not meet this prospect. Tell him you don't think you have enough in common, and move on to the next one.

Do not give out your home telephone number or your name immediately — wait to see if he seems legitimate. You can begin with giving him your cell phone number, as it's a lot easier to change that than it is your home number. As an extra precaution, some women prefer to just get the man's number instead and not divulge theirs.

If your online date wants to meet you, make sure you make it in an open, well-lit area where there will be lots of people around. It's really best to meet for a mid-day coffee or light lunch, and keep the meeting short. *Always* tell someone close to you where you're going, when, and with whom. Provide any information you may have about this date — his name, any physical description you may already know, the make and model of the car he'll be driving, etc. (Naturally, you will have obtained this information from him ahead of time.) Also, someone should have information about the website where you "met" him, as well as his personal I.D. that he uses there. You cannot be too careful. More than likely everything will go well, but don't forget to alert your friend that everything is all right after you return home. One more thing regarding safety: *Never, under any circumstances, get into his car or let him get into yours.* A safe distance in the beginning is a safe beginning!

---

# Remember...

*W*hen "meeting" someone online, don't reveal too much too soon. Do not divulge your full real name, address or any other details until you're certain this person is "okay". And don't ever agree to meet someone in person until you are reasonably sure that it's safe to do so. Even then, meet in an open, well-lit place, and be sure to tell a friend or two where you'll be and with whom you'll be meeting. A safe distance in the beginning is a safe beginning.

---

Once you think you've found Mr. Right, you still need to be cautious. Remember, you were essentially two total strangers meeting through computers. No one introduced you, and you will need to check into his background. If he's not from your general vicinity and you haven't any mutual friends or acquaintances, you can hire a private investigator. Although they can be costly, it may be money well spent. Experience has taught us all that it's better to be safe than sorry.

After you have met your prospect face to face and have actually begun "real" dating as opposed to cyber-dating, all of the normal dating guidelines still apply. Just because you met him through a "new" method, this doesn't mean that some of the "old" wisdom no longer applies. You still need to be cautious and circumspect — and, yes, a little hard-to-get — in the beginning. This means cutting conversations, as well as dates, short. No matter how wonderfully the two of you are getting along, leave him wanting more. Remember that you are not playing games; you are setting boundaries. By doing so, you increase your self-confidence and strengthen your self-esteem, and he will respect you more.

Before we leave cyberspace, there's one more topic we need to mention: chat rooms. I'd stay away from them because at best, they're generally a waste of your time if you are searching for the love of your life. I have read that 30% of the men in chat rooms are married. I have no way of knowing if those statistics are accurate or not, but you can be sure many of the men there *are* married. Your time is better spent on your website, or perhaps a new one, if your current one isn't yielding the results you want.

The age of cyber-dating has definitely arrived. It's far less obscure than it was when we first saw the movie *You've Got Mail*. In that film, Tom Hanks emailed Meg Ryan and a love story unfolded that was a novelty then, but has since become commonplace. Today, there's no reason everyone can't get online and join the Internet dating scene. Will it be fun? It depends on how much time and energy you're willing to give it. Can it be successful? Very. Is it for you? You'll never know if you don't give it a try.

# 39

# DON'T LOOK TO "THE STARS" TO FIND OUT WHAT'S IN YOUR HEART

What's your sign? used to be a notorious come-on line at singles bars. Those days are gone (thank goodness), but astrology is alive and well. In some circles, astrology is more popular than ever, and virtually every magazine and newspaper has an astrology column. For many people, the daily horoscope is nothing more than a pleasant diversion, but there are many who do believe in astrological signs, and wouldn't consider dating someone with a sun sign not in harmony with theirs.

Sue's sun sign is Leo, which is a fire sign (the twelve signs of the Zodiac are divided into four elements: earth, air, fire and water). Sue is a big believer in astrology, and refuses to even consider dating any of the "water signs" — Pisces, Cancer or Scorpio — reasoning that she doesn't want someone to always be trying to "put out my fire". The truth is, Sue had a bad relationship with Ken, a Pisces, fifteen years ago. She happened to read a book on astrology at the time, and she decided her love went sour because Ken was a water sign and she was a fire sign. Actually, he wanted to settle down and get married, and Sue was still somewhat of a party girl in those days. Ken finally left her for a woman who was ready to marry and start a family. Sue isn't bitter about it anymore, and even though she still likes to party once in a while, she's now more than ready to settle down herself. But she still clings to her wariness of those "party-pooping" water signs.

Anyone who knows about horoscopes knows that many factors go into a person's makeup besides his or her sun sign, but that's not the real issue here. The real issue is that Sue needs to get a grip, and realize that her problems aren't in the heavens; they're right here on earth. In the past three months alone, she has passed on fix-ups with four otherwise great guys because — you guessed it, they were the "wrong" sign. I'm sure you're not that extreme, but if you are, this is a friendly reminder once again that you need to lighten up!

There is nothing wrong with reading your daily horoscope in the paper, or even having a professional astrologer draw up a complete horoscope for you. It can be fun, and many find it enlightening as well. When it comes to you and Mr. Right, however, I wouldn't give your respective signs too much weight, especially if they don't appear to be a problem. If you do see problems that you think could be attributed to his "sign", there's no particular harm in reading up on his sign and the combination of his and yours together. You could even learn something about him and yourself. You might enjoy a book called *The Secret Language Of Relationships: Your Complete Personology Guide To Any Relationship With Anyone* by Gary Goldschneider and Joost Elffers. This book seems to have it down to a science, listing every possible combination of birthdays, outlining how the two people will probably get along, and specifying whether they'll be most suitable as friends, spouses, co-workers, etc. Neither a book nor a professional stargazer can tell you everything you need to know about your relationship, however. Relationships are just too complex to be mapped out on a horoscope.

Many of you have spent a lot of time and money on psychics. I don't categorically dismiss them, as I've been to them myself. If you're considering going to one, of course you want to be careful. People in the metaphysical community always say you should approach these matters with an open mind and heart. Well, go with your eyes open too! There are so many different types of psychics, readers, "intuitive counselors" and the like that you can easily be overwhelmed. Some of these people are amazingly insightful, and some are complete frauds. (I know that a hardcore skeptic would say they're all frauds, but I prefer to take a more middle ground.)

In any case, you are always better off if you try listening to your inner self before going to a total stranger. No one knows you as well as you do. If you really feel that the man you are dating is "the one", you don't need someone else to tell you, "It's okay, yes, do it!" If the relationship is a disaster waiting to happen, you do not need to pay someone

$100 or more to tell you, "Run, quickly!" Make up your own mind. You have the tools — you just need to use them. Together with your tools and the skills you have been working on, you'll be able to make the right decision.

## Remember...

*here's nothing particularly wrong with turning to astrology, psychic readings or other "out-there" methods to give you additional insights, but be careful of scam artists. And remember that no astrologer or psychic, no matter how skilled or "intuitive", can tell you what's in your heart and mind. More than likely you already have the tools and the skills to make the right decisions.*

I'm not saying there is no validity to these "otherworldly" methods, but there are lots of pitfalls, not to mention scam artists who are all too willing to take your money in exchange for their dubious insights. You're generally much better off if you take it all with a grain of salt, for ultimately what counts is what's in your heart, and his — not what is in the stars, the cards, or the lines of your palm. ♥

PART Six

# Avoiding Potholes On The Road To Matrimony

# 40

# BREAK FREE OF NEGATIVE DATING PATTERNS (EVEN IF YOU HAVE TO FORCE YOURSELF!)

*H*ave your mother, sister, best friend or therapist ever asked why you go for the same type of man over and over again? Have *you* ever wondered why? Maybe you're crazy about the "bad boy" type who knows how to show you a good time but often treats you poorly. Or, on the opposite end of the scale, perhaps you repeatedly go for meek guys who have absolutely nothing to offer you other than companionship.

It's human nature to repeat patterns; they become comfortable and it's hard to break away from them. No doubt your "bad boy" is exciting and sexy, and he makes you feel sexy too. But he's undependable, he often breaks his word, he breaks dates at the last minute, and you suspect he's running around on you. Still, there's something irresistible about him, and despite the pain he often causes, you've become addicted to the thrills.

What about that sweet, non-threatening, nice guy? He certainly is "safe" — he's there for you unconditionally, and very likely he won't expect much of you. He'll never challenge you to *do* better or *be* better. Let's say you've had an argument with your overbearing boss because you discovered she has been over-billing clients. When you tactfully pointed out this possibility to her (giving her the benefit of the doubt and saying it must have been an error), she lit into you and told you that you didn't know what you were talking about, and had no understanding of the billing system. Once again, she got the better of you, and once again you ended up giving in. Rather than challenging you to stand up for what you think is right, your "nice guy" will tell you he understands why your feelings are hurt. Like an injured little kitten, you'll crawl right into his lap and he'll make you feel better. But do you really feel better? I don't think so — he's there to tell you everything is all right, but you know everything *isn't* all right. He is just telling you what you want to hear.

Actually, I think that by the time a woman reaches her mid-thirties she's much more likely to go for the "safe" type than the bad boy. I was talking recently with Cindy, a woman I've known a relatively short time, and I discussed with her the relationships women have with safe male friends. Cindy said she used to fall into that pattern, too. When she was younger, she dated many men to whom she wasn't particularly attracted, but she liked them well enough to spend time with them. At the time, she didn't realize this was a negative pattern; it was just her "comfort zone". Then she met someone with whom there were real sparks, and they fell passionately in love. She was twenty-six, and even though she had dated lots of guys, including some she *had* been very attracted to, this was really her first true love. Neither one of them was ready to get married, but they moved in together and the relationship lasted several years. Marriage never seemed to come up, but it didn't particularly bother Cindy, because she was happy with things the way they were. The two of them had a lot of fun together, and the sex was pretty good, too.

Unfortunately, he turned out to be emotionally abusive. She says he was never physically violent and the emotional abuse was very subtle — mostly it came in the form of sarcasm — but it hurt her deeply. "After the sparks died down, we discovered that in many ways we really weren't terribly compatible," she said, "but the relationship had become yet another kind of 'comfort zone' and I couldn't bring myself to leave it. Neither could he." Finally she knew one of them would have to leave, so she did.

Before long Cindy began going out with a co-worker with whom she had many things in common. They had fun and a lot of laughs together. The trouble was that even though she was fond of him, she wasn't particularly attracted to him. However, he was so much like the "buddies" she used to date that she soon found herself falling back into her old pattern. Since she was well into her thirties by now, she was starting to feel pressure to get married. In fact, this very nice guy wanted to marry her so she took the leap. She thought it would be a "safe" marriage, even though she wasn't passionately in love with him, or maybe *because* she wasn't passionately in love. "Frankly, I'd had it with the 'love' bit," she said. "I thought I could settle for compatibility and friendship!"

Was she happy? No. Even though she loved this man very much, she wasn't in love with him, and she couldn't get over the sense that something vital was missing from her life. Guess what? It turned out this guy had a hidden dark side (as is the case with some "nice guys"), and he was even more emotionally abusive than her previous partner had been. There were also signs that he might eventually become physically abusive, though he never lifted a hand to her. Talk about patterns, patterns, and more patterns! Yet for years, Cindy closed her eyes to them. It was only when she finally decided to move on with her life — when she became motivated enough to want change — that she was able to recognize her patterns for what they were. She stepped out of her "comfort zones" and, I'm happy to say, she's in a wonderful relationship now. She's passionately in love with Lance, and he with her — and he is about the furthest from abusive that a guy could be, though he's certainly no Milquetoast either. Cindy has even healed the past hurts with her ex-boyfriend and her ex-husband, and is now friends with them. In fact, her current love is great friends with her exes, too!

When I see people making the same mistakes over and over, I want to shout, "Stop!" Of course, it's easier to see it in others than it is in ourselves. That's why I felt this chapter was so important. We all have attractions to certain physical or personality types, but, as we touched on in Chapter 7, if that type has gotten you into trouble several times before, assume it will again. If you've been attracted to handsome, aggressive attorneys and they've given you nothing but grief, stay away from them. If you seem to gravitate again and again toward the same type of strong-willed men, try one who's a bit less opinionated and perhaps more open-minded.

---

## Remember...

*We all have attractions to certain physical or personality types. However, if the type you're attracted to has gotten you into trouble several times before, assume it will do so again.*

---

If you go for the "nice, agreeable" type, it may be harder to convince you that you need to break your pattern. After all, these guys treat you quite well. They're not hurting you, and you're not hurting them... right? Wrong. Don't let yourself be lulled into thinking that what you're doing is harmless. At the very least, you are wasting time — yours and theirs. If you've read Chapter 21, you'll know I am not trying to tell you that "nice" is equivalent to "bad husband material". Of course you want your Mr. Right to be nice. But it takes a lot more than "nice" to make a good marriage. Someone who is sweet and nice and makes you feel good, but offers nothing more than friendship and safety, will not get you anywhere close to marriage. Or if you do get married, but you're not really in love with him, that's even worse. Take it from my friend Cindy, who knows firsthand. She says, "Being married to someone with whom you're not in love is like being dead inside. You do have to 'kill off' a part of yourself, or at least knock it unconscious! But sooner or later, your true feelings will surface and cause trouble."

## Remember...

*Y*ou are probably wasting your time if you think that your relationship with your buddy will lead to marriage at all, much less a happy, healthy marriage. That doesn't mean you have to cut yourself off from a good friend; it just means that you have to move on with your life.

On the other hand, don't take a huge leap in the opposite direction without thinking about it first. Don't make the mistake Cindy made in the story above. For one thing, you could end up with a person who, beneath the surface, is much like those types who got you in trouble. (Patterns are nothing if not insidious.) Or you could even end up with someone worse. I'm sure you've heard the expression, "Out of the frying pan, into the fire." More often than not, though, you just leap out of the frying pan into another frying pan. Your situation may not get worse, but it won't get any better. Frequently we hear of people divorcing, only to marry a similar type, and it often takes them years to admit they could have stayed married to the first one. We all have heard *that* story over and over again.

One of our friends was married for twenty-five years to the same woman. After years of unhappiness and arguing, he came home one day and announced he wanted a divorce. Within a year or two, he married a woman who appeared to be very different from his first wife. After thirty-something years of marriage, he divorced his second wife, and now he says she wasn't any different than his first! As I said, patterns are insidious.

Many experts on human behavior believe patterns go back to the family of origin, and people keep repeating the way they lived with parents and siblings. They continue to try to "work it out" in their adult relationships. For example, a woman who had a cold, distant father, from whom she never received enough love and affection, may end up dating men with similar traits. If she can't get the affection she needs from one man, she moves on to another who is, perhaps, equally cold and unaffectionate. And so it goes, until, ideally, she finds a man who gives her what she needs, and she is no longer driven to seek the unattainable. On the other hand, she may be so accustomed to living without affection that she unconsciously keeps herself from finding a truly affectionate partner. That's an unhappy pattern, to be sure.

No doubt the "family of origin" explanation is valid in many cases, but even if you grew up in a healthy family environment, you still might find negative patterns to be a problem. Let's face it — we all repeat things we shouldn't. Figuring out why we're doing these things is important, but *it won't get us anywhere unless we make the decision to break the pattern.* In Chapter 8 we talk about organizing your life and getting rid of clutter. Certainly some of us are more organized than others, and some are even too organized, but many people, such as myself, have to work at it. I am not naturally organized. I had to break my pattern of disorganization, because it was making me slightly crazy. If I didn't force myself to go through the mail daily, it would build up to the point where I'd never see my desktop. Thankfully, I have built up enough discipline so that I never go to bed unless I've gone through that day's mail — but I had to look at that negative pattern of mine and force myself to meet it head-on.

## Remember:

nce you've detected a negative pattern in your life, it can be helpful to figure out how the pattern started, but you must also make the decision to break out of the pattern. *You may have to force yourself to do it, but it's the only way you're going to find happiness.*

You can take the same approach to dating, and it may indeed take a little "force" at first. If you find yourself attracted to the same "type" over and over — whether it's a physical attribute, a personality type, or both — and you know this attraction never leads you to happy relationships, force yourself to break that pattern. Remember what we've said throughout the book: If what you are doing is not working, you have to try something different. If you can't manage it on your own, ask the help of a friend you trust or, if need be, talk to a therapist about it. The all-important first step is to recognize those negative patterns. Once you do, you can break them. Won't it be glorious to finally be able to say *adios* to the bad boys and the Milquetoasts...and hello to Mr. Right!

# 41

# DON'T LET HIM CONTROL YOU OR TRY TO CHANGE YOU

As discussed in more detail in other chapters, many single women (and men) have a number of unfounded fears or unrealistic expectations about marriage. Sometimes these fears and expectations keep them from making the effort to find someone. Let's say you've overcome your preliminary fears, and have actually met a man who's a real prospect. The two of you just might have a future together. Things are going very well for a while, but then suddenly it seems he's expecting too much of you, or is beginning to exhibit controlling behavior, or is acting in some way that is making some of your original fears resurface. Maybe you were right about men and marriage after all. Well, before you give up on the relationship, give him another chance.

If you think your Mr. Prospect's expectations of you — now and in your future life together — are unrealistic, you have to talk to him about it. For example, if he seems to take it for granted that when you get married, you will be the one to take care of everything on the domestic front, just remind him that running a home and raising a family are mutual responsibilities today. You both need to remember that every marriage is different, and yours may not be at all like your parents' marriages. You're two individuals, influenced by, but in many ways different from, your parents.

Further, neither of you has the right to expect that the other will be the kind of spouse your parents were. Just because his mother was a sweet, gentle June Cleaver-type doesn't mean *you* will be. And just because your father always helped with the laundry, doesn't mean your husband will. The concept of mutual responsibilities doesn't mean that the domestic duties will be split 50/50 all the time. Some women prefer to do all the laundry and would rather their husbands help more in the kitchen. Some women are handy around the house and prefer to do minor home repairs themselves, while their husbands take care of the heavy cleaning. Some couples like to trade off. It doesn't matter, as long as neither of you feels resentful because you think you're doing more than your share. A good marriage — or any other relationship — is whatever the people involved agree upon. Throughout this book the message is to be flexible and open to new possibilities, but since a relationship is a two-way street, you certainly have the right to expect flexibility in your partner as well. The best way to handle potential conflicts about expectations is to sit down and talk about them.

You also have the right to nip controlling behavior in the bud, and let's face it, some men really are controlling. This is not to suggest women can't display that trait — we all know that's not true! (If you know that you're a controlling type, it's never too late to change that behavior. It really does make for a much better relationship, and you will win in the long run.) But this chapter is about men. If you find Mr. Prospect to be too controlling, but everything else seems pretty good, confront him with your feelings. Just don't show weakness by telling him you're upset or you don't think the relationship can work.

Chances are, this isn't the first time he's heard that he's controlling, and if he's showing great potential in all other areas, he may be more receptive to change than you expected. Tell him his controlling behavior is unacceptable. If he wants a lasting relationship, he'll have to deal with the fact that no woman will tolerate controlling behavior.

At this point he has a choice. He can seek professional help, or he can try to fix things on his own. If you think a book about the problem will help, buy one for him and ask him to read it, but suggest that if this doesn't correct the situation, a therapist is the next step. In either case, you should address each issue when it surfaces. Be sure to let him know when you think he's controlling — and be prepared, because he will probably need specific examples in order to be convinced. Let him know that there's a pay-off; remind him that it's just as easy, and even more fun, to make decisions together, so no one feels controlled by the other.

Of course you are walking a fine line here, because if you're giving him books and insisting he read them, or you're telling him he needs to see a therapist, he could very well perceive *that* behavior as controlling. You need to do some soul-searching to ensure that your only motive is to preserve your relationship, not to run his life or "fix" him.

Also make sure you're not confusing "controlling" with performance, responsibility and accountability. Some men are just go-getters by nature. Maybe they believe that the only way to make sure something is done right is to do it themselves. They're used to taking control of most situations. To a certain degree this is admirable, though if you're a strong-willed woman yourself, you might find it hard to deal with at first. It's only when a man consistently ignores or devalues the input of other people, or seems to want to run everyone else's life, that the behavior crosses the line to "controlling".

---

## Remember...

*ake sure you're not confusing "controlling" behavior with performance, accountability and responsibility. Some men are used to taking control of situations because they've had to do so. It's only when a man consistently ignores your input or that of others, or seems to want to run everyone else's life, that his behavior crosses the line to "controlling".*

---

What if he simply doesn't let you be yourself? If you've tried talking with him about controlling behavior and he's still playing Professor Higgins to your Eliza Doolittle, it could be time to move on. No man should want to change you. If he does, and you still continue to date him (or worse, you try to change for him), then you're not recognizing a bad prospect. Get away from him, because he has the wrong woman! A man must love you for who you are. Sure, we can all improve, and we do, but you have to be yourself. If you think you can enter into a marriage pretending to be the person that Mr. Prospect wants you to be, you will become increasingly resentful, and may grow to hate him. The marriage almost certainly will end in divorce. It's just not worth it.

In Chapter 44 we discuss the "red flags" and warning signals that are pretty clear signs a man is not the one for you. Controlling behavior is more of a gray area that can go either way. If a man who is truly controlling is willing to work on the problem, you could have a wonderful future together. If not, at least you will know you did your part to try to fix the situation. There are plenty of good men out there who will let you be yourself. ♥

# DON'T TRY TO CHANGE *HIM*

One of the main points I hope to convey in this book is that finding a husband isn't about a man, it's about you. It's one of those things that cannot be said often enough. We all have the power to change ourselves, and that's what this book is about. Keep in mind that no one else can get us to change, and we cannot (or should not) change ourselves solely for another person. *Similarly, we cannot change another person — not even a prospective spouse.*

A huge mistake many people make is thinking that once they marry, they can get their spouse to change. That statement is gender-neutral, but the truth is that women are more likely to want to change men than vice-versa. In any case, the notion is just plain wrong. Of course there are instances where one spouse has convinced the other spouse to change his or her habits, but it usually is a joint effort. You cannot enter into a marriage thinking it will happen.

When my sister and I began to seriously date our husbands, my mother told us that what we did not like about our husbands when we married them would be the same things we would dislike twenty-five years later. It's only natural to think maybe you'll be different, that you could be one of the few who could actually change someone else! Fortunately we were blessed with a very wise mother, and we knew if she said it, there had to be a reason. Of course people don't usually change, but if they do, it's only because *they* want to. Most people really don't *want* to, and you can't make that happen, so if you get married gambling that you can somehow change your husband, you are probably placing a losing bet. I cannot tell you how often I've heard an engaged woman say, "He'll change after we're married." Ten years later (provided the marriage lasts that long), these women are either still gnashing their teeth over his maddening habit, or they've just resigned themselves to it.

Ashley was engaged to Blake, and the two were very much in love. There was only one little problem, in Ashley's eyes. Blake was a pack rat and a bit of a slob, and Ashley was a "neat freak". She wasn't obsessive about neatness, but she did like order and organization in her life. Blake, on the other hand, didn't care where he threw his clothes, his dirty towels or the daily mail. He did have basic standards of cleanliness and he rinsed the food off of his dishes after he ate, but he let them pile up in the sink for days before he'd finally wash them and put them away. He was completely unwilling to throw away or recycle anything, so his house was filled with old magazines, empty coffee cans, newspapers, used packing material, broken picture frames and a host of other things that "might come in handy some day". This drove Ashley crazy, and she tried on many occasions to tidy up his house. Blake was easygoing and didn't particularly mind (and he loved the fact that she didn't mind washing dishes, a task he hated), but he still wouldn't let her throw anything away. Ashley figured all this would change when they got married and moved into a new place of their own. It would be "out with the old, in with the new" — and the "new" would be neat and orderly.

Do I even have to tell you the rest of this story? Five years and countless arguments later, Ashley and Blake are living in a new house filled with old magazines, empty coffee cans, newspapers, broken picture frames and used packing material. As quickly as Ashley can throw things out, Blake replaces them. She is insanely in love with this man and he really is a great guy. Except for his pack rat problem, she couldn't ask for a better husband, so she has learned to live with clutter. She says she often has dreams of large houses with empty rooms...but it's unlikely that dream will ever be a reality. Ashley is one woman who learned to "live with it". She knows things could have been much worse — she could have been completely intolerant, or Blake could have been a true slob (and, even worse, belligerent about it), and their marriage could have ended in divorce. She feels that all things considered, she's pretty darn lucky, but she did learn the hard way that you can't change someone else.

As insignificant as something may be, if it bothers you before your marriage, chances are it will not get better. What you have to ask yourself is, "Can I live with this? Do I want to live with this?" Because almost assuredly you are going to have to.

---

## Remember...

 f something bothers you about your prospective husband before marriage, chances are it will not get better. You will not be able to change him. Ask yourself, "Can I live with this?"— because you will almost certainly have to!

---

Each of us has definite quirks that probably cannot be changed. We don't even notice most of them, but the ones that are bothersome or even upsetting need addressing before we enter into a long-term relationship. If a man is constantly moody, rest assured, he cannot change. If he goes from extreme highs to extreme lows, he may not be bipolar, but those could be serious personality disorders that are difficult for anyone to live with. If he shows little tolerance and lack of patience in situations where he should be more laid back and understanding, find out why he displays such unappealing behavior. If he's a screamer, uses foul language more than on rare occasions or is bigoted...all these are indicators of what's waiting for you. They will not disappear.

Everyone has something that's annoying to someone else, or vice versa. As discussed elsewhere in this book, there are some annoyances that you can talk about with your prospective Mr. Right, but keep in mind that even if he says he'll change or he promises to work on them, change is not easy. For instance, eating habits are difficult to change. If you're dating a man who chews with his mouth open, chances are he'll continue to do it no matter how many times you remind him not to. If he uses his hands more than his fork and knife, that too is difficult to change at his age. (Just eat at Moroccan restaurants a lot and you'll be okay.) If he swears more than occasionally, it's doubtful he wants to change. Friendly reminders can help, as can sitting down occasionally and talking about those things that bother you, but most men will soon think you're nagging and they'll tune you out.

Realize too that sometimes people *do* make changes specifically for others, but the changes are almost always short-lived. Whether it's quitting drinking or smoking, adopting an exercise routine, or changing one's speech habits, if a person does it solely to please someone else, he may keep the resolution for a while, but almost certainly will resume the old habits before too long. When you make a real change you have to do it for yourself. So if a man "changes" just on a woman's insistence, his changes aren't likely to be long-term. Also ask yourself this: Would you really want someone so pliable that he'd change at your whim? I doubt it. I know I would want someone who's made of stronger stuff than that!

The pros and cons of living together before marriage will no doubt continue to be debated. There have yet to be any statistics that show a lower divorce rate among couples who live together prior to marriage. Nevertheless, living together is a learning experience, and you will quickly learn Mr. Prospect's habits. You'll find out whether or not he picks up his dirty socks and laundry, caps the toothpaste, or rinses his dirty dishes and puts them into the dishwasher. You'll find out whether he is inherently neat and clean or a hopeless slob. He will discover these same things about you, and if you happen to be the one whose habits annoy him, you'll quickly find that out too. There are many ways in which living together is not the same as marriage, but you do learn each other's day-to-day habits, and you can be assured that these won't change, even if you decide to make your union legal.

No doubt, both of you will make many changes and adjustments as your relationship progresses, but don't ever enter into a relationship with the goal of changing the other person. When you find the right man for you, my guess is that he'll be a pretty terrific guy just as he is. I'm sure there will be something about him that you'll want to try to change anyway…but do yourself and him a favor, and resist that impulse! ♥

# 43

# SLOW DOWN WHEN YOU SEE A "CAUTION LIGHT"

*L*earning to read a man's signals is important when you're trying to determine if he is a potential Mr. Right. You have to do more than listen to what he says — you need to pay attention to his *body language* and especially to his *general behavior*. Maybe things would be a lot easier if we could take everything anyone said at face value, but that's not the case. Very often we need to "listen between the lines". This is very important, because if you're attracted to a man, and/or really determined to get married, you will have a tendency to see what you want to see. When you are attached to a positive outcome, it's easy to tune out negative signs.

In the next chapter we'll discuss genuine "warning signals" — the true red flags that tell you the relationship has no future. In this chapter, however, we'll take a look at some signals that aren't necessarily red flags, but nevertheless could be "flashing yellow lights" — signs that you should slow down and proceed with caution. At the very least, you should take a much closer look at the relationship. It is obviously not a comprehensive list but I've covered a few of the more common "types" encountered by single women.

Let's get to the big one first: The man who says he doesn't want to commit. What is he really saying? This is one case where face value is actually pretty accurate. The man who doesn't want to commit is either saying he's afraid of commitment in general, or he's unsure of *you*. If he's genuinely commitment-phobic, you don't want to waste too much time with him, and certainly you don't want to fall for him, because you will only wind up disappointed and hurt. If he comes right out and says he's not interested in a serious, long-term relationship, believe him. Perhaps another woman can get him to change his mind — and maybe you could do it after "working on him" for months or years — but it's a gamble, and the odds are against you here. Do you have years to waste on an unsure bet?

What we're trying to do is get the odds in your favor, eliminating as many obstacles as possible. I can't say it strongly enough: *It is almost always best to believe the man who says he doesn't want to commit.* A relationship with a man like this occasionally turns into marriage, but not often enough to make it worth your while. Oh, I know, everyone knows a story of a woman who ends up marrying one of those commitment-phobic men. There's even a similar story in this book. But those are the rare exceptions, and unless this man is truly a jewel, why not just find someone who's a more likely prospect?

If he isn't necessarily a commitment-phobe but only seems uncertain about making a commitment to you, the relationship could go either way. In Chapter 49 we discuss how and when to bring up the subjects of commitment and marriage. It really shouldn't be a topic of discussion very early in the relationship. However, if a man brings it up at the beginning, and flatly states he's not looking for a permanent relationship, do yourself and him a favor, and take him at his word.

---

## Remember...

*hen a man says he doesn't want to commit, believe him. Odds are he won't change his mind, and you will only end up disappointed and hurt. Some men do change their minds eventually, but why wait? Move on to greener pastures.*

---

Now that we have the commitment-phobes out of the way, let's look at some other potentially negative behavior patterns. What about the polar opposite of the commitment-phobe — the man who comes on strong and sweeps you off your feet? You've only had a couple of dates, and he's already planned your entire future together. This man is definitely trying too hard. If you like him and think you could have a future together, this is not necessarily bad. It's just a signal for you to say, "Let's take things slowly." If he agrees to slow things down and the relationship begins to follow a more natural progression, that's fine. However, if his resolution to slow it down lasts for a day and a half and then he's right back to where he was before, that's reason for caution. Too many of these relationships fizzle out. You could be setting yourself up for a major disappointment, so be cautious and don't let yourself get in too deep.

What about the "last-minute man" — the one who waits until Thursday night to ask you out for Saturday? He has lots of excuses why he's so late in calling. If this is a man you were even remotely considering as a future husband, just say no, even if you have to stay home alone. You could say, "Sorry, I'm busy this weekend, but how about next Saturday?" Certainly there are exceptions — an old friend with whom you occasionally share a nice evening, for example, or a recent widower who may be sitting home, depressed and feeling guilty that he's beginning to date so soon after the loss of his wife. You have to exercise your good judgment in those instances. But here we're talking about men who are well into the dating scene and who are active prospects. If you are in the very early stages of a relationship with a prospective Mr. Right, and he waits until late in the week to call you for a weekend date, don't accept.

Some people might look at this as game playing. I see it as setting boundaries. There's nothing wrong with accepting casual, last-minute invitations once in a while, after the relationship is more serious and the two of you are spending more time together; most men like a woman who can be spontaneous. Nor is there anything wrong with accepting a spur-of-the-moment date with Mr. "Right Now", the guy who's a lot of fun but who isn't husband material. A man with serious intentions, however, is a different story altogether. Early in a relationship, he should be so eager to see you that he wants to pin you down several days in advance, lest someone else grab you. Of course there are those men who are simply desperate and want to monopolize all your time, to "claim" you, as it were, but we're not talking about them here. We're talking about the kind of man you want to marry.

It's true that many men these days are used to having women accept last-minute dates. Therefore, even the most thoughtful, considerate prospect might expect the same of you at first. It's up to you to set him straight right off the bat. If he asks you out late in the week, thank him but say you already have plans. If he tries to continue the conversation, don't be rude, but tell him you're busy and have to go. If he is really a potential Mr. Right, he will get the message. Should he ask you out for the following weekend, or call you early the next week, accept the date. If he waits again, however, write him off. This sounds harsh, but if you are really serious about getting married, you have to be harsh sometimes. A man who really wants to see you will play it your way on this matter. You're not asking him to turn his life upside down, and you're not being selfish — you are simply asking him to be considerate.

When a prospect is sincerely interested in you, he does not need to say much. His actions speak for themselves. He asks you out and then, before he takes you home, he may ask to see you again next Saturday night. Or he calls the next day, says how nice it was, and then asks you out for a second date. Those are all good signs. These post-date and between-date conversations also afford you more opportunities to pick up on his signals. There will be plenty of them, so you need to really listen to what he's saying.

Just a note about phone conversations: Most men dislike them. So if he doesn't talk much on the phone, don't be so quick to think he's sending a signal that he doesn't like you. Although I don't know many women who don't like talking on the phone, men are different. Sure, there are exceptions, but if a prospect has little to say on the phone, it's not necessarily a negative. My husband wasn't a phone talker when we dated, and he still isn't. When we're apart, I want to catch up and talk, but he's no different now than when we dated; he just says after a few minutes, "We'll talk more when we're together!" If you initially connect with a prospect by phone and he's not a "talker", he may come out and say he's not much of a phone person. Believe him. Don't write him off, because he could be quite a talker in person. Give him a chance.

Remember too that some men are shy. We've discussed shyness in other chapters, and I have cautioned you that you should do whatever you can to get over your own shyness, because shy just doesn't "work" for a single woman. On the other hand, I think you should cut a shy man some slack if you really like him. Unfortunately, many women associate male shyness with adolescence, so they cannot quite fathom the notion of a shy man over thirty-five. They may automatically conclude he is either disinterested or gay, and they pass up a wonderful prospect as a result. Or they may acknowledge he's shy, but are convinced that they prefer more aggressive types. You never know what you could be missing if you don't give that shy man a chance!

## Remember...

on't automatically conclude that a man isn't interested in you just because he doesn't like talking on the phone. As difficult as this may be for many women to understand, some men simply aren't "phone talkers" and never will be. Give that "phone-phobic" man a chance — he could be quite a talker in person!

And then there is the "not-quite-masculine" man, which of course isn't the same thing at all as the shy man. I have to mention this type because virtually all single woman have met men that they're not quite sure are 100% masculine. No, they don't cross-dress and they're not gay. They just aren't terribly masculine, and some even have an attitude to cover it up. How can you avoid getting too involved with these men? Some of them, admittedly, may not be all that attractive to you in the first place, so they don't present a problem. When attraction enters into the picture, however, there *is* a problem if you have doubts about his masculinity. He may even be socially and (you suspect) sexually inept, but still, there's that attraction. So how can you find out if the relationship has a future or if it's just another dead end?

Let's face it. By the time a man is in his early thirties, he should have honed his sexual skills. (Hopefully you've honed yours too; we talk about that in a little more detail in Chapter 48.) Not all men are as experienced as you might expect, however. It's hard to believe that in this day of sexual freedom, there are still men who have not had a lot of experience in the bedroom, but they do exist! Sometimes this is just because they're shy or reserved, and as mentioned above, shy isn't necessarily bad. Nor does it mean a man is sexually dysfunctional. In other cases, however, lack of sexual experience *is* a sign of sexual dysfunction or some other problem. If you suspect the man you are dating has such a problem, you do not need to jump into bed with him to confirm your suspicions. There are lots of signals to be wary of. All you need to do is take a closer look at your "suspect".

What are his hobbies? Does he have friends? Most importantly, how does he treat you? If you've met his family, what are they like, and what kind of relationship does he have with them? There are plenty of signs here to alert you if there's a potential problem. There are no hard and fast rules, but the signs do stand out.

If he has trouble with his masculinity, he'll be slow to come on to you. He'll say he's letting you lead the way, or he doesn't want to rush you, but what he's really doing is looking for excuses not to have sex. If sex is important to you, you will probably never be happy with this man.

Another characteristic some of these "less than macho" men display is their tendency to be competitive with you. You'd think that being less masculine, they would be more gentle and caring, but this isn't always the case. These men are trying to show their strength through their speech; this gives them power. They enjoy trying to prove you wrong over a minor point, showing how smart they are. All that does is antagonize you and increase the distance between the two of you.

If you are in doubt about a man's masculinity, how long are you going to hang on for the ride? More than likely, your relationship will not go any place. Understand that this doesn't happen too frequently, but I'm mentioning it so if it happens to you, you will know it's not your fault. Many of these men are good actors in the beginning, but their act wears thin quickly. No doubt they are terribly insecure, but it is not your job to "fix" them. If you have doubts, they are probably valid, so don't waste too much time — again, move on to better prospects.

The reason I'm making a point of telling you about all these signals and signs is to heighten your awareness. The signs are there even from the beginning, but we don't always recognize them. If you haven't seen them early on, these descriptions may help you detect the "flashing yellow light". You may already be a lot more "signal-literate" than you think — just be honest with yourself about the signals you are reading. That way you will save time and lots of anguish, and you will be closer to finding your husband.

# 44

# PAY ATTENTION TO
# REAL "RED FLAGS"

en, as we discussed in the previous chapter, are always sending out signals, both verbal and nonverbal. You need to be willing to look openly and honestly at these signals. In the last chapter, we looked at some signs that might be telling you to "slow down". Here we're going to look at more serious "warning signals". No matter how attractive a man may be, if you detect one of these signals, *do not ignore it*.

After you have met a prospect, there are a few red lights that are almost always signals to run:

1. Too much alcohol or drug consumption.
2. Abuse of any kind, physical or verbal.
3. Cheating and lying.

These will almost certainly never change for the better, and in the case of numbers 2 and 3, they are character flaws — so let someone else deal with them. You are trying to find a husband, not become someone's therapist. Let's discuss these major "warning flags" one by one, and then we'll look at a few others.

*Alcohol and other drugs* speak for themselves. A perfect example is the alcoholic who denies he is an alcoholic, but needs to have his beer first thing in the morning, or has three cans before he goes anywhere. Becoming involved with an active alcoholic is setting yourself up for misery. The signs that a person is a problem drinker will be apparent quite early in the relationship, so keep your eyes open, and don't make excuses for him.

Drug abuse, whether "recreational" or prescription, may be more difficult to detect at first, but if the signs are there, heed them. Unless you do recreational drugs yourself, which of course I don't recommend, you're not going to be happy with this person. You will have nothing but problems — not only emotional, but possibly medical, financial and legal as well. It just isn't worth it. I'm not being moralistic here; I recognize that addiction is a medical problem, but the consequences are far-reaching and affect more people than just the addict. Don't let it be your problem. Do not delude yourself that you're going to be the "rescuer" who gets him to clean up his act. It won't happen, and you will only be more miserable as time goes by.

*Abuse* is without question the worst possible flaw one can possess, and verbal abuse is as bad as physical. Don't make excuses for him. If a man shows any signs of abuse, run quickly. Abuse almost never deserves a second chance. The only time I would say to give a man a second chance is after the very first signs of verbal abuse — provided that he agrees to see a therapist. If he says he did not know that what he said was abusive and he wants to change his behavior, then perhaps a second chance is in order. At the very least you can tell him to work on it and come back in six months. As for physical abuse of any kind, don't listen to an apology or promises that he will never do it again. Either he seeks help immediately, or you're out the door, quickly — and don't look back!

Look at it this way. Early in a relationship, people are generally on their best behavior because they want to impress you. If he is displaying abusive behavior now, what does that tell you? It will almost certainly get worse, not better. Why take a chance?

It probably isn't fair to label people from abusive families, but be very cautious if you meet a man with such a background. As you probably know, patterns of abuse are generally carried on from one generation to the next. There are exceptions, but why risk it? At least be very cautious. If you do happen to begin dating a man who grew up in an abusive home, make sure you date him long enough to see how he handles adverse situations. Remember that you're not looking to become someone's therapist; you want to become someone's wife and life-long equal partner. Nothing you do can make a person emotionally stable. It's difficult and the responsibility is theirs, not yours. There is enough in one's own life to work on; you don't need to help someone else deal with their past.

This doesn't mean you can't be a positive influence on an abusive man who genuinely wants to change. Most cities now offer classes for men who batter females. If you listen to these men talk, you might be surprised to hear many say they weren't aware they were batterers until it was brought to their attention by a woman. Other men admit they knew it was wrong but thought it was the macho way to be. Inside the man who is willing to work on this problem, there may be a very kind, loving soul. If you are certain he is committed to the therapy and shows immediate signs of changing, it could be worth a second chance. But that's all. Remember it may very well be an ongoing battle for him, just like any other bad habit, such as overeating or alcohol consumption. If he's willing to own up to his problem and shows signs of understanding and change, he could turn into a really great guy.

---

## Remember...

*Y*ou *can be a positive influence on a physically or emotionally abusive man who genuinely wants to change — for example, you can suggest counseling — but you can't "fix" him. Most abusive men don't change, and abuse is generally progressive. The best advice...if you meet someone and you suspect he's abusive, RUN!*

---

*Cheating and lying* are related, and in my opinion, both are completely unacceptable. If a man cheats, he shouldn't be married (likewise for a woman). Yes, there have been exceptions. If a man has cheated but has confessed to his wife, asked forgiveness and vowed it will never happen again, the ball is in her court. I feel that under these circumstances, he probably does deserve a second chance. I know I'll be criticized for saying this, but I do believe that in *most* instances everyone deserves a second chance.

However, if you are the one who has cheated, and in your heart you know it will never happen again, why admit it? Go on with your life and forget about it. But be honest with yourself. If you don't think you can be a faithful mate, you shouldn't marry.

Cheating is a form of lying, but lying comes in many forms. Some people, both men and women, lie for no reason at all. It is definitely a character flaw. Why would anyone choose to live a life with someone they cannot trust? If you continually catch the man you're dating in lies, move on; his deceptiveness will always be a thorn in your side.

What if you suspect a man is hiding something — a secret marriage, a criminal past, or not-so-honorable intentions? The short answer is, "If you think he's hiding something, he probably is." When someone is not legitimate, there are always signs. Beware of "too much, too fast", or "too good to be true". Listen to what he's saying; watch him, *read his signals*. As we discussed in Chapter 43, the signals are always there. We just don't always know how to read them.

If he is evasive about anything, that's a major warning sign. For example, if you've been dating a while and you've introduced him to your friends and family, but he's hesitant to have you meet *his* friends or family, he's probably hiding something. Men are not any different from women. If they think they have found a great woman, they want their friends and family to meet her. Also beware of men who are not receptive to spending time with your family and friends. Perhaps they complain that they have little in common with them, or they try to pull you away by telling you you're too close to them. These are all neon signs to run. A good man will want to get to know your family and friends and become a part of their lives.

Unfortunately, many of you have encountered what I feel is the quintessential deception, in which the man doesn't lie — he just fails to tell you the truth: He is married. If it hasn't happened to you, beware, because it could. There are many married men who take advantage of single women. This is their modus operandi: You are out, perhaps at a singles dance. A man walks over and introduces himself; he appears decent, nice looking, softly spoken and a perfect gentleman. You think to yourself that he looks like a pretty good prospect. You spend an hour or two with him, he asks for your phone number, even suggests you meet him after work next week. The clues are not always easy to recognize. The burden of proof is on you. If you have any reason to think a man is married, ask him. I have heard many stories in which the man says, "Yes I'm married," followed by his explanation of why he failed to divulge it earlier: "You didn't ask." Be cautious, move slowly — and if you have any doubts at all, end it quickly.

Whenever you suspect dishonesty in a man, you need to put yourself on full alert. The first rule is to be very aware of what he tells you. Notice I didn't say be concerned or worried — give him the benefit of the doubt at first — just try to be more aware of what he says. If you notice at any time that he has changed his story about anything, you do not need any more proof. He is dishonest.

You can only be deceived if you allow yourself to be, so don't fall into that trap. If you're not sure about a man and you've only been dating him a short time, have someone that you're very close with meet him. You may want to consider hiring a private detective if you're really worried. However, you really don't need a private eye to find out if a man is deceiving you or hiding something — just keep your own eyes (and ears) open. Whatever you do, always listen to your own inner voice and proceed with caution.

---

# Remember…

*Y**ou can only be deceived if you want to be. If a man is continually evasive or you suspect he is being dishonest about something, and you continue to date him, you're asking for trouble. Pay attention to "red flags"!*

---

As with every other aspect of a relationship, honesty works both ways. I am, of course, assuming you are an honest person yourself. We all know that men aren't the only ones who lie and deceive. Many women also practice deception on several levels, from outright lying to telling half-truths (or simply withholding the whole truth). Please know that I'm not referring to discretion about your past, or any of the other cautionary measures one takes with someone they've just met. Circumspection is definitely the way to go early in a relationship. Once you are in a relationship with someone, however, both of you should be honest with each other about your actions and intentions. You cannot expect a man to be honest and forthright if you aren't. As I've said before, if you want a first-class man, you need to be a first-class woman.

Okay, we've gotten the "big three" out of the way, but there are a few other red flags you need to be aware of.

*Personality disorders* are a major warning signal. We all have different personality traits, but any personality trait that is carried to the extreme is classified as a personality disorder. Whether the causes are a biochemical imbalance, a dysfunctional childhood or any other factor, these disorders are serious. If you think you can live with someone with a personality disorder, think long and hard before you make a commitment, because it isn't easy.

A girlfriend of mine was dating a man who had more quirks than most people, and that's putting it mildly. She's a therapist and figured if anyone could be tolerant of his idiosyncrasies it was she. Knowing she couldn't change him, she tried to adjust to his patterns, but after months and months, she realized it was impossible for her to live with someone like that. Ultimately he was diagnosed with obsessive-compulsive disorder, or O.C.D., and was put on medication, but it proved ineffective. After four years, and endless conversations about his unwillingness or inability to change, my friend knew it was time to end the relationship.

Two women I know are married to men with bipolar disorder. There is no doubt that having the disease is unfortunate, but being married to someone who has it is a nightmare. Both of these women have sought outside counseling, which they will probably need as long as they are in their relationships.

I hope I've made the point that any extreme personality disorder is difficult to live with. If my therapist friend with her obsessive-compulsive boyfriend couldn't do it, do you think you can?

*Passive-aggressive behavior* needs a mention here. We have all seen it and we can all identify it. It is displaying passive behavior to get a desired result. For example, a husband asks his wife, "What would you like for dinner tonight?" Her response is that she doesn't care. The husband then says, "How would you like to go for pizza?" His wife says no. The husband suggests hamburgers. Again his wife says no. The husband continues asking and the wife gives the same response. Her passivity, saying she doesn't care what she eats, is in reality aggressive behavior. She does care, but says no to everything her husband suggests, perhaps because she is angry at him about a completely unrelated matter. Or she has learned how to get her way through this manipulating behavior — which, by the way, everyone sees through.

If you think a prospect has these traits, talk about it with him. I'm sure it won't be the first time he's had this conversation. If you're guilty of those traits yourself, own up to it and then do something about it. I know people who admit, sometimes reluctantly and sometimes almost proudly, that they are occasionally guilty of passive-aggressive behavior. Ask them why, and they chuckle, in a rather sadistic way. They know they ultimately get their way without so much as having to ask for it, and they make the other person do all the work. My answer to them is, grow up! You can learn how to verbally express yourself and to communicate in a healthy manner. If you're unsure, read self-help books on the subject, or see a therapist.

*Controlling behavior* is worthy of an entire chapter in itself; see Chapter 41.

I hope it doesn't seem as if I am warning you to expect the worst of every man. You should not start out looking for negatives, because if you do you almost certainly will find them. But neither should you turn a blind eye when you see those flashing warning signals. You absolutely must pay attention to them from the beginning because more than likely, your prospect's negative traits will only get worse, not better, with time. Remember, as we discuss in Chapter 42, you should never marry someone with the expectation that they will change for the better.

Sometimes, however, there is a gray area, and there is a chance that a person may change his behavior or habits. If your prospect does something you find disagreeable, this doesn't necessarily mean you should turn and run without giving him a chance. He may be a genuinely good guy who just isn't aware that what he's doing is bothering you. And he may very well change his behavior, if you bring it to his attention. This is not the same as trying to change him; sometimes people are open to gentle suggestions.

When is the right time to confront him with something that bothers you? Right at the beginning! I'm not saying you should be a whiner or complainer, but you do need to be honest with him.

Let's say you had a successful first date and your prospect, who has a sail boat, asks you to go sailing for your second date. You tell him you're not familiar at all with sailing and, other than being a conscientious bystander, you can offer little assistance. He says not to worry, he can handle most of it himself. So you go out, but before long he's not only asking if you want to help out, he's yelling at you to do this or to do that, and he begins to show impatience because you're not adept with the maneuvers. Wait a minute; you told him up front you know nothing about sailing and didn't think you could be of much help. Presumably you reminded him before you left to go boating, and perhaps as you got on the boat, and now you find yourself reminding him again as he's asking you to help him. If he still doesn't get it after three reminders, take that as a sign that perhaps he's not for you!

Or let's say you've had a few dates with a good prospect, but you've noticed he doesn't show patience in restaurants when the service is less than perfect, or he gets angry when orders don't always arrive as they should. This is a problem with many successful men; they think they can order people around. It is rude and unnecessary. You do not have to stand for that. If all things seem tolerable except this, explain to him that his behavior is embarrassing, and makes you uncomfortable. Like everything in life, we make choices, and he needs to choose another form of behavior: Tolerance. You can use humor if you think that will work. Just say, "Hey, lighten up. This isn't your last meal." If he is habitually rude to the wait staff, sales clerks or other service people, take it as a real red flag. In his book, *Dave Barry Turns 50*, humor columnist Dave Barry wrote a list of things people should know by the time they turn fifty. One of them was, "A person who is nice to you, but rude to the waiter, is not a nice person." I agree!

What if you've had a few dates with a prospect and he has poor table manners, or he lacks good manners in general? There are ways for you to gently suggest that he work on it. Give him a book on etiquette, for example. Be honest, but tactful. Don't be judgmental or controlling; that will scare him off. If your gentle approach doesn't work — well, you need to decide how important good manners are to you.

Or let's say your Mr. Prospect has impeccable manners and treats you like a queen, but there still is something that's keeping you from falling in love with him. Could it possibly be his lifestyle? All right, he doesn't cheat, lie, smoke or drink, but he does live way beyond his means, has poor credit and has charged to the maximum on all his credit cards. If you're someone who prides herself on good credit, has a savings account, and pays her bills on time, do you think you'd be happy with someone like that? Your first impulse might be to say no, but as is often the case, the answer isn't black and white.

If you are dating a man and he has problems such as those cited above (and they are definite problems), be honest with yourself. If those problems didn't exist, could you fall in love with this man? If the answer is yes, then they need to be addressed. If he were willing to turn the finances over to you, for example, would you be willing and capable of handling it? Another option would be for the two of you to sit down and try to budget his income. If you are willing to help and he sincerely wants to change his spending habits, it might work.

## Remember...

*hen talking with a man about traits or habits that bother you, be honest but tactful, and don't be judgmental or controlling. You don't want to scare him off, and you certainly don't want him to perceive you as one of those women who want to change him!*

Whatever the problem is, if you address it honestly and clearly, you will know within a very short time how sincere his efforts are to change. Of course, if his idiosyncrasies or differences are tolerable to you, they won't be a problem. If they are intolerable, ask yourself if you want to live with that the rest of your life, knowing that the chances are he will not or cannot change. That does not mean you have to end the relationship. What is tolerable to one person may not be to another, and if you can make up your mind to accept him and love him as he is, you may have a real chance at a future together.

On the other hand, any of the examples listed above could constitute values, and if you've read Chapter 19, you know the importance of sharing similar values. For example, if having good credit and being financially responsible are core values for you, his financial irresponsibility probably signifies lesser values, and there's a good chance you will never be happy with someone like that. The problem may always be there, and if it is, you will probably find yourselves constantly arguing about priorities.

Just a few words here about financial irresponsibility — it is a bad habit to which many people succumb. It's just another form of instant gratification, and some people never get beyond that need. People have all sorts of excuses, but the bottom line is that they are engaging in immature and irresponsible behavior. The most financially irresponsible person can be helped as long as the desire to get out of the red is stronger than the desire for things. Just don't make excuses for his behavior; he must either own up to it and try to change, or you will become a part of that lifestyle. This is why you really do need to be honest when you ask yourself if you will be able to live happily with someone like that. If he wants to spend money on a new television like the one his best friend just bought, and you're saving for the long-awaited vacation, will you be happy? You have to decide what your priorities and goals are, and work together to reach them.

There are many "warning signals" to watch out for — fortunately, most of them will show up pretty early in a relationship. Keep your eyes and ears open, as well as your heart and mind, and you will avoid all the Mr. Wrongs on your way to finding Mr. Right. ♥

---

## Remember...

*arning signals show up pretty early in a relationship, so you need to be honest with him from the beginning about the things that genuinely bother you. Don't be a whiner or complainer, but confront him openly. That way you'll know if he's willing to change, and you'll have a better basis on which to decide the future of the relationship.*

---

# 45

# WHEN IN DOUBT,
# ASK YOUR FRIENDS

*P*eople can have good judgment when it comes to business, but it doesn't necessarily carry over into their personal lives. Many single people exercise excellent judgment every day of the week, but when it comes to finding a spouse, they are always attracted to the wrong person. In Chapter 40 we talk about negative patterns and how important it is to recognize and break those patterns. Feedback from a friend you respect and trust can help you see them. A reality check from a good friend can also be particularly valuable after you're in a relationship and find yourself overwhelmed with doubts and misgivings. Perhaps you sense something is not quite right about the man you are seeing, or maybe you think he's really okay, but for some reason you are hesitant to marry him.

If you can't figure it out yourself, then by all means ask a friend. Now, to some of you this may seem self-evident. Seeking opinions from friends is second nature to many women. Back in junior high, most of us constantly sought our friends' opinions. "Do you think Billy likes me?" "What do you think of that new boy Matt?" Now that we're all grown up, however, many women keep things to themselves. Either they don't want to "bother" their friends with their problems, or they are just naturally reserved and don't like to open up about their personal lives. In some cases, they know their friend is going to tell them the truth, and it's a truth they don't want to hear or face. I think the latter scenario is the most common.

If you really do think something could be amiss, why not reach out to a friend? Sometimes, just talking about your doubts with someone with whom you feel comfortable, and who generally displays common sense and good judgment, can help you make the right decision. A therapist will generally ask a few key questions, but a good friend can be just as helpful if not more so, and will save you some money. It helps if this friend is already married with a family. They will have a better understanding of your doubts and may have keener insight than your single friends. Don't be afraid of the truth; it might not be as scary as you think. Maybe you're expecting your friend to come back with a long list of negatives, but she or he could very well surprise you by seeing nothing seriously wrong and saying, "Go for it!"

---

## Remember...

 *"reality check" from a good friend can help you decide if your relationship is going in the right direction. A friend who's already married may have keener insight than your single friends.*

---

Possibly you're in the opposite situation to that described above and you're not having any doubts at all. How often have we heard couples say they knew immediately or very soon after meeting their mate that he or she was the one? Even if you're sure he's Mr. Right, it's not a bad idea to ask your friends or family to check out your new prospect before you find yourself too deep into the relationship. It's hard to see the picture when you're in it! When you're too close to any situation, it is very difficult to be objective. Even if you think you're looking at everything rationally, it still pays to get a few opinions very early. You could be avoiding a heartbreak.

Remember that in the beginning, just about everyone is on his or her best behavior, so you may not be able to notice anything unusual. However, if there's a major problem, a third party — someone who's not blinded by attraction to this man — should be able to detect it. There are many signs when someone is less than honest, and we talk about these in other chapters, but some people are better at picking up those signals than others.

Perhaps you haven't had to solicit your friends' advice; maybe they've offered it freely. It's even possible that you find this annoying. But don't tune them out entirely, at least not until you've listened carefully to what they have to tell you. Laura and Sean met the summer after their senior year in a West Coast university, and they dated all through graduate school. None of Laura's friends really liked Sean, but they made an attempt to accept him anyway. However, they told her many times over the years that she should break up with him, because he just wasn't right for her. She didn't listen. At first her parents didn't really like him either, nor did her sisters and brothers. Eventually they too learned to accept him, since it seemed he was there to stay. To everyone's dismay Sean and Laura married two years out of graduate school...and less than one year later they split up. It turned out Sean had been having an affair with another woman, and Laura found out it was far from the first time he'd cheated on her. So that was the end, finally. Laura wishes she had listened to her friends, who all through graduate school had warned her about Sean.

When you are seeking advice from friends, be careful whom you ask. Make sure the person you are asking is a true friend, and is someone to whom you've been a friend as well. Scott moved to an East Coast suburb and decided to look up some college buddies, although he knew he hadn't been particularly nice to one of the guys, Kevin, the last time they were together. They'd been leaving a party where they all had way too much to drink, and Scott deliberately left Kevin there, stranded. He hadn't seen his old pals in over two years but figured by now Kevin must have forgiven him, and probably forgotten about it as well. Was he wrong!

Scott started hanging out with the same group of singles, and one day someone introduced him to a woman. He decided to play it smart and ask one of his drinking buddies if he'd check out this girl. Unfortunately, the buddy he chose to ask was Kevin. Well, Kevin checked her out all right, but he never told Scott what he found out. He gave him the okay sign, saying she was great, everyone liked her and Scott should go for it! Scott began dating her, they fell in love and married — and the marriage didn't last a year. She was a nightmare waiting to happen, and it cost Scott plenty of money and aggravation before he was free from her. You've heard the expression, "Don't get mad, get even." That's what Scott's old friend did!

The opinions of your friends (your true friends, that is) can be invaluable. However, it is important to remember that your friends may not know your prospect intimately and will only be basing their opinion on what they see on the surface. You must still go with your own feelings. Consider what your friends tell you and then decide for yourself. Certainly do not let anyone talk you into or out of any relationship. They may have their own hidden agenda (as Scott found out the hard way). Listen to your inner voice as closely as you do to your friends, and you will make the right decision. ♥

PART *Seven*

# GETTING SERIOUS

# 46

# IF YOU WANT TO BE
# NUMBER 1 TO HIM,
# TREAT *HIM* LIKE NUMBER 1

Many women complain that men don't know how to treat a woman. Let me ask you this: Do you treat a man the way he wants to be treated, or are you always thinking of yourself first?

One of the core messages of this book is that finding a husband is not about the man, it is about *you*. Specifically, it is about your willingness to make the necessary changes to attract the kind of man you want to marry. Once you've found a man who is a "keeper", however, it no longer is just about you. A relationship is not about pleasing yourself; it is about pleasing Mr. Right — who will in turn please you as a result.

Now, before you throw this book into the heap with all those insufferable "how to please your man" bestsellers that have come out over the years, stop! I hope that by now you know I would never suggest you overlook your own needs, or that you be a doormat. I am only suggesting that you need to make an effort to see things from his perspective and think about his wants and needs.

Also notice I did not say that this is about making him happy, nor do I imply that he can make you happy. Another person coming into your life can't make you happy, but if you already are a happy person, he can without a doubt add to your happiness. On the other hand, if you walk around with your head down, looking and feeling as if you have the world's weight upon your shoulders, having a boyfriend or husband will not make all those problems disappear. You will probably just end up making both of you miserable.

So assuming that you're basically a happy person, it's time to turn your focus outward. When you find Mr. Right, you will naturally want to please him. The catch is that if you've been alone for a while, you might find it difficult to put his needs before your own. Many independent women find that this is a challenge. They may simply be used to doing things their way. Many believe that putting a man first means they are being subservient. For some, but not all, this attitude is a holdover from the late sixties and early seventies, when the women's movement emerged on the scene. I believe many good and necessary changes came about as a result of the women's movement, but I also believe some of the old "tried and true" ways are good too, and these have nothing to do with subservience. Recognizing that you are not the only one in the relationship is hardly subservient. In fact, thinking of the other person instead of always thinking of yourself first is downright liberating. And remember that the same works for you. You wouldn't want to date a man who always puts himself first, would you?

I can hear the voices of protest now. After all, women are famous for putting everyone else's needs before their own. Yes, it's true that many married women juggling career, husband and children find they have no time or energy left for themselves. The same is true of harried single mothers (minus the husband, of course), but I am speaking of single women who are a little too accustomed to looking out for number one. There is a huge middle ground between total self-sacrifice and total selfishness.

Many relationships and marriages start out with both partners showing consideration for each other's needs, but after a short time, the couples get so caught up in their daily schedules and family responsibilities that they fail to think of their relationship. Even though they may not be putting themselves first anymore, they're certainly not putting their partner first. That's a bit of a mistake. You can never take your marriage for granted, and once you find yourself in a relationship that could lead to marriage, treat it with the same care as you would a marriage. Think of your relationship as you would a newborn baby or a very young child. Both need constant attention and nurturance to grow and cannot be neglected.

Kerri and Ryan had a short marriage, the first for both of them. They were engaged after only having dated a few months. Although they didn't marry for nearly another year, their relationship went downhill from the moment she got her ring. Kerri was busy with graduate school, and when she wasn't studying or in the library, she spent the remainder of her time planning their wedding. They never really got to know one another well. If they had, they probably would not have gone through with the wedding. Of course, for every story like this there's one to counter it. There are couples who meet, date only a matter of weeks or a few months before they get engaged, marry soon after, and have a very happy marriage. The difference is that they enter into their marriage caring about each other, looking out for each other's needs, and not putting themselves first.

I recognize that for many of you, "putting him first" will come naturally at this stage. Most women are nurturers by nature. Furthermore, most of us want to put our best foot forward early in a relationship, and it's easy to find new and creative ways to please our partner. However, this principle of putting him first applies not just early on, but throughout your relationship. It is those little "niceties" that keep a relationship warm and alive, no matter how many years you've been together. *You can never stop thinking of the other person. You can never take your relationship for granted.* Established relationships need just as much, if not more, "care and feeding" than new ones.

---

## Remember...

 hink of a new relationship as you would a newborn baby or a very young child; give it constant care and attention so it can grow. Once you enter into a relationship that could lead to marriage, treat it with the same care as you would a marriage.

---

It might even help if you remind yourself that there are lots of women out there, and if you don't want to care for and nurture your partner, there will be more women knocking down his door, ready to take your place. That is a fact. I admit this may be a negative reason, but sometimes a little negative reinforcement works when nothing else does. There are, of course, many positive reasons to put him first. Ultimately you benefit, because if you make him feel special, he will want to please you. It's really a very simple formula.

I suspect some of you reading this are disagreeing with me. All I can ask is that you try these suggestions and then see if you still disagree.

When you have met a prospect and he's turning into a potential Mr. Right, do everything you can to make him feel special. He will interpret all those niceties as "she's wonderful to me!" Listen to him, and let him see that you really care about the person he is, not just about what he can do for you. Learn about his tastes in music and movies, books and food. Find out his stance on political and social issues, and his philosophy about life. Be considerate of him. On a date, do the things he wants to do, at least once in a while. (Is this beginning to sound like that old Dusty Springfield hit, "Wishing and Hoping"? Like I said, the old ways are sometimes good ways!)

You must also always let him know that you appreciate him and the things he does for you. Never forget to thank him, whether he's holding a door open for you or bringing you fresh-brewed coffee in the morning. Even if he's done it dozens of times, thank him *every* time. The power of "thank you" goes a long way!

Little domestic touches here and there are great too, as long as you don't get too heavy-handed with them early in the relationship. (We discussed this in Chapter 13.) You don't want to come across as desperate or obvious, and you certainly don't want to scare him away, but there are all sorts of creative, thoughtful things you can do. Bake him something, or cook him a simple dinner. It doesn't have to be a romantic candlelight dinner, and really shouldn't be the first time. Something easy and informal — even a picnic lunch, weather permitting— will almost certainly please him.

While we're on the subject, I have a few words of wisdom for the "domestically challenged" among you. Believe it or not, there are women who can sew on a button, sew an open seam in an emergency and even — gasp! — iron clothes if they have to. Doing so doesn't mean you're trying to be a perfect 1950s housewife. It just means you're capable in any situation. And don't get upset, because I've told men the same thing: At least learn how to sew on a button. The point here is that it doesn't take a lot to impress a man. If he's in need and you can help out, you will go up a few notches. It's still true that most people choose extensions of their own parents — men look for their mothers and women look for their fathers. Men want a woman they can depend on, not a little girl. If a button falls off his shirt, why not offer to sew it back on? If he's ripped the seat of his pants, tell him to take them off and you'll fix them. You won't do a perfect job, but good enough until he can get to the tailor!

## Remember...

ake care of your boyfriend, make him feel special...and he won't have to look any further.

A final aspect of considering his needs and wants is not always having to have the last word, and not always needing to be right. Would you rather be happy or right? Forget that dubious bit of wisdom in *Love Story* back in the seventies; love does sometimes mean having to say, "I'm sorry" or "You're right." Men like to joke that letting the woman have the last word, or just giving up and telling her she's right, is the only way to keep peace in a relationship. This is really pretty condescending to women, but unfortunately, there is some truth to it; we do often like to "be right" and have the last word. Well, it's up to you to break that stereotype. This doesn't mean you should be conciliatory when you think he's wrong or is being unreasonable. It certainly doesn't mean you shouldn't present your side in an argument or conflict. Just don't be so attached to being right that you refuse to even look at his side. You might come to the conclusion that he *is* right once in a while!

Looking out for Mr. Right's wants and needs may be an old-fashioned concept, but believe me, it still works today. Putting him first will add a new and wonderful dimension to your life as well as his. ♥

# BE A GOOD FRIEND
# TO HIS FAMILY

A fter you've met your Mr. Right, sooner or later you're going to meet his family. If marriage is in your future, it is essential to develop a good relationship with them. As is the case with your circle of friends and acquaintances, you don't have to like or love everything about each and every one of your future husband's relatives, but you do have to give them a chance, and hope they will do the same for you.

"Family" can encompass a broad range of people. Maybe your Mr. Right is an only child with only one surviving parent and no other close relatives, in which case the "obstacle course" probably won't seem nearly so formidable. On the other hand, you could find yourself overwhelmed by a boisterous crowd of parents, grandparents, siblings, aunts, uncles, cousins and assorted close friends of the family, much like the hapless young man in *My Big Fat Greek Wedding*. Your prospective husband may also have children from a previous marriage or marriages. When you marry him, for better or worse, you are marrying all of these people.

With all of these new relatives comes a whole new set of family dynamics. The term "family dynamics" refers to the way family members relate to and interact with each other. Divorce and remarriage, the birth order of siblings, the presence or absence of grandparents or other relatives in the household — these are just a few factors that influence family dynamics. There is a wealth of literature on the subject, and it is far beyond the scope of this book to elaborate. Suffice to say that every family is different — and no matter how similar his background is to yours, when you meet his family you will most likely encounter behavior, as well as customs and traditions, that will be unlike yours. The same applies to him when he meets your family. You both need to keep in mind that each family has had years to establish their personal style, and although theirs may differ from yours, it doesn't make one right or wrong. Chances are, when their families melded together, they took some from one family's side and some from the other family's side to establish their own family traditions. History repeats itself, and if your relationship becomes a marriage, that's how new traditions and customs are formed — each family decides what they like best about the other family's, and then adds some of their own thoughts and ideas.

Holidays, in particular, can be a real challenge when you're getting used to "new" ways, but they can also provide you with a wonderful chance to prove your willingness to be a friend to his family. When the first big holidays arrive, try to go to both family gatherings. (In case of divorces, try to attend as many as possible — that is, if the families live nearby. If not, then try Thanksgiving with one family and Christmas, New Year's or Easter with the other family.) It's important that you rotate holidays/families and make every effort to be "fair". You will want to meet as many of the other family members as possible if you're going to be celebrating holidays together. Without a doubt, you will have some new routines to get used to, but that's part of the fun! One family may eat at noon, the other at four o'clock in the afternoon. One family may prefer a seated dinner, another a buffet. Some families open gifts Christmas Eve, other families prefer to do it Christmas Day. Whatever the customs are, try to be accommodating. It makes you a congenial and appealing person, someone these new family members will enjoy being with. It doesn't matter what their style is, it is *his* family and you need to respect it. Keep an open mind and be non-judgmental. Of course, you should expect him to show your family the same consideration. It's all part of the art of compromise that is so important in every relationship. Remember that even though each of you may have celebrated holidays one way your entire life, it doesn't mean that's the *only* way.

On those first visits, try to introduce as many people as possible to each other, and try to make everyone comfortable. You want his family to feel as if you're already one of them, and you want your family to feel the same way about him. The most important thing to keep in mind is that holidays can be very stressful, so do anything you can to prevent any uncomfortable situations. (A good rule of thumb is that if you think you may be hurting someone's feelings, you probably are. This is true any time, but it goes double for holidays, so be extra careful at these times.)

Dealing with each other's families can be a challenge all year round, not just at the holidays. We all know about the classic mother-in-law "problems" many women have. Mothers-in-law have been given a bad rap for years and it's time for women (and men too, for that matter) to grow up! There are some exceptions of course, but almost every parent wants her or his children to be happy. If you've met a man who is close with his mother, she does not have to be a threat to you, nor do you have to be jealous of her. She is not your enemy. To deliberately create a situation where you come between your boyfriend and his mother is terribly harmful to all concerned. You have everything to gain by being a good friend to his mother — and if a man is a good son (or a good grandson), he will probably be a good husband.

---

## Remember...

*olidays can be especially challenging when a relationship is new and you're just getting to know each other's families. Make every effort to spend as much time as possible with both families, and try to make everyone comfortable with each other.*

---

If your prospective husband has siblings, of course you want to be nice to them too. You may end up developing very close friendships with them. I have to warn you, though, that if he turns out not to be Mr. Right after all, you may lose a good friend or two. I know of more than one woman who felt badly that she could no longer be friendly with her ex's sisters, mother, or other relative. It does happen, but it's a risk you have to be willing to take.

Unfortunately, many women have a "double standard" where their prospective husband's family is concerned. They are close with their own families but seem to resent their husband being close with his. If you have these tendencies, ask yourself why. Your husband is entitled to the same relationship with his family as you have with yours, and once again, remember, you have more to *gain* by being congenial and loving to all of them.

Even if your Mr. Right is estranged from his family, they are still part of him, and vice-versa. You never know when they might reappear in his life, so you need to be prepared for all possibilities. I know of women who have entered into relationships with men who have children from former marriages but who had been out of their lives for years. These women learned that circumstances change, sometimes drastically, and the unexpected happens. When children or other relatives resurface, they can bring all kinds of problems. Of course the reverse can also happen — their reappearance can result in wonderful reunions as well. You really have to be prepared for anything, and be willing to go the extra mile to be a friend to even the most "difficult" family member. Your relationship is worth it.

Your relationships with Mr. Right's family can be some of the most rewarding you will ever have. Get to know them, get to love them if possible, but at the very least, try to be their friend — and not only will you win points with them, but you will be adding immeasurable satisfaction to your own life. ♥

# REALIZE THAT WITH SEX, TIMING IS EVERYTHING

Elsewhere I mention that some people just make better decisions than others. Here is a perfect example: You haven't had sex for a while, at least not "good sex", and this new prospect wants it on the first date. Of course you can say yes, and many women do, despite the risk of sexually transmitted diseases. The better decision is to say no. Old-fashioned as it may sound, you're more likely to end up walking down the aisle if you avoid jumping into bed too soon. Sex isn't necessary — or advisable — on the first, second or even the third date. If he tries to change your mind, just tell him you're not ready, but you will let him know when you are.

Intimacy does not come from sex alone. In fact, having sex too soon in a relationship can ruin any chances for true intimacy. There will be plenty of opportunities if this relationship develops, so it's best to take it slowly. "Less is more" — particularly when it comes to sexual activity early in a relationship. On the other hand, if one of you absolutely cannot wait and the other agrees…well, you have to use your judgment. But keep in mind that the longer you refrain, the more objective you will be about seeing him as he really is. No matter how rational or adept a woman may be at handling her emotions, having sex (even "casual" sex) makes her emotionally vulnerable. Once she has opened her heart to a man, she is more likely to be in denial should he begin to display any serious character defects.

Women have sex for all sorts of reasons that may have nothing to do with lust...or love. Many single women are simply hungry, perhaps even starved, for touch. Since non-sexual touching doesn't seem to be in the average single man's repertoire, some of these women feel that sex is their only option for satisfying their deep need for touch. Other women jump into bed too soon because they have low self-esteem, and feel that sex is all they have to offer a man.

Too many women use sex as "bait" or even as a weapon. "Making him wait for it" is a power ploy used by many women, and not surprisingly, most men resent it. (Needless to say, they wield the ultimate "power" when they go to bed with a woman, promise, "I'll call you", and then disappear from her life forever.) Naturally, I am not recommending that anyone adopt such a callous attitude towards sex, but unfortunately, people do.

You can't control other people's attitudes, but you can make an effort not to be cynical or insensitive yourself, no matter how many negative experiences you have had in the past with having sex too soon or not soon enough. Don't think of delaying sex with your potential Mr. Right as a strategy, think of it as a way of protecting yourself from potential hurt. Because that is exactly what it is.

Although I didn't grow up in the sexual revolution, I am a modern thinking woman. Most likely you're not a virgin, and you know the score. But no matter how much you love sex and like this guy, having sex too early in the relationship is simply not the best decision if you want a serious, long-term relationship. The odds are against you. The short-term pleasure you get will quickly fade, to be replaced by guilt or the feeling of having been used. He may decide that he has "gotten what he wants" and it's time to move on to the next woman. Sex has been around a long time, but some things never change. You may argue, "Well, if he's just going to leave me after we have sex anyway, why not have it sooner than later?" That's a defeatist sentiment, but if you think he's going to walk after sex, you probably fear he's going to walk anyway — and you really will feel a lot better about yourself if he leaves without having had it! If he has more time to get to know you and love you before you go to bed with him, there's a much better chance that he'll want to stick around for good.

What if he gets angry with you for saying no? That's not necessarily a sign you should write him off. He's probably just used to women going to bed with him on the first or second date. If he really likes you and wants to pursue a relationship with you, however, he will respect your wishes on this matter. If not, he's probably not your Mr. Right.

---

# Remember...

 t's better to wait and get to know something about the other person before you have sex. You could end up with great sex and little else, and you won't feel good about yourself.

---

So let's say you have thought about it and have decided you *don't* want to wait. In this you're certainly not unique (are you reading between the lines here?); most single men will tell you that many women have become much more aggressive when it comes to sex on the first or second date. Some men say they don't mind, but believe it or not, there are those who do. Before you start unbuttoning his shirt or taking off his shoes, ask him what he wants. Most men can't say no, and probably want to have sex as much as you do. But don't take it for granted that he's a sex machine, always ready for action. He may be a perfectly normal, lusty guy who has good reasons for wanting to wait — such as a desire for you to get to know each other better. If so, I'd say you've found yourself a gem. Remember, it's always wiser to take it slowly. Early in the relationship, it is better to err on the side of "not doing enough" than "doing too much, too soon".

For some women, taking it slowly isn't a problem because they're ambivalent about having sex in the first place. They lack self-confidence because they're out of practice, or have problems with their body image, or any number of other reasons. If you this describes you, I'm hoping that you've been doing what you need to do to improve your self-image and your confidence. Beyond that, as with so many other issues discussed in this book...*lighten up!* Get to know this wonderful man and let him get to know you — and sex will happen when it happens. It may even be awkward at first but don't worry, it will improve as your relationship grows.

In Chapter 43 I mention that men should have honed their sexual skills by their early thirties. (As also noted in that chapter, there are exceptions; some men are simply shyer or "slower", but aren't necessarily sexually dysfunctional.) Our society places a lot of emphasis on men's sexual prowess, but it goes without saying that women need to be good sex partners as well. We are long past the era where the burden of "performance" is solely on the man. Women must share the responsibility for the couple's sex life. Most men these days are well aware that they need to be considerate lovers, and most of them really do try. Still, men aren't mind readers, and learning to communicate your sexual needs to him in a gentle and non-threatening way is one of the finest "arts" you can learn. Equally important, you must be sensitive to *his* needs. That's all part of "treating him like Number 1", as we discuss in Chapter 46. Of course, if there's plenty of sexual chemistry between the two of you, wanting to please each other will come naturally. Even so, learning each other's most intimate needs takes time and effort. The rewards, however, are immeasurable!

I would be remiss if I didn't remind you that today everyone needs to practice "safe sex". You should *never* have unprotected sex unless both you and your partner have been tested for AIDS and other sexually transmitted diseases.

Enjoying sex with your partner is important to your relationship. Communicating your wants and desires with each other is also very important. Take your time, even if you have made a practice before of having sex on the second or third date. First try to find out how much you like this man, and how much he likes you. And when you're both ready...then go for it, with no holds barred. ♥

# 49

# KNOW WHEN AND HOW TO APPROACH THE SUBJECTS OF COMMITMENT & MARRIAGE

*A*ll right, you're pretty secure in your relationship and you think he may just be the one, but for some reason, he hasn't asked you to marry him yet. Or maybe you're not quite to the point where you've decided he's Mr. Right, but he's certainly Mr. Possible, and you're wondering when and how to bring up the subject of commitment and marriage. You don't want to scare him off, but you certainly don't want to wait around for years when you could be looking for other prospects. The sooner you can determine if your relationship is on the "marriage track", the better.

When it comes to men, commitment and marriage, there are lots of "types" out there, but most of them fall into a few major categories. There are those who really don't care if they marry or not — and some of these are good prospects. There are those who say they're "ready" for marriage, but just "haven't found the right one" yet. (Maybe they need to read this book!) Then there are those who just want to date and not commit, and as we've discussed in Chapter 43, you're better off not wasting your time with those men.

Some men will talk about marriage early on in a relationship, while others avoid the topic altogether. Some will let you know they're open to marriage, but they're not yet sure if you are Ms. Right. However, there are some men who know you're not Ms. Right immediately, but they're comfortable in the relationship and aren't ready to say good-bye. The latter can be extraordinarily frustrating, because you can end up hanging on for months, or even years, living on false hopes. Don't let it happen to you.

By the time a man is in his mid-forties, if he hasn't been married, or at least engaged, you could be in for a tough time. He's been independent for so long that it may be difficult for him to move over and make room in his life for someone else. There are some exceptions, of course. Doctors or other professionals who put their lives on hold while getting their education and training are one exception. There are also men who decided to return to college for an advanced degree, and were saddled with new college loans and had to start all over again. Sooner or later, most of these men find room in their lives for a wife.

Many women are hesitant to bring up the subject of marriage, perhaps because they've known so many commitment-phobic men who turn pale at the very thought of walking down the aisle. There is absolutely nothing wrong with your talking about your desire to marry. Think of it this way. There are many women, especially those in their late forties and early fifties, who do not want to get married. They have successful careers and enough friends and family to occupy their free time, but they still desire to have a man in their lives — they just don't want to marry. These women have no problem telling a man they have recently connected with that they are *not* interested in marriage. They want a long-lasting relationship, but marriage is out for them. Well, you can be just as honest: You are looking for a long-lasting relationship — and you *definitely* have not ruled out marriage!

If you see from the beginning that this man may become Mr. Right, what is the best way to approach the subject of marriage, and how soon can you start? You have to do it in steps — obviously you don't want to jump the gun. You certainly don't want to broach the subject while one or both of you are still dating others. Exclusivity is the first requirement, and he may very well be the first one to announce he's no longer interested in dating anyone else. That's a great first step. You can either agree or not respond, unless of course he asks you how you feel about dating him exclusively. If that's the case, don't play games — be honest. Usually the desire for exclusive dating is mutual, so there shouldn't be a problem. Remember that if he's a good prospect, he is looking for the same thing as you are — a lasting permanent relationship. Hopefully, he's tired of playing games.

Once you're dating exclusively — and that could happen as soon as the fifth or sixth date (or even earlier) — how do you move ahead to the next step? Don't wait too long to send out feelers. You should already have shared your histories about some of your former relationships; it's not inappropriate to do that by the third or fourth date. If he hasn't at least hinted of his future plans by the time you have decided to date exclusively, it is perfectly fine if you bring up the topic in a very informal, non-threatening manner. At this point in your relationship you are not seeking a commitment, you just want to know how he feels about permanent relationships. You can ask him how close he came to getting engaged in his previous relationship(s). Did he discuss marriage at all? This is a good way to get much needed information. It's not one hundred percent accurate, but it's a good indicator. When he responds, this is as good a time as any to ask him what he wants, especially if you think there may be a problem later on. Does he plan on marrying, or is he afraid of marriage? Remember to be gentle about it. After all, you are just asking a question. Don't make him feel as if you're backing him into a corner. If he becomes flustered or tongue-tied, he may have a commitment problem, but I wouldn't write him off yet. There still may be hope for him, especially if you think he's a really good prospect.

Now let's say you've been dating your potential Mr. Right for a few months, and everything seems to have fallen right into place. You're dating exclusively, you've met his friends and he's met yours, and perhaps you've met each other's families as well. He said he *does* want to get married someday and have children, and may even have asked how you feel about that. If you are still interested in starting a family, you have that in common. Things are looking good — your goals are in sync with his!

Now what? It's still too soon for you to worry if he doesn't come out and talk about the two of you spending the rest of your lives together, but it isn't too soon to find out if he's moving in that direction. There are several signs which indicate what he's thinking.

One good indicator is his participation in your social life. Does he make most of the suggestions or plans, do the two of you share in it, or do you make all the plans? Like almost everything in a marriage, the task of making social arrangements should be shared at this point. How does he feel about spending time with your friends and family? This is not a definite sign, but he may be less inclined to spend time with your family if he thinks he's being scrutinized. How does he feel about your spending time with *his* family? Don't be pushy, but do show an interest in getting to know his family and friends. If his family is close by, suggest going out with them for a Sunday drive or dinner. Should he seem reluctant to have you meet them, this could be a warning sign. We discuss this in more detail in Chapter 44. If he brings you to his family gatherings, you'll have a great opportunity to observe how he is with his family, how well they interact, and of course, whether or not they seem to like you. His mother may even give you the high sign, but I have to warn you that if he's not interested in marriage, she won't be able to change his mind. Regardless, be as nice as you can be to his parents, and show them you're the warm, friendly caring person that you sincerely are.

What if everything is going fine — you're spending a lot of time together, you're visiting with each other's family and friends, and it seems clear to you that he's "the one" — but he still hasn't popped the question? Some women have had success giving their boyfriend an ultimatum. Personally, I don't like ultimatums, but sometimes that is the only way to move on with your life. At the very least, you need to lay your cards on the table at some point. If after four or five months — six at the most — he hasn't mentioned the possibility of the two of you getting married, perhaps you should bring it up. Why waste any more time? In your mind you can have a plan — an approximate date, a suggested location, or any other details you can offer that will nudge him to commit.

## Remember...

on't settle for a "permanent boyfriend" if what you really want is a husband. Give him time, and don't try to rush him into a commitment he isn't ready to make — but don't let him keep you waiting forever, either! You have to know when to move on.

Ask him how he feels about your relationship. If he responds by telling you how crazy he is about you, tell him that you know he loves you, there's no doubt about that. Tell him, however, that it's time to discuss any doubts he may have about your relationship. If his doubts seem valid, then of course you both need to address them and see if they can be easily resolved. However, you should also find out why he failed to discuss these issues with you earlier. If you hadn't brought up the subject of marriage, when was he planning on discussing them with you? If his "issues" are lame, they may just be an excuse not to commit. Ask him for more specifics; he may be looking for a way out and doesn't know how to do it nicely.

Some people recommend dating at least a year before marriage is seriously discussed. A year is a good guideline if you're in your twenties, or even your early thirties. But when you're older, a year is a long time to wait before marriage is even brought up, especially if this is your first marriage. Here's a suggested timeline, but remember, it is just a guide; nothing is hard and fast.

1. If you think a man could be a good prospect, within a short time it's only natural to discuss your goals for the relationship. At this point, you will just be discussing marriage in a general sense. If you met him on a web site, he probably said he's looking for a long-term, permanent relationship. In most instances, talk about marriage will follow a natural progression, but since many of these men may be commitment phobic, a woman needs a huge amount of patience. Approach the subject casually but with conviction — but remember, try not to scare him.

2. Between four to six months, there should be a deeper commitment and more serious talk about marriage. It's best if he brings it up, but if not, you can. If he raises the subject of marriage, don't take that as a premature proposal. How many relationships don't make it back to home plate because something, after a few months, just doesn't seem right? Don't take anything for granted at this point.

3. There is nothing certain in life, and six months hardly seems like a long enough time to decide if you want to spend the rest of your life with someone, but it's a "guesstimate" of when you can expect to talk about marriage. At some point, you may have to force the issue. As I mentioned before, I normally don't like the idea of delivering an ultimatum, but sometimes it is necessary. (The catch is that you have to be prepared to follow through with your ultimatum.) If he is still noncommittal after your discussion with him about future plans, tell him you won't wait around for him to make up his mind. He may take offense and make himself out to be the injured party. Ignore it — it's just an act. Tell him that you need to have a commitment from him,

or you're going to move on. You can tell him immediately or wait a few weeks, but why prolong it? Remind him that you have a great relationship going, and then ask him how he'd feel if he lost you. If he says he doesn't want to live without you, then ask him directly what his intentions are. Don't let him get away with being evasive.

4. If he doesn't seem totally averse to marriage, but just seems doubtful or uncertain, ask him what his doubts are and ask for examples. If he dismisses them as minor, or says there aren't any problems with your relationship, then say, "Well…?" He'll probably say, "Well, what?'" At that point you can say, "Honey, I'm not sure how you feel about me. If you don't want to live the rest of your life with me, be honest. You know how I feel about you —I think we have a wonderful relationship here. I don't know what you're looking for. Maybe you don't want to plan for the future, but I do." Unless he gets down on his knees and asks you to marry him, tell him to think about it — but he'd better think quickly. Don't beg, cry or show any expression other than a smile (if you can force one) and a twinkle in your eye, as if to say, "If you don't commit, you'll be passing up someone really wonderful!" The longer you date without a commitment from him, the less chance you have of marrying. At least this way, you have a fifty/ fifty chance he will propose.

5. Keep in mind your six-month commitment is not necessarily about an engagement ring, but remember that you are looking for marriage, not a permanent boyfriend. Once you're beyond your mid to late thirties, time is of the essence. Why should you wait around for a commitment? You laid your cards out on the table soon after you began dating; it's not too soon to expect a serious commitment. You need to know where he stands. He doesn't have to ask you to marry him yet (though it would be nice!), but you should know his intentions. If he is still unwilling to even make a commitment, now may be the time to say good bye.

There are two forms of commitment. Initially, it is a commitment of exclusivity, which, if your relationship is on the "marriage track", comes soon after you begin dating. The next commitment is for your future. It may not be accompanied by a marriage proposal immediately, but there should be a clear indication that a proposal is forthcoming. Even then, it's not out of line for you to ask him to give you an idea of when you can expect that proposal.

6. If after a year he still has not agreed to set a wedding date, be cautious; this is probably a signal that you simply are not on the same track. He may sincerely believe he has made a commitment to you, but obviously you and he have a difference of opinion on the meaning of "commitment". It is time to move on. Don't waste another minute!

---

## Remember...

*hen you're on the "marriage track" there are two levels of commitment. Initially there is a commitment of exclusivity, and then a commitment for the future, which ultimately translates to a marriage proposal. At that point, it is not out of line for you to ask him to commit to an actual time frame, if he hasn't already.*

---

Of course, this guide is only a generality. Your "timeline" may be shorter or longer. In the end, you have to go with your gut feeling. Whatever you do, don't settle for a permanent boyfriend if what you really want is a husband!

As I've noted before, when it comes to the prospect of marriage, men aren't any different from women. They get just as eager and excited as we do when they think they may have met "the one". You don't want to give up too soon, and by all means you should give him every chance, but you have to know when to call it quits. He can be a wonderful guy but still not be *your* Mr. Right. At least you will have the satisfaction of knowing you've given it your best effort. If you see that marriage is not in the cards, thank him for having shared part of his life with you. Say goodbye and mean it. And then, when you're ready...go out and try again!

# 50

## ONCE YOU'VE FOUND YOUR "KEEPER", HELP OTHERS FIND THEIRS

*M*any years ago, I mentioned to a married friend of mine that a mutual friend's daughter was searching for her Mr. Right. I suggested she ask her married children if perhaps they knew of eligible men. Her response to me was, "Who am I to play God!" Well, after I caught my breath, I told her how shocked I was that she would have an attitude like that. It was so foreign to my way of thinking that today, when I recall the conversation, it still astounds me.

Is it playing with fate to help others find true love? Hardly! Perhaps you're unsure, or you may even happen to agree with my girlfriend's response. The truth is that introducing two people is neither taking control of, nor trying to change, someone else's destiny. It's simply an introduction. Introducing two people is far removed from trying to change someone's destiny.

Some twenty years ago, when dating services were just becoming popular, I was asked to help start a dating service for singles. One of our city's prominent businessmen approached me, together with two other women, to start a dating service with paid memberships. Previously, there had been many informal gatherings specifically for singles, and this man felt we were naturals for running a dating service. For various reasons, we were forced to call off the project just as we were about to launch it, but there is no doubt in my mind it would have been successful! Just the idea of introducing two prospects and possibly making a "match" was exciting, and we were all disappointed when we had to cancel it. Were we playing God? Not by a long shot, we were just doing our part to help others find a little happiness. It still gives me joy to think about the possibility.

A few years ago, I introduced a friend of my daughter's to a recently separated friend of mine. I knew before I ever introduced them that it would be a perfect match. In many ways they seemed an unlikely pair, but from the very moment that my friend called me and said his wife had left him, I knew my daughter's friend would be a great match for him. However, I waited until his divorce was final to say anything to either one of them. His wife was also my friend, and I didn't want to jump the gun or hurt anyone's feelings. I did put some "feelers" out, though. I had my daughter ask her friend if she would be interested in meeting a really great guy, and she said yes. I did nothing more at that time; I just waited. One day my friend called me, and in the course of the conversation, he happened to mention that he was ready to meet someone. I felt he was hinting, so I said, "Not until your divorce is final!" He replied, "That's what I'm calling to tell you! It *is* final." So I said, "Well, yes, as a matter of fact I do have someone in mind." You can guess the very happy ending to this story. They met, they hit it off, they married, and to this day they both thank me every chance they get.

What a great feeling it is to have been responsible for two people falling in love and finding happiness. That reminds me of the significance of the message: There is no greater gift than the gift of giving. When I was young, I always thought that was something fund raisers said when they were looking for donations. Years later I realized exactly what the gift of giving was all about.

If I could, I'd send this message to every married couple, especially those who married after thirty-five: **Single people need to continue making new acquaintances, and it is the responsibility of every married person to introduce their single friends to as many people as possible.** I would remind them that not everyone to whom one introduces a friend has to be a potential match. On the contrary, singles need to meet a variety of single and married people of both sexes. (The chapters on "friend collecting" (Chapter 35) and "fix-ups" (Chapter 36) explain why this is so important.)

Call your married friends and read this chapter to them, or copy it and send it to them. While you're at it, send a reminder to everyone on your e-mail list, married or single. Every opportunity I have, I ask people if they have single friends, and if so, are they introducing them to their friends? I almost always hear the same response; they never gave it a thought. Here are the facts: The numbers of single people today are increasing, and the majority of heterosexual singles want to marry. They need their friends' help.

---

## Remember...

*elping others find happiness is one of the greatest gifts you can offer. After you've found your true love (or even before), don't be afraid to fix up your single friends.*

---

I am very aware that if you are still single and searching for a husband yourself, helping someone else find their Mr. (or Ms.) Right may be the last thing on your mind. That's perfectly understandable. I realize that at this point in your life, you need to concentrate primarily on your own quest, but I am asking you to think ahead. You see, I'm operating under the assumption that you *will* find your Mr. Right. Once you do, don't hesitate to fix up your single friends. Go out of your way to do what you can to help them — after all, it wasn't that long ago that you were in their shoes!

You might even consider trying to fix up one of your friends with a man you've dated in the past, but in whom you are no longer interested. (There are even websites where women recommend their former boyfriends!) If he was a great guy but just wasn't "the one" for you, there's a chance he and your friend could really hit it off. I know many women fiercely resist such fix-ups. They still feel possessive of the man, even though they're no longer dating him. It's common for people to begrudge others that which they can no longer use, but that is selfish. So try to let go of the idea that this ex-boyfriend still "belongs" to you, and concentrate instead on the fact that you want your friends to find happiness.

If a couple does marry as a result of your introduction, it will give you more pleasure than you could imagine. The most wonderful gift you can give in life is to help create a union of marriage. After you have met your Mr. Right, and may be headed down the aisle, never forget that "There but for the grace of God go I." Once you have found the love of your life, the greatest thing you can do is help others find theirs. ♥

# AND FINALLY...

Our son married just days before his fortieth birthday. Where did he meet his wife? On an Internet dating website. Was she worth waiting for? You bet! Sooner or later, everyone who wants to marry does marry — it just takes some longer than others.

You will never be younger than you are today. Don't wait until tomorrow to begin making the easy, subtle changes we've talked about in this book. Remember to practice the changes, put them into motion, and you'll see almost instant results. Practice equals changes, and changes equal results. It doesn't get much easier than that!

If you are feeling insecure for any reason...if you haven't had a date in a year or more...if you haven't registered on an Internet dating website because you've been out of the dating scene for so long you've lost your nerve...here's a solution. The next time you are ready to go out, and your hair, clothes and makeup look great, take a moment to look in the mirror and have a talk with yourself. Remind yourself that there is nothing you can't do and no hurdle you cannot clear. You are as smart, as pretty, as kind, caring and capable as any other woman out there. You have all the tools you need to conquer any doubt and fear. Smile at yourself, and go out the door with a twinkle in your eyes and a new attitude. You will be on the road to matrimony more quickly than you had ever thought. That wonderful man will be mesmerized by you; he'll be drawn in by your self-confidence. And soon you will realize that you have finally found your "keeper". Who said miracles can't happen? They do every day; sometimes, we just need to give them a little help!

Don't ever give up, because that wonderful, loving man is out there looking for you. All you have to do is make it a little bit easier for him to find you. The road may have been rough, but if the journey takes you over the hills and into beautiful pastures, why not hang on — you'll see it will have been well worth the ride.

# I Want To Hear From You...

I want to hear from my readers! Tell me all about your successes and failures on the road to finding Mr. Right, and feel free to share your questions, comments and concerns. Send me an e-mail at myra@findingakeeper.com. I'm looking forward to hearing from you!

*Myra*

# Places And Ways
## To Meet New People —
### A "Quick List"

You never know when and where Mr. Right (or even your new best girl-friend!) will be...

♦ Leave your car at home and take public transportation.
♦ Change your lunch locations.
♦ Stop at a variety of different Starbucks or other coffee houses.
♦ Visit museums.
♦ Go to gallery openings.
♦ Join seasonal organizations, such as garden clubs.
♦ Go on home and garden tours.
♦ Attend Happy Hours specifically geared for singles about your age.
♦ Accept all invitations to weddings, bar and bat mitzvahs, baby namings, and the like. Even funerals can be a good place to meet someone, provided, of course, that you're not too obvious!
♦ Keep your eyes open in supermarkets, drug stores, dry cleaners, take-out places and the like — after all, single men have to eat and do their laundry too!
♦ Join a fitness club, or go along with a friend for a free trial.
♦ Don't forget running stores, sporting goods stores and other fitness-related outlets.
♦ Check out your church, synagogue or other places that are religiously affiliated.
♦ Sign up for classes at the local YMCA, Jewish Community Center, Asian Center, etc.
♦ Take a cooking class — try different locations and different types of classes.
♦ Take a photography class. You don't necessarily need to buy an expensive camera. (Check out the requirements first.)
♦ Don't overlook adult learning centers and other venues that offer continuing education classes, such as junior and community colleges.

- Dance lessons are a must for femininity, grace and self-confidence. Remember that men take lessons too! Be sure to attend the group dances that the studios offer.
- Participate in a community or local theatre.
- Take a CPR survival class (it's only one day or evening, and it's usually a mass event).
- Travel agencies sometimes offer open houses — you may be able to book a great vacation *and* find Mr. Right.
- Volunteer for the Arts...opera, symphony, ballet, international festivals or other special events.
- Wear or hold something that may be an eye-catcher, such as an unusual colored handbag or something else that will call attention to you.
- Buy a new book or carry one that will attract someone else's attention. I've frequently asked someone about the book they were reading. It's a wonderful way to start a conversation. (Just don't be too intrusive if you see he's truly engrossed in his book. Know how to take a hint.)
- Compliment everyone you speak to — the checkout people in the supermarket, salespeople in the stores, etc. — everyone you come in contact with. There is always something you can think of to say, something positive to notice. Compliment them on their nice demeanor, their pretty eyes or smile, their efficiency, their speedy manner, their, hands, their handwriting, even their voice.
- Speak to people waiting to board your plane and the people near you on the plane. Again, don't be too intrusive — if it's clear that they'd rather not converse, respect that.
- If you're standing in line for anything, at the very least striking up a conversation with someone who's also waiting makes the time pass more quickly. Of course, always use discretion.
- Pretend you're looking to buy a new car and scope out the salesmen in the showrooms. If you really *are* looking to buy a new car, your work is that much easier!
- Check out the waiting room for car service, or the service people in your automobile dealership.
- Consider joining, or at least going to a meeting of, any professional organization that may be affiliated with your job/career.
- Attend a convention or meeting that's job related.

- Don't forget bookstores! Most of them have special areas that are great for socializing as well as browsing, and many have coffee areas attached. Most bookstores also offer special events all year round. Make a note on your calendar and attend the book-signings; there are always lots of people at these events with whom you may share a special interest — photography, art, the newest novels, best sellers, etc.
- Cancel your newspaper subscription — or at least the Sunday edition — and pick up the paper in a variety of locations.
- If you need to buy a gift for a man, look in the men's department of the better stores. As a matter of fact, whenever you're shopping, take some time to scope out the men's departments or men's stores, especially on the first day or two of a sale.
- Walk in the park, and even change parks once in a while. Just be sure you're in a relatively safe one, and always in daylight hours when others are there.
- If you have a dog, walking with your dog will always attract other dog lovers and they'll stop and visit. Again, change parks once in a while. If you don't have a dog, ask a friend who has one to go walking with you, and take the dog along.
- While waiting for a hair appointment, manicure, etc., visit with the people around you. You never know who might have a son, brother or cousin who would be just perfect for you. At the very least, these are great places to meet a new girlfriend. (I happen to know lots of women who have become good friends with women they met at these places.)
- Work on someone's political campaign when they're running for office.
- Join the reunion committee for your college or high school.
- Attend any and all reunions — high school, college, even family. You never know who your long-lost cousin might know.
- If you have nieces and nephews, offer to take them to their parties, games, etc. It's a good way to meet new people. The new acquaintances will probably ask if you're married. Tell them you're not, then proceed to let them know that you're looking to meet someone — and if they think of someone they can call your niece or nephew's mom or dad. Be sure to thank them for keeping you in mind!

- Visit the library, not just to check out books, but to check out any functions they may offer.
- Work on any city-wide events — they always need volunteers.
- Work on a charity event – they always need more volunteers, and many of the women heading the committees are very well connected; they know everyone!
- Attend every event you're invited to (if you can afford it, and of course if you have the time).

I'm sure you can think of many more places, and many more things to do. This list is just to get you started. Look at it frequently and I bet you'll never run out of inspiration and motivation.

Good luck, and don't forget to have fun!

# ABOUT THE AUTHOR

Myra Kaplan and her husband Gene live in Texas. Although this is her first published book, she has been writing for many years. A native of Schenectady, New York, Myra and her husband married in 1962. They lived in Albany, New York until 1976 when they moved to Texas, where they have been ever since. Gene is a retired stockbroker, and when he and Myra are not traveling they're at home with their two dogs. They have two grown children.